PREACHING AND ITS PARTNERS

PREACHING AND THEOLOGY

Preaching and Its Partners
A series edited by Paul Scott Wilson

PREACHING AND THEOLOGY

James F. Kay

CHALICE
PRESS

ST. LOUIS, MISSOURI

Cover design: Michael A. Domínguez
Cover art: © 1998 Artville
Interior design: Wynn Younker/Elizabeth Wright
Art direction: Michael A. Domínguez

Visit Chalice Press on the World Wide Web at
www.chalicepress.com

10 9 8 7 6 5 4 3 2 1   07 08 09 10 11 12

Library of Congress Cataloging–in–Publication Data

Kay, James (James F.).
    Preaching and theology / James Kay.
        p. cm.
    ISBN 978-0-8272-2991-4
    1. Preaching. 2. Bible–Hermeneutics. 3. Theology. I. Title.
    BV4211.3.K39 2008
    251–dc22   2007038683

Printed in the United States of America

Contents

For
Fleming Rutledge

PREFACE

"You poor preachers. You only have words!" This reproach rings truer of the Christian pulpit than a certain defensiveness might otherwise allow. Yes, we preachers work largely with words. And words are problematic. Sometimes they seem scarcely up to the job. Sometimes they wander and hide from their subject matter–or get lost. Through repeated use and overuse their meanings cease to challenge us to further reflection or needed action. Sometimes preachers browbeat or manipulate their hearers through words, what Karl Barth (1886–1968) once called "the gospel at gun-point."[1] And words can cease to house truth and shelter deception. No less than ourselves, words are fallen into the grips of a power, traditionally termed sin, that corrupts them and kills them even while enticing them into its service and frequently in the name of religion or God.

For this reason, thinking critically and theologically is necessary for preaching to proceed with honesty, integrity, and faithfulness to the Christian message. Yet for many people, including many preachers, pastors, and professors, theology is itself a negative word–and not always for negative reasons. Recently, at the American Academy of Religion meeting in Philadelphia, a leading Christian scholar forcefully urged in the interest of world peace that we leave "theology" behind and find our common ground with other faiths in "spirituality." The point, of course, is an old one, namely, that faith, in this case taken as "piety," always precedes its theological formulation in doctrines and creeds. Yet even this view presupposes a theological anthropology where words vocalize, but do not constitute, our experience–questionable for a tradition in which "the Word" is said to be "in the beginning." And it is also through words, perhaps only through words in the broadest and deepest sense, that we encounter what the apostle Paul calls "the gospel of God" (Rom. 1:1), that is, the glad news that originates with God, and which is "the power of God unto salvation" (Rom. 1:1, 16). Amid all the easy talk rolling off our affable tongues on Sunday morning, there sit people in desperate need, perhaps more desperate than they recognize. Given these stakes, we preachers are called to do more from the pulpit than bandy about bromides or "code words," even great ones like "the gospel." The test for faithful preaching cannot simply be "Lord, Lord" talk, as our Lord himself warns us (Mt. 7:21); neither will the mantra, "The

vii

Bible says . . ." suffice, as our Lord's own struggle with the scripture-spouting Tempter reminds us (Mt. 4:1–11). So, insofar as the God of the gospel is of concern to preaching, theology–that is, thinking about what we are saying and doing in light of this God–is unavoidable. This book attempts to show how and why this is true; how and why theology matters for preaching; and how and why preaching matters for theology.

You will soon discover that I speak of a distinct theological "frame of reference" in relation to those afforded by rhetoric and poetics. This is my way of signaling that there are three principal ways by which sustained reflection on preaching has historically proceeded, almost always in dialogue or debate with each other, since the issues at stake are not trivial. Naturally, things are more complicated than schemas and typologies allow. There are many possible theological positions within a general theological frame of reference, just as there are multiple points of view operative in rhetoric and poetics. I was tempted, therefore, to write a descriptive "cookbook" listing in cafeteria style all the current entrées for reader sampling. On further reflection, this seemed to be an evasion of my responsibility to give the reader a more richly textured account of God as the Subject of preaching, and to guide the reader through sometimes complex arguments advanced in major positions. As a result, many other topics and perspectives have had to remain on the sideboards. I have attempted to indicate something of the theological diversity of homiletics in the bibliography, where you will find books and articles representing a variety of views, including many that could not be adequately treated here.

I owe a number of debts to my conversation partners who over the years directly and indirectly contributed to this book. They include Christian Andrews, Charles L. Bartow, Allan Hugh Cole Jr., Robert DiSalle, Nancy J. Duff, Karlfried Froehlich, Thomas W. Gillespie, Angela Dienhart Hancock, Charles B. ("Chip") Hardwick, Elsie Anne McKee, Hughes Oliphant Old, J. Louis Martyn, Christopher Morse, the late Richard A. Norris Jr., George L. Parsenios, and Paul E. Rorem. None of these colleagues should be held responsible for my views or errors. To Paul Scott Wilson, general editor of the series, Preaching and Its Partners, I owe a large measure of thanks for his patience, persistence, and goodwill in seeing me through this project amid the delays and detours of my various administrative assignments. Thanks are also due to Trent Butler, Pablo A. Jiménez, Gail Stobaugh, and Lisa Scronce of Chalice Press for their encouraging spirit and editorial suggestions.

I welcome this opportunity to thank my students who have heard some of this material in courses in homiletics and theology at Princeton Theological Seminary. I also thank its Board of Trustees, former President Thomas W. Gillespie, former Dean James F. Armstrong, President Iain R. Torrance, and Dean Darrell L. Guder for facilitating a generous sabbatical and research leave that enabled me to complete this book. To Sally Brown, Cleophus J. LaRue, J. Randall Nichols, and Kristin Saldine go my appreciation for assuming extra institutional burdens during my leave. Faculty Secretary, Lois F. Haydu, has been of untiring assistance to me and my colleagues for nearly two decades at Princeton Theological Seminary, enabling all of us to balance our administrative, teaching, and writing projects. So, once again, Lois, thank you for everything. I also wish to acknowledge with gratitude the encouragement of Thomas E. Brown, who kept me attentive to the task at hand.

Unless otherwise indicated, all citations from the Bible are given in the text of the *New Revised Standard Version* (NRSV). All translations from the German language, unless otherwise indicated, are my own.

Since my doctoral days at Union Theological Seminary in New York, Fleming Rutledge has been a loyal friend and colleague. Above all, she is a faithful minister of the Word of God amid the changing seasons of the theological climate. To her this book is dedicated.

INTRODUCTION

Frames of Reference

You may have discovered, if you delve into books on preaching, a recurring term, "frames of reference." For example, in *As One without Authority*, Fred Craddock rejects a rigid dichotomy between the "Word of God" and the "word of man" by appealing to "the hermeneutical frame of reference" where "all the words we know are human words."[1] James Forbes, in his Beecher Lectures, can characterize "the anointing of the Holy Spirit for preaching effectiveness" as relating to "the highest frame of reference."[2] For his part, André Resner Jr. employs "frames of reference" throughout his study, *Preacher and Cross,* to compare and contrast homiletical theorists who take a "rhetorical" approach to preaching from those who take a "theological" route. Their differences over the role they assign to God are traceable to their distinctive "frames of reference."[3]

Hollywood has recently caught up with homiletics in seeing the possibilities of organizing an entire motion picture around distinctive frames of reference. In the opening scene of *Crash*, Graham, played by Don Cheadle, says in the aftermath of his traffic accident, "It's the sense of touch…in LA nobody touches you. We're always behind this metal and glass. I think we miss that touch so much that we crash into each other just so we feel something." His girlfriend and passenger, Rita, played by Jennifer Esposito, replies, "Graham, I think we got rear-ended. I think we spun around twice. And somewhere in there one of us lost our frame of reference–and I am going to go look for it."[4] We may wonder what precisely Rita is going to find. What is a frame of reference, and why would knowing be helpful for preaching?

The term "reference frame" or "frame of reference" is not native to homiletics or to theology. Physicists coined it in the late nineteenth century in rendering accounts of celestial mechanics ultimately derived from Copernican theory. This theory had successfully challenged the dominant Ptolemaic theory in the early sixteenth century by replacing the earth with the sun as the center of all motion in the then-known universe. Subsequent reflection led to the recognition that either the earth or the sun could serve equally well "as merely possible points of view from which the motions of the celestial bodies could be described." Indeed, Galileo demonstrated that "mechanical experiments will have the same results in a system in uniform motion that they have in a system at rest." Thus, the descriptions and predictions of celestial mechanics are possible regardless of one's "point of view" or frame of reference, and none can be regarded as necessarily or intrinsically privileged. Nevertheless, assuming uniformity of motion, all points of view lead to equivalent calculations of motion. Therefore, as Leibniz recognized, neither the Copernican nor the Ptolemaic theory is "true," rather, "both are merely possible hypothetical interpretations of the same relative motions...differing in their arbitrary choices of a resting point or origin, but agreeing on the relative positions of bodies at any moment and their changing relative distances through time." Once one adopts a "point of view," that is, an inertial or originating frame of reference, then all motion in the universe can be calculated in relation to it.[5]

While Einsteinian physics largely dispensed with frames of reference as incompatible with its theory of general relativity, the concept has nevertheless passed into widespread use. It recognizes that reality claims are always perspectival. They are not "true" in themselves, but they are "valid" for certain purposes. They are best understood as relative descriptions of equivalent value, dependent on one's viewpoint. Whereas in classic physics "frames of reference" denoted arbitrarily chosen points of view that still secured exactly equivalent measurements of motion, as now employed in common parlance, frames of reference are taken for arbitrarily chosen or inherited viewpoints that ordinarily lead to varying conclusions, even incommensurable ones, and to which a dogmatic relativism assigns equivalent value.

Moving from physics to preaching, we could likewise say there is no universal discourse regarding preaching. This is something any pastor or professor who follows the homiletical literature, even from afar, knows well. Nevertheless, within the known universe of preaching, certain traditional points of view, even "fixed stars," orient either oneself or the discipline of homiletics, to the purposes, tasks, and means of preaching. It behooves preachers to know the stars by which they are guided in making judgments about their sermons. Some would claim that none of these points of view can be exclusive of the others; they are simply different ways of viewing the phenomenon or practice of preaching. In this sense, they are all arbitrarily chosen and relative descriptions of equivalent value, thereby giving the "whatever works" or the "anything goes" approaches to preaching something close to hermeneutical respectability. Generally, however, some normative claim is usually assumed or made that the adopted frame of reference, while not exclusive, is superior to its competitors–at least for certain purposes.

Three competing frames of reference currently inform homiletics. By "homiletics," from the German *Homiletik*, a discipline is designated that refers to sustained academic reflection on the practice of preaching.[6] The most venerable frame of reference for this reflection, at least in the Anglo-American tradition, is rhetoric, which has proven dominant since the Scottish Enlightenment. Over the last thirty years, poetics has emerged to challenge quite successfully the hegemony of rhetoric in homiletical theory. The third frame of reference, which has traditionally, but not exclusively, been given more prominence in German-language than in North American homiletics, is explicitly theological, and it is the frame of reference privileged in this book.

Rhetoric, poetics, and theology can each lay historical and homiletical claim to partnership with preaching. Because each of these three frameworks can mean so many things, it may be helpful to indicate some distinctions. For example, one tendency among some homiletical theorists is to expand the meaning of rhetoric from the study of "the available means of persuasion,"[7] principally in oral discourse, to embrace more broadly "effective text production, text interpretation, and text analysis."[8] In this understanding, rhetoric includes hermeneutics, literary criticism, and even poetics. Similarly, one homiletical theorist broadens the meaning of poetics from a theory of aesthetics or artistic production that treats the formal properties of literary texts to "the character of our articulation of reality as it arises from our historically conditioned imaginative construction of the world."[9] Here poetics has been broadly transposed into general hermeneutics and, if the essay from which this quote is taken is any indication, perhaps rhetoric as well. For the purposes of this book, I hug rather more closely to the classic meanings of rhetoric and poetics, not simply for the pedagogical and topological purposes of presentation, but because the more classic meanings and uses of rhetoric and poetics are vigorously–sometimes rigorously–alive in the "rules of art" commended to preachers.

The term "theology" is not found in the Bible, but first appears in Plato's *Republic* in order to designate those myths that record the words of the gods. "Theologians," are originally the poets who interpret these myths through allegory and typology. Later, Aristotle employs the word "theology" to distinguish and devalue it from philosophical science. In a kind of "demythologization," Aristotle also coins the adjective "theological" in order to refer to the science that treats the first cause, *theos* or God, the unmoved mover and origin of all things. Over time, the word "theology" began to designate the science of first principles, so that eventually it came to refer to the discourse of the philosophers as distinct from the poets. Clement of Alexandria (c. 150) was the first church father to use the word "theology," in part to designate the knowledge of eternal truth. Although Clement introduced the term into Christian vocabulary, it was Origen (c. 185–c. 254) who sharpened it as reflection on the saving mystery of the Word and on the relation of the Father and the Son.[10]

The Christian tradition has also understood "theology" as "Word of God," in the sense of "coming from God" or "by God." Dionysius the Pseudo-Aereopagite (ca. 500), among other writers in the patristic period, uses the term "theology" to refer to scripture, and therefore understands their human authors as "theologians."[11] In addition, "theology," or more precisely, "theologies," are the words, that is, praises, Christians address to God.[12] "It is indeed a traditional dictum in Eastern Christianity that the true theologian is the person who prays."[13] Furthermore, "theology" can be taken in the sense of our talk about God, based on the Word of God encountered in scripture.[14] In this sense, the "theologian" is one who speaks of God or of divine things, God's spokesperson. Thus, the Christian tradition understands "theology" in three distinct ways: as "words from God," as "words to God," and as "words about God."

When we pray to God and when we witness to God, we are theologians in the proper and primary sense. Preaching, whether the proclaiming "of God" or as witness "to God" therefore counts as theology, but so is the subsequent reflection "about God" that continually arises from this announcement and witness.[15] It is thus one of the tasks of "academic theology," as practiced within the Christian tradition since the founding of the medieval universities, to think "about God" systematically in reference to scripture, to prayer, and to preaching. The point of this stepping back from these more primary forms of theology is not some kind of neutral disengagement from them, but rather to understand and test how our prayers and our preaching may be faithful and fitting to the Christian message or gospel "in accordance with the scriptures" (1 Cor. 15:3–4). Preaching and theology are thus inescapable partners. Since preaching funds academic theology, both by generating constructive knowledge through participatory practice and by providing data for critical testing, and since academic theology serves as both a coach and critic for preaching, academic theology and preaching may be said to be, in a positive sense, completely codependent on each other.

For this reason, I argue that a particular theological frame of reference, honoring the speaking God of scripture as the ultimate Agent of preaching, is necessary and primary both for a proper understanding of preaching as a Christian practice as well as for the vitality and even "progress" of academic or systematic theology. I recognize, as I hope my readers do, that this is not the only perspective on preaching or on theology known to the Christian tradition. It grows out of specific communities where the proclamation of the Word is taken as one of the marks of the true church,[16] and where systematic theologies have as one of their primary aims the assistance of preachers in their weekly task of sermon preparation and scriptural exposition. I draw heavily in this book on theologies that take their orientation from the concept of the Word of God in relation to the task of preaching. I therefore resist homiletical proposals that lop off a theological frame of reference, deem it as only an "option" among possible points of view, or subordinate its comprehensive claims and concerns to either rhetoric or poetics taken as sovereign. Nevertheless, I also argue *on theological grounds* for the validity and assistance afforded by rhetoric and poetics with respect to preaching, amid reactive assertions of their irrelevance.[17] These distinct, but related, points of view contribute a unique angle of vision to our understanding of preaching. By better understanding how influential rhetoricians and narrative artists come to the task of preaching from their distinctive frames of reference, we can also better assess why theology still matters so decisively for this practice—and why preaching still matters so decisively for theology. To those who may have lost or never found their theological frame of reference, I invite you to join me in "going to look for it."

1

PREACHING AS THE WORD OF GOD

In his Beecher Lectures, Gardner Taylor confesses that "measured by almost any gauge preaching is a presumptuous business."[1] Taylor goes on to say that if preaching "does not have some sanctions beyond human reckoning, then it is indeed, rash and audacious for one person to dare to stand up before or among other people and declare that he or she brings from the Eternal God a message." Who, we might ask, would be presumptuous enough to engage in this activity, if in fact it were not commanded by God? Yet isn't Taylor's claim that preaching has "some sanctions beyond human reckoning" itself presumptuous? And does not this sanctioning of preaching by an appeal to sources "beyond human reckoning" make preaching more, not less, presumptuous? Indeed, what could be more presumptuous, if not dangerous, than to regard preaching itself as "Word of God"?

Danger notwithstanding, this Christian claim comes to sharpest theological expression during the Reformation era. In 1566, Heinrich Bullinger (1504–1575), Huldrych Zwingli's (1484–1531) successor in Zürich, published a Confession of Faith. With the possible exception of the Heidelberg Catechism, this document, now known as the Second Helvetic Confession, is the most widely adopted and authoritative of all continental Reformed confessions.[2] In a famous marginal heading, the Confession declares, "The Preaching of the Word of God Is the

7

Word of God [*Praedicatio verbi Dei est verbum Dei*]" (5.004). This may well be the most influential theological sentence ever written about preaching. Before unpacking further its meaning and implications, it is important to note that since the pontificate of Paul VI, who reigned from 1963–1978 in the wake of Vatican II, the Roman Church has also issued a number of official statements on preaching which bring that communion's positions on the theology of preaching much closer to those of the Reformation.[3] Nevertheless, what a risk the Western Church takes by its high valuation of preaching! If Gerhard Ebeling (1912–2001) is correct "that man is by nature a fanatic,"[4] then it must also be acknowledged that the history of preaching provides confirmation of this thesis in the terrible events at Münster in 1530, at Salem in the 1690s, and continuing down into our own time as the names of Jonestown (1978) and Waco (1993) recall. Mayhem and even murder can result whenever preachers speak as though the Word of God were on their lips. Precisely to protect the church and its witness from fanaticism and other departures from the gospel, both Rome and magisterial Protestantism have historically hedged both scripture-reading and preaching with liturgical and legal (canonical, confessional, or constitutional) controls. Such controls do not guarantee fidelity to the gospel, as renewal and reformatory movements often demonstrate, but they no doubt restrain unconscionable excesses that might otherwise occur.

From the more skeptical traditions of the theological left, which have greatly influenced modern theology since Immanuel Kant (1724–1804), the answer to the question, "Who speaks for God?," might be, "No one!," as one of my Unitarian classmates once declared in a sermon (thereby indicating that even his "anti-dogmatic" dogmatic claim could not itself be taken for gospel truth.) Perhaps, more generously, the Enlightenment would answer the question, "Who speaks for God?," by replying, "Only those for whom 'God' signifies a reality that corresponds to universally accepted canons of rationality." Granting that such canons actually exist, a questioned assumption in our postmodern period, no one might be able to speak for God simply on logical grounds. For example, Ebeling discusses the possibility that the concept "Word of God" is self-contradictory. "'Word,'" he writes, "exists for us only as human word." Therefore, he asks, "Do we not in all honesty have to choose between meaning 'word' but then not claiming God for it, or meaning 'God' but then not ascribing a word to him?"[5] If the term "Word of God" enshrines a non sequitur, then preaching understood as "Word of God" would simply be nonsense squared.

Can preaching, then, ever be styled "Word of God"? If, historically, Western Christianity risks fueling fanaticism by retaining such a claim, the Enlightenment finds it an intolerable formula of dogmatic illusion and delusion. In light of these difficulties, it is significant to find a theologian such as Rebecca Chopp calling for "a reconsideration of proclamation and the Word."[6] As a feminist theologian, she is perhaps more aware than many of the tragic consequences of both fanaticism and dogmatism for the life of our churches. Thus, her call for a feminist engagement with the Protestant "Word of God" tradition is a significant development in recent theology. She writes,

> Historically, Protestant theologies placed the Word at the center of their reflection, understanding theology's purpose to relate God's Word to the world. But contemporary Protestant theology contains hardly any reflection on the theological status of proclamation or of the Word, an absence which perhaps contributes to the general malaise in Protestant theology or to what Jürgen Moltmann has called the dual crisis of identity and relevance. If Protestant theology has any identity to find, or more to my interests, if Protestant theology has anything to contribute to Christian theology and Christianity in general, such a contribution requires a reconsideration of proclamation and the Word. Is the identity of Protestant theology and Protestant Christianity secured only through institutional affiliation, or *is there some meaning in the Reformation insistence that God is revealed, experienced, and present in the proclaimed Word?*[7]

To Chopp's question, many Christians continue to answer, "Yes." Thinking about this question is one of the tasks of this book.

When we ask in what sense "God is revealed, experienced, and present in the proclaimed Word," we try to think critically in order to test a claim that historically has characterized Protestant understandings of preaching. Without such thinking and testing, faith and its practices can degenerate into fanaticism or delusion. Christians are called to neither. Both are excluded by the command of Jesus Christ to "love the Lord your God with all your heart, and with all your soul, and with all your might" [Deut. 6:5] and "your neighbor as yourself" [Lev. 19:18] (Mt. 22:37–39 //). While preaching is not necessarily coterminous with dogmatics or systematic theology, nevertheless, in the words of Gerhard Ebeling, "Theology is necessary in order to make preaching as hard for the preacher as it has to be."[8] Conversely, "Preaching is necessary to make theology as hard for the theologian as it has to be."[9] Preaching is too dangerous to be undertaken glibly or lightly without thinking about what you are saying and doing. Likewise, theology is too dangerous to be so undertaken apart from prayer, scripture, and the practice of preaching.

Disputed Questions

In *Not Every Spirit: A Dogmatics of Christian Disbelief,* Christopher Morse organizes his reflections on the doctrine of the "Word of God" with reference to six dimensions of Christian teaching on this topic.[10] These six dimensions are distilled from or suggested by 2 Corinthians 4:6, where Paul writes, "For it is the God who said, 'Let light shine out of darkness,' who has shone in our hearts to give the light of the knowledge of the glory of God in the face of Jesus Christ."

First, Paul makes the claim that God speaks: "It is the God who said..." The God of Christian faith is the speaking God. The God whose thoughts are not our thoughts and whose ways are not our ways (cf. Isa. 55:8) is nevertheless the God who "spoke to our ancestors in many and various ways by the prophets, but in these last days...has spoken to us by a Son" (Heb. 1:1–2).

How are we to understand this claim? Does God speak in Hebrew or in Greek? Does God have a mouth, a tongue, and some vocal chords? When we say, "God speaks," are *we* speaking univocally, analogically, symbolically, or metaphorically? When we hear, "Thus, says the Lord!," is such talk simply human hubris, projecting on to the canopy of transcendence a preacher's subjective states or wishes? As Morse observes, "Not only prophets and saints, but also the psychotic and the drugged, report hearing voices from God."[11] In the words of Lily Tomlin's quip, "Whenever we talk to God, we call it prayer. But when God talks to us, we call it schizophrenia." If Paul is right that God speaks, then we need to become clear not only about what we mean by this claim but "what a faithful affirmation that God speaks does *not* mean."[12]

Second, not only does God speak, but God speaks through scripture. Paul identifies the speaking God with the One who said, "Let light shine out of darkness," melding Genesis 1:3a and Isaiah 9:2b. That God speaks through the holy scriptures is common to Christian teaching, whether Eastern or Western, both Roman Catholic and Protestant.[13]

Nevertheless, this common claim raises some uncommon difficulties, as Morse again notes. For example, doesn't the identification of the Word of God with the Bible run the risk of reification, that is, of making God into a thing or an object, namely, a book? In this case, the Bible functions as a sort of linguistic golden calf. Moreover, is the claim that God speaks through scripture an exclusive one? Does God only speak through the presently accepted canonical books of the Christian Bible? Could we not read other inspired books in public worship in the expectation that through them God will speak to us? Why not supplement the Bible with a feminist collection of writings as Rosemary Ruether once urged?[14] Why not create a "new" New Testament, incorporating gnostic writings and other gospels, and excising apocalyptic elements, as Robert Funk (1926–2005) proposed?[15] Is God's speaking really confined to something as parochial as the ecclesial canon of the Christian scriptures? Confronted as we are by such contemporary constructs and phenomena as weapons of mass destruction, stem-cell research and cloning, growing evidence of extraterrestrial life forms, not to mention pervasive religious and cultural pluralism, is not the God of our Bible, like Baal of old, now rendered silent by all these developments?

Third, God's Word for Paul is not dead, but alive; not impotent, but powerful; God's Word is God's act. God's Word, that commanded "the Light" to come forth, accomplishes God's will.[16] Of this Word, the New Testament says that it "is at work" (1 Thess. 2:13); that it can "spread rapidly" (2 Thess. 3.1); "increases" (Acts 6:7; 12:4 et al.); and, "bears fruit" (Col. 1:6). Moreover, it "endures forever" (1 Pet. 1:25, alluding to Isa. 40:8).[17] God's Word "is not merely descriptive but causal (Jer. 1:1–10; Heb. 4:12–13)."[18] Thus, God's Word is more than simply an "informative utterance." To recall the term used by linguistic philosophers, God's Word is a "performative utterance," that is, a "speech act." God's Word does not simply describe an already existing state of affairs we might know on grounds other than God's Word. Rather, God's Word creates, institutes, and accomplishes a new state of affairs.

Here, many more theological questions arise for our thinking and testing. What does it mean to say "God acts"? More particularly, what does it mean to say "God acts linguistically," that is, through language? Does God's active Word disrupt or violate the laws of nature, or the laws of nature as we know them? Rudolf Bultmann (1884–1976), for example, who held to a doctrine of the Word of God, denied that this Word, when interpreted for existence in the event of proclamation, would contest reality descriptions based on the scientific method.[19] Moreover, what does God's Word do anyway? Does God's Word act in history to remove injustice and oppression? When news came that the United States Supreme Court had ruled bus segregation unconstitutional, the cry, "God Almighty has spoken from Washington!" was actually heard in a Montgomery courtroom. Will God have spoken yet again from Washington, if Roe v. Wade is overturned? Did the Word of God overthrow apartheid in South Africa; topple Communism in Eastern Europe; stamp out black slavery in the United States? If so, are we saying that God's active Word, which brings about a new state of affairs is publicly accessible, historically demonstrable, or empirically evident with a little honest effort?

Fourth, Paul speaks of the God "who has shone in our hearts." In classic Reformed theology, the external Word of God which encounters us through the Holy Scriptures, when read or proclaimed, is said to be confirmed by the "inner illumination" of the Holy Spirit. This is the dogmatic reason why many Reformed liturgies offer a prayer for illumination by the Holy Spirit before the reading or expounding of the scriptures. The Reformed tradition holds that ordinarily there is never an internal witness to the Word of God without the accompanying witness of the external Word of God.[20] Conversely, therefore, "there is no Word of God from without that is not confirmed from within by the Holy Spirit."[21] We may take this as a paraphrase of Paul's claim that "no one can say 'Jesus is Lord' except by the Holy Spirit" (1 Cor. 12:3). Naked appeals either to one's own experience apart from the external Word, or to the external Word apart from the inner witness of the Spirit, both miss the mark. Perhaps that is why so many Christians are talking past each other as they debate disputed questions in the church today.

If God the Holy Spirit confirms the Word of God read and proclaimed, then what role, if any, does the preacher play in the event of God's Word? Can preachers evoke or confirm the Word of God? Do they make the Word of God "come alive"? Do they "bring it home"? Can they get in the way of this Word–or nullify it? If the answer to these questions is ultimately no, then isn't today's homiletical preoccupation with hermeneutics, rhetoric, and poetics, really a well-meaning but ultimately futile, if not blasphemous, attempt to usurp the work of the Holy Spirit?[22] If only the Holy Spirit confirms the external Word of God, then why are we taking or teaching courses in preaching and homiletics?[23]

Fifth, God's Word gives "the light of the knowledge of the glory of God." The God who speaks, and who speaks through the Holy Scriptures, acting both externally as Speaker and internally as Illuminator, brings us the knowledge of his glory. Thus, all talk of and about God in the Christian context presupposes revelation. God's Word reveals God's glory. God's Word conveys knowledge of God.

But what form does this knowledge of God take? If the knowledge of God's glory comes to us through the Holy Scriptures, does it not thereby necessarily occur in such forms as historical accounts, as yesterday's liberals and today's evangelical conservatives like to insist; or through mythological frameworks and motifs, as Bultmann claims; or, more fashionably today, through evocative parables, realistic stories, or narrative plots, as some homiletical theorists claim? But what kind of knowledge does such history, myth, parable, or narrative convey? Is knowledge of God akin to that of character identity as portrayed by novelists? Or, is the knowledge of God conveyed by propositions of a cognitive sort, so that God's Word is essentially a collection of facts culled from the Bible, as Charles Hodge (1797–1878) might say?[24] Or, is knowledge of God more mystical, personal, or existential, deeply connected to our self-understanding? Does knowledge of God conveyed by God's Word aim to inform us–or to transform us?

Sixth, Paul claims that the knowledge of God communicated by the Word of God comes to focus "in the face of Jesus Christ." In this way, the Christian tradition comes to identify Jesus Christ as the Word of God, the Eternal Logos, who at a particular time and place became a real human being.

But in a world of many religions, and many far more ancient than Christianity, does not such a claim represent intolerance? Is the claim that God speaks in Jesus Christ an exclusive claim? Does it mean that God is not, or cannot be, known apart from or independently of Jesus Christ? If the answer to that question is yes, then doesn't this answer represent a missionary and Western imperialism at variance with the love commandment of Jesus himself? To use "Logos language," although we could substitute the "Sophia language" with which it is closely connected (cf. 1 Cor. 1:24; 1:30; Col. 2:3), is the Logos enfleshed only in Jesus? Could the Logos or divine Sophia enfleshed in Jesus also be enfleshed in other religions, or in other religious personalities, who, like Jesus, bear the Word and Wisdom of God? To what degree should Christian preaching of the Word of God lead our congregations to confess Jesus Christ? "Is the face of Jesus Christ the only face of God?"[25]

God speaks. God speaks through scripture. God's Word accomplishes God's will. God's external Word is confirmed by the inner illumination of the Holy Spirit. God's Word conveys knowledge of God. This knowledge of God is found "in the face of Jesus Christ." However presumptuous or audacious these claims may seem, they are not peripheral but central to the Christian message, and, therefore to its proclamation. They become intensified whenever, as at the Reformation and in twentieth-century theologies of the Word, they become linked to the practice of preaching. If God speaks through the scriptures to convey and accomplish God's will, then God also speaks and so acts when those same scriptures are truly expounded and enacted in sermon and sacrament.

The Threefold Word of God

In the New Testament, the term "Word of God" (*logos tou theou*) is used to denote both Jesus Christ (Rev. 19:13, cf. Jn. 1:1, 14; 1 Jn. 1:1) and the message of, or the witness to, Jesus Christ, that we also call "the gospel" or "the kerygma" (see 1 Thess. 2:13; 1 Cor. 14:36; 2 Cor. 2:17; 4:2; Acts 4:29,31; Rev. 1:9; 3:8, etc.). If it is true Jesus never begins his own preaching or teaching with the prophetic words, "Thus says the Lord," that is probably because the Gospel writers understood Jesus as himself God's Word. As the Book of Hebrews puts it, "God spoke to our ancestors in many and various ways by the prophets; but in these last days...has spoken to us by a Son" (1:1–2). *Deus dixit.* God has spoken. Jesus Christ is the Word from on high who "lived among us." But we only know this claim through the witness to Jesus Christ that we call the holy scriptures, especially when this apostolic and prophetic witness is rereleased for us in church proclamation. There is thus a threefold form by which the one Word of God comes into the world and all the way down to the likes of us: The Logos–enfleshed in Jesus Christ, attested in scripture, and proclaimed today in sermon and sacrament. The relationship between these three forms of the one Word of God, that is the Word Incarnate, written, and proclaimed is expounded in the first chapter of the Second Helvetic Confession.[26]

The Word of God and God

Three times in as many paragraphs, the Second Helvetic Confession declares that scripture is "the Word of God" (5.001, 5.003). If we ask on what grounds, we find no mention of "the inspiration of the recording process" or "the providential preservation of the text from impurity" as in the later Westminster Confession.[27] Rather, the Second Helvetic Confession gives this initial reason why scripture is to be taken as the Word of God: "For [*Nam/Denn*, introducing an explanation] God himself spoke to the fathers, prophets, apostles, and still speaks to us through [*per*] the Holy Scriptures" (5.001; cf. 5.059, "*viva vox Domini*").

Here, God is understood as Speaker. God is the speaking God. The God who once addressed human beings "still speaks to us."

Before there were any holy scriptures, there was the God who said, "Let there be light." Similarly, long before there was what we call "the New Testament," there was Emmanuel–God with us. So according to the Book of Hebrews, "God…in these last days…has spoken to us by a Son" (1:1–2). The God of Christian faith, the God of whom the holy scriptures tell is God the Speaker, whose speech or Word expresses his will.

The Word of God and Scripture

If God's Word belongs to God before it is recorded or attested in scripture, then God's Word, for Bullinger, is never automatically or mechanically in one-to-one correspondence with Bible verses printed on a page.[28] The scriptures are regarded *as* the Word of God only in the sense that this Word occurs *through* them. Scripture is thus termed "God's Word" because it is the *instrument* or the *medium* through which God addresses us. In making the distinction between the Divine Speaker and the means or instrument of his speaking to us, Bullinger honors the Creator-creature distinction in the event of God's self-revelation. The scriptures are not God. Composed in human words, they are the instrument by which God communicates his Word, that is, his will and intention.[29]

Among the functions of scripture identified by the Second Helvetic Confession is "the confirmation of doctrines" (5.003). Therefore, in confirming the doctrine that scripture is the Word of God, Bullinger appeals to scripture. Four proof texts are cited:

1. We also constantly give thanks to God for this, that when you received the word of God that you heard from us, you accepted it not as a human word but as what it really is, God's word, which is also at work in you believers. (1 Thess. 2:13)

2. "Very truly, I tell you, whoever receives one whom I send receives me; and whoever receives me receives him who sent me." (Jn. 13:20)

3. "…for it is not you who speak, but the Spirit of your Father speaking through you." (Mt. 10:20)

4. "Whoever listens to you listens to me, and whoever rejects you rejects me, and whoever rejects me rejects the one who sent me." (Lk 10:16)

Taken together, these four passages synoptically indicate that what Paul calls "the word of God" in 1 Thessalonians 2:13 is actually human speech that, without ceasing to be human speech, is also heard by its listeners as address from the Triune God, through the persons of the Father, Son, and Holy Spirit.[30] Scripture is the record or rhetorical artifact witnessing to such previous speaking and hearing. In this witnessing capacity, scripture becomes the means by which God is revealed as the speaking God. Only in this witnessing capacity, does scripture show itself as the written Word of God. In this utterly human witness and utterly creaturely form the living God is confessed as speaking to us today. In this connection, Edward A. Dowey (1918–2003) comments that for Bullinger "the Bible is not presented as primarily an ancient deposit of faith, but as instrumental to the present work of the Spirit in the church."[31] For this reason, God's Word or Jesus Christ is not only a past historical event of some 2000 years ago. God's Word is not trapped in the first century A.D. or confined to the biological life span of the historical Jesus. Rather, God's Word is continually taking flesh among us whenever and wherever the message or good news of Jesus Christ is proclaimed in the power of the Holy Spirit.

Yet, even if this is the case, why do we specifically need preaching? Why can't the scriptures simply be read, or chanted, or studied by the church, if in fact, they are the means through which God speaks to us today? If the scriptures so sovereignly reveal the will and way of God, why interpose another layer of human witness over that of the scriptures? Doesn't preaching simply obscure the clarity of God's Word as it comes to us through this original or primary witness? This is a recurring question in the history of the church that has surfaced with surprising regularity and variety as witness the old dispute between Puritans and Anglicans over the necessity of preaching in the liturgical assembly, in the debates between fundamentalists and modernists over the authority of scripture, and, more recently, in the claims of postliberalism that "the gospel narrative" as a "realistic" one has the inherent power to reveal the identity and, hence, presence of Jesus Christ.

The Word of God and Preaching

As we have noted, Bullinger identifies scripture as Word of God because it is the instrument of the Divine Speaker and not because there is a one-to-one correspondence between the literary or rhetorical artifact we call the Bible and the Actor or Agent of "God the Speaker." Bearing in mind this distinction, in what sense can preaching be taken as "Word of God"?

First, what do we mean by preaching? When Bullinger claims that "the preaching of the Word of God is the Word of God," the term translated here as "preaching" (Lat. *predicatio*; Ger. *Predigt*) generally can refer to the pulpit exposition of the holy scriptures. Indeed, this is clearly what the context of the Confession has in mind, for Bullinger states explicitly, "Wherefore when this Word of God is now preached in the church by preachers lawfully called, we believe that the very Word of God is proclaimed, and received by the faithful; and that neither any other Word of God is to be invented nor is to be expected from heaven" (5.004).

Edward Dowey, canvassing Bullinger's discussion in chapters one, thirteen, fourteen, and especially eighteen of the Confession, finds:

> almost synonymous use of preaching (as the sermon ...), teaching ..., doctrine ..., exposition of Scripture ..., and various other expressions. Whatever the precise form, preaching is the verbal communication or proclamation (*annunciare*, ...) of the Gospel and appears as a middle term or means (*mediante praedicante evangelii*, ...) between Christ and Faith. It is an 'outward' means of the Spirit's 'inward' work....At its center preaching is the exercise of the power of the keys or absolution..., and it embraces also exhortation, comfort, and discipline....Preaching, thus conceived, is the primary task of the ministry and the ordinary means by which the Spirit brings about and nourishes all aspects of faith in the believer.[32]

Two comments on this comprehensive definition of preaching are warranted.

First, preaching is not restricted to, but does include, pulpit discourse. In its broadest sense preaching is everything the church says and does in proclaiming the gospel. As a multidimensional practice, preaching embraces pastoral care, catechesis, and church discipline. Thus in its broadest sense, preaching here is more than sermonic discourse; it is the comprehensive proclamation and announcement of the Christian message in word and act.

Despite this expansive definition of preaching, Bullinger does restrict its practice to the official witness of those duly charged with specific responsibility for the ministry of the Word. While Bullinger holds, with Martin Luther (1483–1546) and John Calvin (1509–1564), that all Christians are priests and are therefore called to the work of intercessory prayer, he denies, over against Anabaptism, that all Christians are ministers of the Word (5.153). Here, we see an ecclesiological concern that preaching not be undertaken by self-appointment, the potential gateway to unaccountable authority and fanatical disorder, but rather only by those "lawfully called"

(5.004). Today, this claim is again disputed as the entrepreneurial and charismatic patterns of emerging renewal movements, following those of an earlier pietism and revivalism, together with economic pressures on small congregations, challenge both the "clerical model" of leadership and the requirement of an educated ministry trained in the traditions of academic theology.

Nevertheless, Bullinger does not make his confessional claim, "The Preaching of the Word of God is the Word of God" (5.004), on the basis of the intrinsic power of the church or its officers. Bullinger does *not* say that "preaching is the Word of God," and he is not saying "to encounter preaching is to encounter God" as William H. Willimon mistranslates.[33] Such claims can only be affirmed under very specific conditions. Otherwise, they could be taken to mean that anything a preacher or minister says in his or her official capacity is to be identified as such with the living voice of God. That would represent hierarchical prelacy in the worst sense!

Preaching is the Word of God if, and only if, it preaches the Word of God, that is, the scriptures as witnesses to the will and way of God. If what I say in my official capacity as a minister, whether in the pulpit, in the counseling session, or in a business meeting of the church is contrary to the Word of God, that is, the gospel of Jesus Christ witnessed in scripture, then I am not proclaiming the Word of God, but only my own opinions. One of the purposes of ordination, in the Reformed understanding, is to protect the church from a ministry that is not a servant of the Word of God, but seeks to impose on the church "another gospel" (Gal. 1:7) or another God than that attested in scripture. While Bullinger calls both preaching and scripture, "Word of God," while both preaching and scripture are the means or instruments through which God still speaks today, (and while we know this, in part, because the scriptures tell us so), all preaching must be governed and, hence, tested, by the scriptural witness. In other words, there is an instrumental equality between scripture and preaching. Both are equally instruments of the Divine Speaker, but there is not a normative equality. The scriptural Word of God must govern our preaching if that preaching is to be received as "Word of God."[34] In this capacity, scripture provides the basis and norm for further human speech that will, by the inner testimony of the Holy Spirit, be heard yet again as address from God. For this reason, the proclamation or exposition of scripture, and not simply its recitation, is also the Word of God. This exposition of scripture must itself be normed by the gospel to which the scriptures witness, a principle known as "the rule of faith and love" (5.010).

We would misunderstand the scriptural norm as to what is and is not the Word of God if we assume it is simply a matter of quoting Bible verses. After all, the devil himself can do that, as the temptation of Jesus reminds us (Mt. 4:1–11). By "the rule of faith and love," first formulated by Augustine (354–430), proper interpretation of the scriptures will accord with the summary of the Law given by our Lord (Mt. 22:37–39 //) and with the apostolic faith formatively summarized in the Apostles' Creed.[35] Whatever in the practice of the church, including its interpretation of scripture and its preaching, is congruent with the love of God and of our neighbor and consistent with the apostolic faith is scriptural. Likewise, whatever in the practice of the church, including its interpretation of scripture and its preaching, is contrary to the love of God and of our neighbor and denies the apostolic faith is unscriptural, even if, following the devil, such practice quotes scripture, chapter and verse.

Moreover, whether in regard to scripture or preaching, the "inner illumination" of the Holy Spirit, is essential for hearing and believing the Word (5.006). As Dowey elaborates, drawing on Bullinger's sermons collected under the title of *Decades*, God accommodates his speaking "to human frailty through the outer speaking and writing of the patriarchs, apostles, and the ministers of the church: the 'external' means….[T]he fruitful and effective hearing that results [is] by virtue of the Spirit's 'inner' work. The relation, thus of the 'outer' to the 'inner' again proves to be that of means to end."[36] That is to say, only God can speak God's Word. Only God can reveal God. But in so choosing to address us, God uses the utterly frail and human speech of his witnesses, including those of preachers. But the source of salvation is not our frail human words–however evocative–in their own wisdom and power. The source of our hearing, and, therefore, of our saving faith, is God, who shines in our hearts by the power of his Spirit.

Preaching and Scripture

Why do the scriptures *require* preaching? Why can't the venerable church practice of reading the scriptures within the liturgical assembly suffice for our salvation? The scriptures themselves show that their own witness to the gospel occurs not simply through their reading or recitation, but in the act of their interpretation, that is, in their exposition and application. Jesus does not simply read verses from Isaiah in the synagogue in Nazareth. He preaches: "Today this scripture has been fulfilled in your hearing" (Lk. 4:21). The Risen Lord does not simply read the scriptures on the road to Emmaus. He preaches: "Then beginning with Moses and all the prophets, he interpreted to them the things about himself in all the scriptures" (Lk. 24:27). Peter, on the Day of Pentecost, does not simply read from the Book of Joel or from the Psalms. He preaches: "Let the entire house of Israel know with certainty that God has made him both Lord and Messiah, this Jesus whom you crucified" (Acts 2:36). If the reading of scripture alone ordinarily sufficed as the saving means of grace, then the Ethiopian eunuch might still be in his chariot scratching his head over the fifty-third chapter of Isaiah. But what did the Spirit say to Philip? "'Go over to this chariot and join it.' So Philip ran up to it and heard him reading the prophet Isaiah. He asked, 'Do you understand what you are reading?' He replied, 'How can I, unless some one guides me?...About whom, may I ask you, does the prophet say this, about himself or about someone else?' Then Philip opened his mouth, and beginning with this scripture he told him the good news of Jesus" (Acts 8:30–39).

Notice that in each case the scriptures serve as the rhetorical artifact for a subsequent act of preaching. *Preaching arises, so the scriptures teach us, because the meaning of the scriptures is not obvious but requires and demands interpretation.* As Fred Craddock comments, "Interpretation is not an alien and abusive intrusion upon the Scriptures. The problem of honest and relevant interpretation of texts is imbedded within the Bible itself and is not to be looked upon as an exercise post-biblical in origin."[37] Because God wills to address us, here and now, in our time and in our place, in situations of which the original biblical writers could have no knowledge, if God's Word is to continue as an event in the present, then there must be interpretation of the holy scriptures as they themselves indicate. Since God accommodates his present speaking to ever-new situations and occasions, one form this accommodation takes is preaching. But it is preaching that interprets not simply our age and its wants, or our own opinions or wisdom, but rather the Wisdom and the Word that God has spoken to the prophets and apostles who have gone before us; that Wisdom and Word whose name is Jesus Christ. Thus, scripture norms preaching; scripture has no normative role in the church apart from its continuing interpretation in preaching.

While couched in the traditional language of Christian dogmatics and symbolics, the contemporary pertinence of the Second Helvetic Confession to theological discussion today can be seen from the provocative way it conceives of the relation between preaching and scripture.

First, the continuing existence of preaching as a church practice and the persistence in the church of the office of the preacher (under whatever name) arises from the fact that scriptures require interpretation. The perspicuity of scripture, of which the Reformation spoke, does not remove the Bible's enigmas, and it certainly does not permit the abandonment of the practice or office of preaching.

Over the centuries, critics of the church have variously portrayed the Christian scriptures as too Jewish, too anti-Jewish, too anti-scientific, too anti-democratic, too pro-slavery, too anti-gay, and, what is more, as too patriarchal and too androcentric. As a result of such allegations, various hermeneutic strategies have been urged and, sometimes, tried. For example, some Christians have abandoned the liturgical use of the Bible altogether (traditional Quakers); others have supplemented the canonical writings with newer collections (Mormons); others have excised offensive passages (Marcion, Thomas Jefferson, "German-Christians"); others have altered the scriptures periphrastically making them in turn, more "evangelical," as in *The Living Bible*, or, less "patriarchal" as in *The Inclusive Language Lectionary*. All of these strategies assume that the Bible is too alien or too dangerous to be turned loose in the church, a fear not unknown, as we have seen, to both Roman Catholicism and the magisterial Reformation.

Prodded in every generation to recognize the scandalous character of its scriptures, when measured by changing and contemporary climates of opinion, the church has generally done so while proceeding with basic trust in its canonical writings. This trustworthiness derives from the promise of God and the testimony of God's people that, in the words of Bullinger, God "still speaks to us through the Holy Scriptures." For this reason, the hermeneutical problem of the church's canonical texts is handled in Christianity by *interpreting* them through preaching and teaching, rather than by excising or otherwise supplementing them. The very presence of the preaching office in the church (as in the synagogue before it) is a hermeneutical marker that no simple or complete identification exists between the Word of God and the Bible. Only the Holy Spirit can establish the correspondence between the Word of God and the human witness. To the degree that the correspondence occurs, through the inner illumination of the Holy Spirit, it does so in the act of interpretation. The fact that the church has historically required *preachers,* and not simply lectors or cantors, is a reminder that because the Bible comes to us historically, its texts demand interpretation and not simply recitation or reiteration. In this way, the practice of preaching and the office of preaching stand as a countersign against biblicism whether in the form of theological fundamentalism, which identifies the Bible as the Word of God in a hypostatic or univocal sense, or in the form of a narratological theory that assigns to the scriptures the power to "absorb our world," or to render the identity, and, hence, presence, of Jesus Christ. By contrast, the Second Helvetic Confession strongly suggests that God never gives Godself to us, even in the scriptures, in such a way that God would become our prisoner or that preaching would become superfluous. The fact that the preaching office exists for the purpose of scriptural interpretation makes its own case against biblicism, even if the interpreter currently occupying it is a full-throated fundamentalist or a more modulated postliberal.

There is a further sense in which the practice of preaching relates to the role of scripture in the life of the church. Given Bullinger's instrumental understanding of scripture as the means through which the divine Word ordinarily addresses us, we can also draw the conclusion that only those portions of the Bible that are proclaimed and heard in the life of the church are functioning as scripture. What counts as scripture in the practice of the church is determined largely by the Bible passages that are in fact preached. Simply having an iconic, open Bible on a pulpit does not mean that it is functioning as scripture in the life of a congregation. For example, if there is no preaching or teaching from the Ten Commandments, then they disappear from our lives and our churches and from the scriptural canon itself, even if those commandments remain officially in our printed Bibles or on our courthouse walls. Large chunks of scripture are never expounded in our churches. They have simply dropped out of the canon in any concrete sense.

This was brought home to me a few years ago when a student asked me if it was permissible to preach a sermon based on the Old Testament from the main pulpit, or whether sermons based on the Old Testament should be delivered from the smaller lectern in a divided chancel. "Forgive my asking," she continued, "but in eighteen years, I have never heard a sermon from the Old Testament." No truncated Marcionite or "German-Christian" Bible was likely to be discovered in this student's church, but if there is no preaching from the Old Testament, it can cease to function formatively in our lives and churches, even if remaining officially in our Bibles. Moreover, simply reading or reciting the Old Testament cannot make up for the need to interpret it in "the face of Jesus Christ."

In this regard, certain trends prompted by of the ecumenical liturgical renewal movement are disquieting. The widespread custom that the sermon always be based on the Gospel reading, that the Psalms never be used as lections for exposition, and that no deviation from the Revised Common Lectionary be countenanced, all need to be questioned in light of the continuing need for scriptural interpretation. The scriptures themselves call forth this hermeneutical responsibility, and it is necessitated by the ever new and shifting cultural situations in which these scriptures will yet witness to the Word of God.

Our exposition of the Second Helvetic Confession as a key document for construing and assessing perennial theological perspectives on preaching makes possible a concluding paraphrase of its central claim that "the preaching of the Word of God is the Word of God." In light of our discussion, we can amplify this claim as follows: When the canonical scriptures (i.e., the Word of God written) are interpreted for the contemporary situation in light of their subject matter (i.e., the Word of God or Jesus Christ), then we can trust the divine promise and Spirit (attested by scripture) that in this ordinary, but ordered, activity of the church, God is still speaking to us today (i.e., the Word of God proclaimed).

In taking the bold step of declaring that "the preaching of the Word of God is the Word of God," Bullinger confesses that the ultimate subject matter of preaching is neither the preacher nor even the sermon, but the Word of God or Jesus Christ, to whom preacher and sermon witness in the company of the church. Nevertheless, this Word wills to address its hearers through the utterly human words of the preacher and the sermon. Without denigrating human agency, or creaturely means, including what it terms "pious eloquence" (5.150), the Second Helvetic Confession consistently holds that the ultimate Agent of the Word of God rightly preached is the divine Speaker. In this way, Bullinger's formative theology of preaching raises the issue of "double agency," or how God's act and the human act in preaching are related. In my judgment, this is a question of which many a sermon and much homiletical theory falter–dominated as they are by rhetorical or poetic frames of reference. Thus, as we proceed to explore how theology functions as a partner of preaching, we need to begin with some theological questions and perspectives that are often overlooked or, at best, assumed in many homiletical textbooks. I know of no more important question to ask than "What is the gospel, and why is it preached?" To that question, at the heart of a theological frame of reference, we now turn.

2

THE GOSPEL OF
GOD WITH US

Standard histories usually identify among precursors and contexts of Christian preaching both Israel's prophets and the synagogue's liturgy.[1] It is in the synagogue that the Torah and the prophetic books are read and expounded every Sabbath. Jesus, too, stood in the prophetic and rabbinic tradition of Israel, teaching in the synagogues and proclaiming the gospel or good news of the imminent Kingdom of God. Nevertheless, Jesus was not the first Christian preacher–and not simply because he lived and died as a Jew and not as a Christian. Rather, "the apostles and prophets" were the first "Christian" preachers in the earliest church. The Book of Ephesians speaks of the church as "the household of God, built upon the foundation of the apostles and prophets, with Christ Jesus himself as the cornerstone" (2:19b–20). That we know anything at all about Jesus and his preaching, and about his destiny as the Christ of God, is largely due to these women and men, both Jews and Gentiles, whose own words and deeds recalled those of Jesus and thereby preserved them in what became the canonical Gospels of "the New Testament." Thus, even though "Jesus came into Galilee, preaching the gospel of God" (Mk. 1:14, RSV), the same "gospel of God" for which the apostle Paul was "set apart" (Rom. 1:1), the message of the earthly Jesus and that of the subsequent apostles and prophets, while genetically related, must be materially distinguished by virtue of Jesus' destiny as the crucified and risen Lord.

The Gospel: In Hand and at Hand

The Gospel as Transmitted Tradition

What is the gospel? One answer is given in terms of transmitted tradition in Paul's first letter to the Corinthians 15:1–8:

> Now I would remind you, brothers and sisters of the good news [*to euangelion* =the gospel] that I proclaimed [*euengelisamen* = "gospeled"] to you, which you in turn received, in which you also stand, through which also you are being saved, if you hold firmly to the message [*logos*] that I proclaimed [*euengelisamen* = "gospeled"] to you–unless you have come to believe in vain. For I handed on to you as of first importance what I in turn had received: that Christ died for our sins in accordance with the scriptures, and that he was buried, and that he was raised on the third day in accordance with the scriptures, and that he appeared to Cephas, then to the twelve. Then he appeared to more than five hundred brothers and sisters at one time, most of whom are still alive, though some have died. Then he appeared to James, to all the apostles. Last of all, as to one untimely born, he appeared also to me.

Here Paul speaks of "handing over" to the Corinthians what was once "handed over" to him: the glad tiding(s) or good news concerning the death and subsequent appearances of Christ. Paul reminds us that we do not invent the gospel. It is "the gospel of God," that is, it originates with God–not with us (1 Thess. 2:2, 8, 9; 2 Cor. 11:7; Rom. 1:1, 15:16). The gospel we proclaim was "handed over" to us by the proclamation of others. We "receive" it. We "hold fast" to it. We are "being saved" by it. But we do not invent it! To belong to Christ is to "stand" within this apostolic tradition of good news.[2]

Paul characterizes this good news by the noun "gospel" and the verbal form "gospeled" so that the good news is not only "the message" proclaimed, but entails the act of proclaiming it. The gospel embraces both word and act. Paul elsewhere uses another term for this same activity, forms of the Greek verb *keryssein*, "to herald, to proclaim," (as in 2 Cor. 4:5), of which the noun is *kerygma*, meaning "proclamation" or "preaching." As with our English word preaching, so "kerygma" can refer either to the act of preaching (1 Cor. 2:4) or to the content of what is preached, if you will, the "preachment" (1 Cor. 15:12).[3] For this reason, Bultmann uses the term kerygma to identify the summaries of the gospel sprinkled throughout Paul's letters. As kerygma, the message is "authorized, prescribed proclamation, a sovereign edict."[4] What is summarized or assumed in every case is a cross-resurrection message bespeaking the destiny of Jesus Christ. In addition to 1 Corinthians 15:3–8, the New Testament offers summaries of the gospel in 1 Thessalonians 4:14; 2 Corinthians 5:15 and 13:3–4; Romans 4:25; 6:10; 8:34; 10:9; and 14:9, and the Christ-hymn of Philippians 2. These passages all summarize what has been transmitted or handed over through proclamation.[5]

Nevertheless, in Bultmann's view, and contrary to Karl Barth, "the word of proclamation is no mere report about historical incidents" or "teaching...which could simply be regarded as true without any transformation of the hearer's own existence. For the word is kerygma, personal address [*Anrede*], demand [*Forderung*], and promise [*Verheissung*], it is the very act of divine grace."[6] This word, calling for obedience to God's will and announcing God's grace, is directed to the listener's conscience (*syneidesis*, 2 Cor. 4:2; 5:11), which it presupposes, and, as such, requires from the listener a decision. Therefore, revelation is never simply information. For example, I can attend a university lecture on the topic of "love" and gain information as that topic has been researched by the social and human sciences. Yet that is a very different kind of communication from hearing someone say to me, "I love you." The latter declaration, which is analogous to the promise of the gospel, requires from me a decision, a response, whether positive or negative, that involves my existence. For Bultmann, every time, the gospel is truly preached it constitutes such an hour of decision.

Paul's use of the term kerygma, with its connotation of a pre-scribed proclamation, by definition "requires authorized messengers, *kerykes, apostoloi* [heralds, apostles] (Rom. 10:13–17)."[7] Paul pictures the preacher as a herald sent running ahead of the royal entourage to proclaim the monarch's mandates or announce the monarch's imminent arrival. Heralds do not proclaim themselves (2 Cor. 4:5), they proclaim only what their sovereign authorizes. Through the mouth of the herald the monarch speaks, much as an ambassador conveys authoritative messages from a head of state (cf. 2 Cor. 5:20). This is the way the gospel of God is transmitted, through oral proclamation announcing the destiny of Jesus Christ in relation to our own.

Does this mean the gospel of God is simply a matter of repeating or regurgitating, perhaps word for word, the kerygmatic formulations of the New Testament? Are "ambassadors for Christ" (2 Cor. 5:20) simply God's megaphones? This is the charge often made against "the herald model" of preaching.[8] Paul again proves instructive by directing our attention not only to the foundational cross-resurrection kerygma of the apostles, but to the subsequent preaching of the prophets who interpret this kerygma to the gathered church. In his study of early Christian prophecy, Thomas W. Gillespie confirms Adolf von Harnack's (1851–1930) thesis, prompted by the discovery of an early church order, the *Didache*, that "the prophets were the primary preachers of the early Christian congregations,"[9] and Gillespie further shows that prophecy was Spirit-inspired interpretation of the theological and ethical implications of the apostolic kerygma. In other words, prophetic speech was neither confined to a verbatim repetition of a kerygmatic formula, nor characterized by ecstatic and oracular speech; rather, it was an extended discourse of a sermonic kind. In contrast to the ecstatic speaking in tongues, Paul declares "those who prophesy speak to other people for their upbuilding [*oikodomeo* = edification] and encouragement [*paraklesis* = urging, exhortation] and consolation [*paramythia* = comfort, encouragement]" (1 Cor. 14:3). In this, arguably the oldest definition of Christian preaching, both *paraklesis* and *paramythia* indicate the prophet as one who is "engaged in contextual proclamation of a pastoral kind."[10] Thus, "Prophecy explicates the gospel in terms of its theological and ethical implications within the life-situation of the congregation."[11] Moreover, Gillespie argues that in 1 Corinthians 15 we have an instance of a prophetic sermon that takes for its "text" the traditional kerygma (vv. 3ff.).[12] Whatever the fate of this bold hypothesis, the general point still stands. Paul's letters to the churches invariably unpack the foundational apostolic kergyma in sustained prophetic discourse in relation to the contingencies and contexts of the particular congregations he is addressing. This is true whether he is disputing with those Corinthian prophets who deny the resurrection of the dead (1 Cor. 15:12), exhorting his beloved Philippians to look "to the interests of others" (2:4–5), or comforting the Thessalonians "that you may not grieve as others do who have no hope" (1 Thess. 4:13).

Thus, true preaching of the gospel is always Spirit-directed interpretation of the cross-resurrection kerygma, drawing out its implications and pertinence for contemporary situations. When the kerygma disappears from preaching, we are simply in the realm of moralism or advice-giving. On the other hand, when the kerygma is routinely invoked as a mantra, devoid of theological interpretation and criticism, it functions "ideologically" as a "system of propositional truths independent of the situation, a superstructure no longer relevant to praxis, to the situation, to the real questions of life."[13] As my colleague

Christiaan Beker (1922–1999) used to say, the gospel is always a word "on target." It is, to use again Bultmann's term, *Anrede*, literally a "speaking to," that authoritatively addresses and summons its hearers, but always within the context of their situation and mindful of "the real questions of life." In this hermeneutical way, the church continues to be built and rebuilt "upon the foundation of the apostles and prophets, with Christ Jesus himself as the cornerstone" (Eph. 2:20).

The Gospel as God's Invasive Inbreaking

So far, we have been examining the gospel of God as transmitted apostolic tradition "handed on" through a chain of witnesses attesting to Christ's saving significance (1 Cor. 15:1–8). In this sense, the gospel may be said to be the "word" or "message" with which the church has been "entrusted" (2 Cor. 5:19), something which is, therefore, "in hand" and which the church must "hold firmly" (1 Cor. 15:2). Nevertheless, this is only one dimension of the gospel.

In one of Paul's earliest letters, that to the churches of Galatia, the apostle emphasizes another aspect of the originating gospel, highlighting its character as something God is doing, and not simply something we are transmitting. He writes, "For I want you to know, brothers and sisters, that the gospel [*to euangelion*] that was proclaimed [*euangelisthen*, lit. "gospeled"] by me is not of human origin; for I did not receive it from a human source, nor was I taught it, but I received it through a revelation [*di apokalypseos*] of Jesus Christ" (Gal. 1:11–12). "With these words, writes J. Louis Martyn, "we are taken into the strange new world of apocalyptic."[14]

As with the Jesus of the Synoptic Gospels (e.g., Mt. 12:32; 13:47–49a; Lk. 18:28–30; cf. Mk. 10:30), so Paul's teaching and preaching assume the dualism of "two ages" dividing the world's career between the reign of evil and the reign of God, a common motif in apocalyptic eschatology. For example, Paul asks the schismatic Corinthians, "Where is the debater of this age?" (1 Cor. 1:20), before speaking of "a wisdom of this age or the rulers of this age, who are doomed to perish" (1 Cor. 2:6; cf. 2:8; 3:18). "This age" stands in contrast to the calling of the Corinthians "on whom the ends of the ages have come" (1 Cor. 10:11). According to Paul, in the destiny of Jesus as the Christ of God a decisive, indeed, cosmic event of salvation has taken place "to set us free from the present evil age" (Gal. 1:4). This cosmic act of redemption, which Jesus expects, has, for Paul, already begun. God has acted, in the destiny of Jesus as the Christ, to rescue us from the enslaving and oppressing power(s) of the present evil age.

Galatians 3:23–26 expresses this "turn of the ages" wrought by the advent of Christ: "Now before faith came, we were imprisoned and guarded under the law until faith would be revealed ["apocalypsed," *apokalyphthenai*]. Therefore the law was our disciplinarian until Christ came, so that we might be justified by faith. But now that faith has come [*elthouses*], we are no longer subject to a disciplinarian, for in Christ Jesus you are all children of God through faith." As Martyn notes, the verb *apokalyphthenai*, "to be apocalypsed," is explicated by *elthouses,* from *erchomai*, "to come on the scene." Thus, an "apocalypse" is not simply a revelation or "unveiling" of the mysterious unknown, as is typical in "apocalypses" as a literary genre; rather, Paul's language tells of God breaking onto the scene of this age to subdue the power(s) of evil. In Martyn's words, "it shows that Paul's apocalyptic theology–especially in Galatians–is focused on the motif of invasive movement from beyond."[15]

Turning from Galatians to 2 Corinthians, if we ask Paul when this invasive incursion began marking the juncture or conflict of the ages, his answer points to the death of Jesus Christ: "We are convinced that one has died for all; therefore all have died. And he died for all, so that those who live might live no longer for themselves, but for him who died and was raised for them" (2 Cor. 5:14–15). What conclusion should be drawn? "From now on, therefore, we regard no one from a human point of view [*kata sarka*, 'according to the flesh']; even though we once knew Christ from a human point of view [*kata sarka*], we know him no longer in that way" (2 Cor. 5:16). Heard in context, "From now on, therefore" is not referring to some moment of conversion, whether Paul's or others', but to the more decisive and universal turning point that "one has died for all." From that axial moment and first casualty of God's invasive action, there has come on the scene a new way of living ("no longer for themselves" [v. 15]) and a new way of knowing ("no longer according to the flesh" [v. 16]). Both are so radically opposite to "this age" (2 Cor. 4:4, NIV) that Paul, perhaps echoing Isaiah (42:9; 43:18–19; 48:6; and 65:17–18) can exclaim, "So if anyone is in Christ, there is a new creation: everything old has passed away; see, everything has become new!" (2 Cor. 5:17; cf. Gal. 6:15). God's reconciling act in Christ does not prop up or reform the old creation, it aims to overthrow it and replace it by a new one.

What is this *kata-sarka* way of knowing that has been put to death on the cross of Christ? It is a perceiving of others divorced from their destiny as beloved of God, that is, as those for whom Christ died and was raised. It is also a perceiving of Christ divorced from his destiny as the one who died and was raised for all. Hence, as Bultmann so clearly recognized, the futility of all quests for "the historical Jesus," insofar as these *kata-sarka* reconstructions proclaim as "saving" one known apart from his cross and resurrection. "So if anyone is in Christ" (2 Cor. 4:17), that is under his power and enlisted into his service, there is a new way of perceiving and proceeding, namely according to the Lord (2 Cor. 11:17), according to love (Rom. 14:15), or "according to the Spirit" (Rom. 8:4–5).

In Corinthians, Paul characterized the contrast between these antithetical ways of knowing dividing the Corinthians into two camps as "spiritual" and "unspiritual" (1 Cor. 2:6–16). But when the Corinthians attempt to demonstrate the power of their spirituality by manifestations of ecstasy (cf. 2 Cor. 5:12), while remaining in competitive patterns of communal life, their perceiving of the gospel is shown to be *kata sarka*, still bound to the dominant perspectives of the old age. This spirit, for all its exuberance, stands in opposition rather than orientation toward the love of Christ "who died for all." At the juncture of the ages, the crucial test of all our God-talk and earthly ethics, let alone our pulpit "eloquence," is not whether they demonstrate their power in ecstatic spirituality (cf. 2 Cor. 5:13), but whether they proclaim the cross of Christ as God's power to extinguish whatever prevents us from knowing and serving those in need (5:14–15). Such proclamation, in words and deeds, is a defining hallmark of authentic and apostolic ministry of the gospel.[16]

Both this ministry (2 Cor. 5:18) and its "message [lit. *logos*, 'word'] of reconciliation" (2 Cor. 5:19) have been entrusted "to us" (*hemin*, v. 18; *en hemin*, v. 19), indicating here not only Paul but also his coworkers, if not the whole church. In verse 18a, Paul redescribes the message of the redemptive event (previously stated in 2 Cor. 5:15) as an act of God, "who through Christ reconciled us to himself." Paul then explains this act in more detail as "not counting their trespasses against them" (v. 19a), which parallels his later discussion of reconciliation as the purging of sins wrought by God through the death of his Son (Rom. 5:1–11). If God's love discounts our trespasses, verse 21 immediately reminds us that this is only accomplished through divine judgment, an annihilating no, but one which God himself bears in Christ: "For our sake he [God] made him [Christ] to be sin who knew no sin, so that in him we might become the righteousness of God." Thus the word of reconciliation at the heart of Christian preaching is none other than "the word of the cross" (1 Cor. 1:18, RSV), which is "the word of life" (Phil. 2:16).

With respect to the content of the gospel we are entrusted to proclaim, several preliminary points, all of which require further interpretation, can be made on the basis Paul's discussion. First, whatever human actions led to the death of Jesus Christ, in this death God was at work to bring forth new life "for all." Second, God did not need to be reconciled to the world; it is we who stood "helplessly" mired in hostility to God; and it is God who acted in love for us "while we still were sinners" (Rom. 5:8), "while we were enemies" (Rom. 5:10), and "reconciled us to himself" (2 Cor. 5:18). Third, God did not respond to our evil with evil, to our enmity with enmity, to our lovelessness with lovelessness, or to our violence with violence. God rejected all these old-world patterns and practices by overcoming them in a sovereign love that suffered unto death–and unto new life. Fourth, the "word of reconciliation" entrusted to the church is not the conciliatory imperative, "Let's all get along!" Rather, it is the indispensable indicative proclaiming the reconciliation God has accomplished in Christ. The only basis for all pulpit promptings to "be reconciled to God" (2 Cor. 5:20) is that God has *already* "reconciled us to himself through Christ" (2 Cor. 5:18). Pleading the former without proclaiming the latter exchanges the enlivening gospel of God for the deadening moralism of a hectoring harangue.

Notice further that 2 Corinthians 5:18–19 predicates two acts of God: (1) reconciling through Christ, restated as "not counting their trespasses," and (2) giving the "ministry of reconciliation," restated as the "message [*logos*, lit. 'word'] of reconciliation." The question arises whether these two acts are sequential, as Barth maintained, or "simultaneous," that is, as two sides of one eschatological event, as Bultmann held.[17] To say that God simultaneously instituted the deed and the word of reconciliation is to claim the event of the cross and the word of the cross as soteriologically synonymous. In other words, there has never been a Jesus Christ who is savingly present apart from the proclamation of the kerygma. To state the matter positively, on the basis of this simultaneous institution by God, Jesus Christ is savingly present or "at hand" whenever the word announcing his cross and resurrection as God's act on our behalf is proclaimed. For this reason, faith in Jesus Christ and faith in the word (or kerygma or gospel) proclaiming him are, for Paul, one and the same (cf. 1 Cor. 1:21; 2:4–5; 15:2, 11, 14; Gal. 2:16; Phil. 1:27, 29; Rom. 10:14). While we cannot restrict God's saving work to the explicit proclamation of the gospel, we can affirm that in this proclamation, "God is making his appeal through us" (2 Cor. 5:20). This conviction is the basis of Paul's confidence in his apostolic ministry of the word. Heard today as God's promise to us, it renews our own confidence that "a day of salvation," anticipated by Isaiah 49:8, now dawns and is "at hand" in the ministry of the word (2 Cor. 6:2).

Thus, Paul likens his vocation not to "peddlers of God's word" (2 Cor. 2:17), but to heralds or envoys with a message from God: "So we are ambassadors for Christ, since God is making his appeal through us; we entreat you on behalf of Christ, be reconciled to God" (2 Cor. 5:20); and, "we urge you also not to accept the grace of God in vain" (6:1). Paul does not invent the gospel of God's reconciling act in Christ's cross and resurrection, and neither do we. As "ambassadors for Christ," God entrusts us with a message not of our own invention, namely, "the gospel of God." The message is to be delivered not only to the world but also to the church entrusted with it. As Paul's entreaties to the Corinthians show, the church never moves beyond its own need to hear the message of reconciliation that it bears to others. It is needed and new every morning! Through the words of his ambassadors, God is now making his appeal, uttering his own creative Word bringing forth life out of death, and thereby constituting and reconstituting cruciform communities of the new creation. These bridgeheads established by God's invasive action into a world dominated by evil are themselves held by former prisoners now impelled and constrained by the love of Christ.

Here we come to a very important point often overlooked in homiletical theory today. From the point of view of the gospel, God is not simply the topic of a sermon, "in hand" as a matter of transmitted tradition, but God is also "at hand" as the acting Subject of that preaching announcing the eschatological saving event disclosed by the cross of Jesus Christ. This is the pattern we find in Paul's letters. As Bultmann observes, the eschatological event can be predicated either of Christ or of the contemporary word proclaiming him. This is not to say that the cross-resurrection kerygma itself "suffered under Pontius Pilate, was crucified, dead, and buried"! Rather, what is meant is that with respect to their saving benefits, the event of Jesus Christ is synonymous with the event of Jesus Christ proclaimed. "As the Christ event is the eschatological event which ends the old aeon and begins the new, so the same is true of the preaching of the apostle: 'Behold now is the acceptable time; behold now is the day of salvation' (2 Cor. 6:2)."[18] Hence, "as Christ can be called the 'power' (*dynamis*) of God (1 Cor. 1:24), so also the preaching itself, the 'gospel' is 'a power of God for salvation to everyone who has faith,' (Rom. 1:16)."[19] Likewise, Paul can name Christ "our righteousness" (1 Cor. 1:30) and the gospel proclaiming him "the righteousness of

God" (Rom. 1:17).[20] By bestowing the same eschatological predicates on kerygmatic preaching that he gives to Christ, namely, "power" and "righteousness," Paul testifies to the soteriological synonymy of Christ and the kerygma.[21]

In Paul's thought, then, the apocalyptic event of the cross–God's invasive coming on the scene in power to redeem those enslaved by the present evil age–continues to be "at hand" in the proclamation and proclaimers of that event. The effecting of life and death, salvation and judgment, spreads not only from the cross of Jesus Christ, but from the proclaiming of its word on the lips and in the lives of its heralds (2 Cor. 2:14–16). As Alexandra R. Brown puts it, "Paul has located the power of the cross not simply in the past event itself but in the present Word about the event that continually re-presents it to the reader," and, we might add, hearer.[22] The word of the cross effects the same death to the construals and patterns of the old age and the resultant awakening to those of the new as the original cross-event itself. "See, now is the acceptable time; see, now is the day of salvation!" (2 Cor. 6:2).

Karl Barth: From the Words to the Word

Even as Bultmann was rediscovering in academic contexts the essentially eschatological message of the New Testament kerygma, Karl Barth, as the village parson of Safenwil, Switzerland, was forced to rethink, "What is preaching?–not How does one *do* it? But How *can* one do it?"[23] To this question, occasioned by the cultural crisis of the First World War, Barth brought an answer that literally changed the subject of homiletics. As reformulated by Barth, the subject of a sermon is nothing other than the subject matter of the Christian faith, namely, the Word of God, or God in the act and event of self-revelation. For Barth, God is not primarily a doctrine or "subject of religion" on which preachers expound. Rather, God is the Subject of a sermon; not simply as its topic, but as its *Agent.* The effectual orator in the pulpit is God. Only when God speaks is preaching real preaching, that is, proclamation of the Word of God.[24]

Within this new theological frame of reference, rhetorical considerations seemingly become mute or moot, for rhetoric cannot package or deliver the living God. Simply put, if the human words of a sermon are to become God's Word, then God must make them so. It is not in the preacher's power to speak God's Word, for the power of rhetoric is not the power of the gospel.[25] The world crisis of 1914–1918–and beyond–made clear to Barth that everything human, including our rhetoric at its best, falls under the dominion of death. Preaching, as a rhetorical act, is powerless to bring either the world or even its own words to life. Preaching can only be undertaken because God has commanded us to preach the Word, through which God has promised to raise the dead, including our words. Preaching proceeds on the basis of this divine command and promise. But as "pulpit eloquence," preaching neither possesses the new creation nor has the power to deliver it, because death circumscribes all eloquence. For this reason, Barth's colleague and early collaborator, Eduard Thurneysen (1888–1978) declares, with a nod to Friedrich Nietzsche (1844–1900), "The pulpit must be the grave of all human words…"; hence, the "first rule" of preaching: "*Keine Beredsamkeit!*" "*No eloquence!*"[26] Preaching begins where eloquence ends.

This turning point or revolution in preaching theory means that homiletics is no longer a species of rhetoric but a subfield of dogmatics. The frame of reference has axially shifted from rhetoric to theology. Given these polemics, Barth seems to drive "a stake into the heart of rhetoric."[27] While he is often taken in this way, I think it is more accurate to say that Barth stakes a dogmatic claim over rhetoric. He re-situates its perennial concerns within a theological frame of reference. What is rejected is not rhetoric, as such, but an autonomous rhetoric, theologically ungoverned, that claims for its eloquence the power to make God real for people. If we examine Barth's own lectures on homiletics given in Bonn in 1932–1933, it becomes apparent that he does attend to rhetoric. Here, Barth circles back from his original question of a decade earlier, "How *can* one preach?" to the question, "How does one *do* it?" What is new is Barth's attempt to derive this rhetorical "How," from the dogmatic "What," or, better, "Who," so that rhetoric is taken captive by the Word of God and impressed into its service.[28]

Barth's resulting homiletics rejects the sermon as a persuasive oration calling either for the decision of faith or for right conduct. Whereas Bultmann orients preaching around the term kerygma, entailing a summons to decision, Barth prefers *epangelia* (verb, *epangellomai*), widely used in the New Testament (e.g., Gal. 3:16–17; 2 Cor. 1:20; Rom 9:4) to refer to God's "promise," as something "announced," and, in Barth's view, without connoting any human decision.[29] For Barth, the only decision that finally matters is God's decision to elect creaturely humanity in Jesus Christ–and to elect the creaturely words that bear witness to this event. The purpose of preaching is to announce this good news that the scriptures promise.[30] Any "persuading" that may occur, or any "enlightening" that is a saving illumination, can only be attributed to the divine Speaker and that hearing of the Word of God wrought by the Holy Spirit.[31] Humanly speaking, preaching is an informative utterance; but, with respect to God, preaching is a performative utterance. Only God can persuasively perform the gospel and make significant to the hearer what the human herald signifies.[32]

For Barth, Jesus Christ, or God-with-us, is the Subject of all preaching.[33] Barth is not thinking of Jesus Christ as a sermonic topic, but as a sermonic Agent: "Not the word, 'Christ,' not some sort of description of Christ, but solely the event of God with us in Christ, Immanuel, God with us–this is the central point of all preaching."[34] Likewise, this event of Jesus Christ is the subject matter or ultimate context of every scriptural text. Jesus Christ is the one to whom the scriptures bear witness (Jn. 5:39), and for this reason preaching turns to them as the basis for its own witness.[35] Nevertheless, Barth rejects the rhetorical attempt to derive a subject for a sermon, other than Jesus Christ, from any particular text itself. Barth not only rejects topical preaching, whether catechetical, ethical, or occasional, but he also rejects expository preaching, if by that is meant extracting a subject or *scopus* from a pericope, which is then structured, expounded, and applied. Such textual preaching misses the true context of all scripture, namely, Jesus Christ, to whom it witnesses.[36] This kind of expository preaching represents a "bondage to the letter," a misuse of the Bible as a source rather than as a witness; it privileges the text over its context, its reference over its referent.[37] In other words, the only preaching Barth recognizes as worthy of the name is the self-proclamation of the Word of God.

But what rhetorical forms honor such preaching? For Barth, it is the expository form, but only in the sense that a sermon either follows the sequence of thought or contours of expression in the scriptural text, or it makes the text's center of gravity its own.[38] Exegeting these scriptural passages means attending to the specificity and interrelatedness of their form and content but always in light of their theological context. This enables a sermon to follow what Barth calls "the way of witness."[39] This way of witness, "the train of thought," or "distinctive movement of thought in a text," varies tremendously within the Bible.[40] Preachers, therefore, should "construct the corpus of the sermon in repetition of the text's own rhythm and with due regard to the proportions discerned by exegesis."[41] Preachers should honor this variety in scripture and never compose sermons according to some predetermined rhetorical or poetic pattern (whether a thematic sermon with "three points and a poem," a classically constructed oration that proceeds from an introduction to a conclusion, a two-step exposition-application model, a law-gospel pattern, or a formulaic plotted sequence.) The variety of scriptural forms simply defies such prefabricated templates. On the other hand, when homiletics maintains dogmatic clarity about the ultimate subject matter of preaching, the pulpit will not flounder in biblicism, overwhelmed by the tyranny of a text.[42]

Sermon: "The Church of Jesus Christ"; Text: Romans 15:5–13

Karl Barth preached this sermon on December 10, 1933 at an Advent service for the university congregation gathered in the Schlosskirche in Bonn. The larger context of the sermon was the continuing attempt by the pro-Nazi "German Christian" party of the Evangelical (Protestant) Church to exclude Jews from church office through adopting the "Aryan paragraph" which had already barred them by law from the German civil service.[43]

Barth begins his sermon with telling, but indirect, allusions to the crisis confronting the church, and immediately progresses to the scriptural text in the space of one long sentence:

> Dear friends! The church of Jesus Christ is a company, a troop, a gathering–a "congregation"…which is held together not by common interests, nor by common blood, and not even by common opinions and convictions, but by the fact that in it again and again–not to be silenced, nor counterfeited, nor confused with any other sound–that voice rings out which we hear at the beginning and again at the end of our text: "*May the God of patience and of consolation give to you…!" May the God of hope fill you…!*" The voice which thus speaks to us,…is–in the words of the Apostle Paul–the voice of God's own Word, from which the church of Jesus Christ is born, from which she must again and again be fed, and from which alone she can live. *God* knows who God is; and in his Word he *tells* us: he is the God who gives patience, consolation, and hope. *God* knows that we need him like nothing else, and yet have no power over him; and in his Word he tells us that, he collects and pulls our thinking and willing together and to himself so that we must plead: "May *he* give to us! May *he* fill us![44]

Note here Barth's theological concentration. Instead of turning anthropologically to the Christian "virtues" of patience, consolation, and hope, a perfect possibility for a three-point exhortation in a time of crisis, Barth sees these "virtues" as identity descriptions *of God* who is the source of these charisms. One marvels at how carefully Barth attends to the divine subject matter of his text. Without mentioning the Aryan laws, the "German Christians," or the Nazi party, Barth immediately defines the church not in national or racial terms, but as the place where God's own voice rings out through the voice of the apostle, and, therefore, through the voice of the proclaimed scriptural word. This reframes the church primarily as the event of the revelation of the Word of God, rather than as an institution, particularly of the state.

Barth does not extract a central theme or proposition from the text and then develop and illustrate it through some standard form of rhetorical arrangement. Likewise, Barth does not proceed with a topical sermon on "the Jewish question." The shape of the sermon largely follows the contours of the text in its train of thought; it mentions "points," but they are not rhetorically patterned or symmetrically developed, and they scarcely break the continuing flow of the sermon. The exposition is not verse by verse or word by word in any wooden sense; in fact, Barth never cites the verse numbers when he quotes from the text. Noting that this passage from Romans begins and ends with prayer, Barth, too, begins the sermon with a prologue concluding with an invocation, and he closes his sermon with a call to prayer. Barth is clearly teaching his congregation the Christian, as opposed to Nazi, stance toward the Jews, but he does this by adherence to the scriptural word and without direct reference to any contemporary events, illustrations, stories, or anecdotes.

The heart of the sermon comes directly from what Barth presumably regards as the center of gravity of the text:

> "*Christ hath become a servant of the Circumcision for the sake of the truth of God, to confirm the promises which came unto the Fathers.*" That is: Christ belonged to the people of Israel. *This* peoples['] blood was in his veins[,] the blood of the Son of God. He took on the nature of this people when he took on humanity, not for the sake of this people, or because of the advantage of its blood and race, but for the sake of the truth, viz. for the sake of demonstrating the truthfulness and faithfulness of God…Jesus Christ became a *Jew*. He said once of himself, that to the lost sheep of the house of Israel and only to them was he sent (Mt. 15:24, cf. 10:5–6). That means for us, who are not Israel, a locked door. If it is nevertheless open, if Christ nevertheless belongs to us too as we to him, then it must once again be true in a special sense that "Christ hath received us unto the praise of God."[45]

In this context of divine election, Barth offers the only example in the entire sermon, apart from other passages of scripture. Frederick the Great (1712–1786) asked his personal physician whether he could give an irrefutable argument for the existence of God. The reply: "Your Majesty, the Jews!" In this way, Barth brings from the court of Prussia's greatest ruler testimony of the Jews as the continuing and indelible sign of God's election, something not lost on a congregation in the Third Reich.

Barth holds off on the Pauline imperative "Therefore receive one another," until expounding the indicative of Christ having "received us unto the praise of God." Here proper exposition of the indicative of divine election reverses the actual word order of the text, as the true Subject of the text, the Elect One, Jesus Christ, breaks through the language of the text:

> "As Christ has received us to the praise of God, so '*receive one another.*' That is a law which may not be evaded. That is a command, and indeed a strict and inexorable command. But the Gentiles and the Jews, all those received by Christ, who praise God for mercy's sake, fulfill this command. They receive each other. "To receive one another": that means, to see each other as Christ sees us. He sees us all as covenant-breakers, but also as those with whom God will nevertheless keep his covenant. He sees us in our pious and worldly godlessness, but also as those to whom the kingdom of God has come near. He sees us as Jews struggling with the true God and as Gentiles at peace with false gods, but he also sees us both united as "children of the living God" [Hos. 2:1].[46]

Here, we see the triumph of God's startling election of the godless that creates the church and reconfigures the customary relations between Jew and Gentile, both of whom fall far short of their calling. For Barth, the indicative of the gracious covenant always frames, precedes, and enables the imperatives of divine command, so that even in expounding the imperative, Barth uses the indicative language of God's gracious electing activity. To be seen as Christ sees us–and sees us all–is to know we are sinners *and* elected by the "God who has come near."

A Role for Rhetoric?

As our sketch of Barth's homiletical theory and the companion overview of his sermon indicate, Barth's theological framework explicitly treats the subject, the purpose, and the form of a sermon. In this way, he creates a theological rhetoric (and, perhaps, by his close attention to the unfolding thought of a given text, may even imply a theological poetics). Barth boldly shapes the principles of pulpit rhetoric by appeal to theological criteria. This is further illustrated by his notorious rejection "in principle" of typical sermon introductions.[47] Barth argues on theological grounds that introductions mistakenly suggest a "point of contact [*Anknüpfungspunkt*] for an analogue in us which can be a point of entry for the Word of God."[48] Nevertheless, Barth can also give his students rhetorical guidance on "practical, or if one will, *psychological grounds.*"[49] On these grounds, he also denounces introductions as "a waste of time"; they distract listeners and diminish the attentiveness already present when the preacher begins; and, they often use a quotation or illustration that causes listeners' minds to wander.[50] While Barth's rhetorical advice on this question, as well as others, accords with his doctrine of revelation, it does not arise from that doctrine, as such, but presumably issues from his own experience as a preacher and listener of sermons. Moreover, despite his dogmatic strictures, Barth did introduce at least some of his sermons, at times rather extensively.[51] These contradictions in Barth's own position and practice raise the question whether his theological frame of reference is adequate for homiletics. If it were, why would Barth himself deviate from it?

By the 1960s, something of a rebellion was simmering within the Barthian ranks. Hans-Dieter Bastian, for example, found Barth's dialectic between the Word and the words "irreplaceably significant and effective" in pastorally reassuring uncertain preachers about the worthiness of their weekly task.[52] Nevertheless, because Barth developed his theological framework from the standpoint of the preacher and the Bible, the hearers of the Word in their "real situation" drop out of the equation.[53] In Bastian's judgment, "The dogmatic passage, which begins with the Bible text and terminates in the sermon, consistently overlooks that spoken communication moves beyond the preacher to the hearer and that it may be examined in terms of its effects or non-effects."[54] But this is precisely the kind of rhetorical inquiry and guidance for which dogmatic theology is ill-equipped, as witness Barth's own ad hoc advice to would-be preachers. Another frame of reference, an explicitly rhetorical one, is also needed.[55]

In other words, can a theological frame of reference that honors God as the Subject, or ultimate Agent, of true preaching also provide a basis for recognizing rhetoric, and, we might add, poetics, as legitimate, if subordinate, partners?

Rudolf Bultmann and Demythologization

While holding as high a view of preaching as Barth, Bultmann still sensed more strongly as a New Testament scholar trained in the historical-critical and form-critical methods of exegesis, as well as the comparative study of ancient texts, the gap between the world picture of the Bible and the modern world picture. For Bultmann, believing in Jesus Christ as one's Lord and Savior does not require assenting to the pre-scientific cosmology presupposed by the New Testament's kerygmatic formulations. Christian faith is neither a leap out of modernity, nor a retreat from intellectual honesty. One does not have to profess the mythical frameworks and formulas of yesterday in order to proclaim and confess Jesus Christ today. Thus, the aim of Bultmann's theology is to show how the church can responsibly embrace and preach the Christian faith in a modern age whose canons of knowledge are shaped by science.[56]

This apologetic aim shows the kinship between Bultmann's thought and that of Protestant liberalism. Indeed, Bultmann learned from his liberal professors that the New Testament accounts of Jesus intertwine historical sources and traditions with mythical motifs widely found throughout the ancient Near East and Graeco-Roman world. With this discovery, liberalism sought to unbind the historical Jesus from the constrictions of myth by eliminating them from its dogmatics and preaching. These included a number of traditional tenets such as Jesus' virgin birth, vicarious atonement, and bodily resurrection. No longer handicapped by these orthodox "absurdities," liberalism was free to emphasize the incomparable personality of the historical Jesus and to join him in proclaiming a Kingdom of God progressively developing within the historical process. Faith was interpreted to mean coming under the redeeming influence of Jesus' personality as it continues to guide humankind towards the realization of God's rule in human affairs.

Bultmann believed liberalism was right to distinguish between the historical and mythical elements in the New Testament, but he went on to show where, with the best of intentions, it had gone wrong. The error was in its failure to recognize that the saving significance of Jesus is never understood in the New Testament in a historicist sense, as a fulfillment of the world's latent possibilities; rather, it understands Jesus in an eschatological sense, as one whose coming marks the final judgment or end of the world. This is expressed in the apocalyptic language of Paul's cross-resurrection message or kerygma (which the Synoptic Gospels narrate) and in the gnostic-derived concepts and framework of the Fourth Gospel, which tell of the divine Logos who comes into the world "from above." In other words, while the Jewish prophet Jesus of Nazareth, who proclaimed the Kingdom of God, is the historical presupposition of Christianity, it is the proclaimed destiny of this Jesus as crucified and risen, or God's eschatological salvation event, that is the real source and norm of Christian faith. The proclaimer (of the Kingdom) has become the proclaimed (of the church), and Christian faith only arises from this latter proclamation. Therefore, when the liberals eliminated apocalyptic and gnostic myth from their portrayals of Jesus, they unwittingly eliminated the eschatological essence of the Christian faith and, hence, the significance of Jesus for salvation.

The resultant problem was how the church could continue to proclaim its eschatological understanding of salvation when that understanding was expressed in mythological language. In Bultmann's judgment, this is not simply an academic problem but goes straight to the heart of what it means to preach the gospel. His solution, offered on behalf of preaching, was to argue for an existentialist interpretation of New Testament eschatology. The point is not to eliminate the Christ-myth that expressed Jesus saving destiny, but to translate it so that it could truly be heard as a call to authentic existence. This apologetic aim led Bultmann to advocate his famous hermeneutical program known as "demythologization."

This program assumes that the real referent of New Testament mythology is not the objectivized realities of which it literally speaks–heaven, hell, Satan, atoning sacrifice, reanimated corpses, or virgin births–but rather the understanding of existence that such mythological constructs symbolize. Thus, interpreters of the New Testament, especially preachers of the gospel, must proceed by translating outmoded cosmological categories into modern existentialist ones. For example, Paul's mythology of the cosmic powers, which the cross of Christ overcomes (1 Cor. 2:6–8; cf. Col. 2:13–15), is a way of speaking of one's bondage to the norms and patterns of this world, to the past, and to vain attempts to secure existence ever threatened by suffering and death. Hence, to be "crucified with Christ" (Gal. 2:19–20; 5:24; 6:14) means to accept God's judgment on our worldly dependence and to accept God's freedom to embrace the future without fear of death.

The word that judges our past and extinguishes our old life is simultaneously the word that recreates us; it is "the power of God unto salvation" (Rom. 1:16). Faith means entering here and now into eschatological existence, into love for our neighbors, and into the freedom of no longer being determined by the power of death. This message or "the word of the cross" (1 Cor.1:18, RSV) is thus "the word of life" (Phil. 2:16). The resurrection of Jesus is not about the resuscitation of a corpse. Such mythological language, rooted in Jewish apocalyptic, is really a way of saying that when the church proclaims the word of the cross as an appeal for authentic existence, as a call for the decision of faith, the word comes alive in its hearers and effects in them the very judgment and grace it proclaims. Jesus' resurrection is simply a first-century way of symbolizing the performative power of the Christian message in effecting in the listener the crisis of decision on behalf of authentic existence. This is why Bultmann could agree with the formulation, hurled at him in criticism, "Jesus has risen into the kerygma." The resurrection becomes saving when it is understood not simply on the literal plane as something that happened to Jesus, but as the symbol for the performative power of the proclaimed gospel awakening the rise of faith in the believer. Through his translation of cosmological categories into existentialist ones, Bultmann shows how the Christ-myth can be proclaimed and encountered today as the Christ-event. Thus, Bultmann may be reckoned among the greatest allegorical interpreters of the Bible since Origen.[57]

Sermon on Matthew 11:2–6

Bultmann preached this Advent sermon on December 11, 1938, barely a month after *Kristallnacht* in which state-sponsored terrorism of Germany's Jews led to the murder of scores, the looting of 7,500 shops, and the destruction of nearly 200 synagogues, all with no immediate protest from the leaders of the Christian churches. Bultmann preached not far from where the synagogue in Marburg lay in ruin.[58]

"Advent, the time of preparation for the Feast of the Nativity, the incarnation of the Word, confronts us with the question: How shall I receive the Lord." Following this key first sentence that identifies the existential issue at stake, Bultmann gives a quick reprise of his Advent lectionary text, focusing on John the Baptist's question regarding Jesus, "Are you he who is to come?" Taking John's question for his theme, the sermon goes on to develop it in two movements. In the first, John's question functions to reveal the world as standing outside of God's rule, and therefore under God's judgment, (but also the world as secretly longing for God's rule all the same). In the second movement of the sermon, John's question is taken as pointing to the coming of the Word of grace to the believer. We thus have a Lutheran law-gospel sermonic structure, paralleling the apocalyptic dualism of the two ages, and with the message preached as a call for the decision of faith.

These excerpts come from the first of this two-part sermon:

What is implied in the phrase "the One who is to come?"...

The question flows from Messianic hope. Hence we ourselves can ask such a question only if such a hope is alive in us. It is a question which has no meaning for all those who are satisfied with the world as it is...

[I]n so far as they are not, they live in the belief that it lies in their own hands to give the world the form which they consider right...And in this struggle which is now engaged, it is being said: what is the origin of such a hope? It originates with Israel and the Jews! With Jewish prophets and dreamers! All that is essentially foreign to our own way of life.

We must not allow ourselves to be led astray by such voices even if the picture they draw were true. But it is not true...All over the earth there has always been the living hope in return of paradise, a restoration of a golden age, when there was no pain and wrong on earth....

Christians realize that whenever any system is established in this world, however noble and lofty its aims and however much it may be inspired by the will to good, it is only possible through sheer power, and that in the process of setting up any secular order, whether nationally or internationally, human beings are sacrificed and crushed...That is the way things inevitably go in this world. But Christians refuse to be satisfied with this inevitability; they feel as a painful burden the sorrows and tears of those to whom violence is done. And if this is the unalterable way of things in this world, if the secular government is a way which always leads through blood and tears, then we conclude that this very fact is a sign that the dominion of men is never the dominion of God nor can it ever lead to the dominion of God.

Christians know above all, however, when they honestly reflect on their own personal lives, that in their own hearts the strife between good and evil is unending, that they never completely master evil, that repeatedly the power of the lie triumphs over the will to truthfulness...And Christians do not speak lightly of God because they cannot name Him without fear...They know that God is a holy God who is not mocked. They are aware that they cannot of their own will power free themselves from the toils of evil in which they are caught, and thus they look for a release and redemption from above. They look for the One who is to come.

The strong apocalyptic dualism recognized by this sermon is striking. Simply calling it "Jewish" cannot dismiss this schema since, as Bultmann takes care to point out, messianic hope is historically and geographically widespread.[59] The two ages are sharply contrasted, between the way the world works and always has, between the political order and the dominion of God, and between what God wills as right and true. While the cosmological dualism of Jewish apocalyptic is largely taken in an ethical sense, thereby enabling social and cultural criticism, it also detaches the political order as the scene of God's present activity. Bultmann employs the language of power to characterize the dominion of evil and the dominion of God–insofar as God is able to free individuals crying for redemption from the evil in which they are enmeshed.

Despite the events of recent days, there is no reference to either the Nazis or *Kristallnacht,* a restraint reinforced by totalitarian political conditions, but one which also accords with Bultmann's understanding that these features of his contemporary world are symptomatic of the perennial power of sin rather than its exceptional sources. Yet, as with Barth's sermon of five years earlier, the anti-Nazi subtext is evident. Bultmann uses the diatribe, reminiscent of Paul's letter to the Romans, to quote typical anti-Jewish propaganda, in order to refute it. Speaking of Christians as those who "feel as a painful burden the sorrows and tears of those to whom violence is done," must be taken as Bultmann's public acknowledgment of the persecution of the Jewish community.

In the second half of the sermon, in which the gospel is proclaimed, we encounter Bultmann's program of demythologization or existentialist interpretation of the kerygma:

> Is Jesus Christ in truth the One in whom all our hopes and longings find their fulfilment? Is He the one who brings in the kingdom of peace?

> We notice, first, Jesus gives no direct answer. He says neither yes nor no. He refers the questioner to things which he can see and hear; and thus the latter must himself win the answer to his own question; he must himself decide.

> But secondly, there must have been a certain state of affairs with regard to Him, arousing a certain reaction towards Him,

so that the grounds for a considered judgment were there. And what is this state of affairs? The picture is suggested in the words: "The blind see." Jesus points to His mighty deeds, which we are accustomed to call His miracles.

Miracles, properly speaking, are only those events which essentially cannot be classified within natural and historical sequences, and which in the natural historical process stand out as arousing the sentiments of wonder, astonishment and repulsion. A miracle of such a kind is–quite simply–every straightforward manifestation of Christian love, which strikes us, shames us, convulses our being, and yet quickens us.

A miracle is in fact every deed…and every event which takes place where the Spirit and mind of Christ hold sway. And where does Christ hold sway? Wherever the Word of the Gospel is preached and heard in faith. And for this reason the most important element in the answer of Jesus, and in the light of which alone the other affirmations are intelligible, is this: the poor have good news preached to them…

The poor; that is to say, those who suffer in this visible world and who wait for the world to come. And what is the message preached to them? It may be summed up in one word: freedom from the present world. The Gospel has the power to free us from the oppression of the world, because it is the message of God's grace and the forgiveness of sins. It tells us that we become free from the world and from ourselves, when we honestly and unreservedly commit ourselves to God who assures us of His grace, in the word and the person of Jesus Christ…

Those who believe in the One who is to come are lifted out of the flux of time into the transcendence of eternity; they have truth, purity, and fullness of life; as pain and death have no further power to reduce them to despair, so the evil around them and within them can no longer make them afraid. It is engulfed in the full tide of divine grace…

And just because the coming of Jesus is not merely an event taking its place in past history, but an event which spells the end of all history, for them the One who has come is always at the same time the One who is to come and will be so to the end of the world and of time.

From this excerpt, we see that the miraculous character of salvation ("the blind see"), traditionally taken as a supernatural event disrupting the laws of nature, is transposed by Bultmann into the disruptive power of the Word of God in which we personally encounter divine love and grace, even where there is no empirical evidence of its transformative power. It is in this "demythologized" sense, that Bultmann can retain the language of miracle and find its chief and true locus in the preaching of the gospel. Salvation is largely understood as freedom from the present evil age, not in the sense of political liberation, but in the sense of inward detachment "from the flux of time" so that the believer is placed in a new position, that of eternity, vis-à-vis the old age, and no longer determined therefore by its malignant power. From Bultmann's standpoint, the gospel thus affords the believer an opening, a space in the world for a decision: Shall I remain behind in an existence determined by death and disposing me to fear and despair; or, shall I cross over to an authentic existence trusting in the power of God and therefore reoriented to "truth, purity, and fullness of life"?

Conclusion

This chapter has sought to set forth "the gospel of God with us," by beginning with the earliest kerygmatic summaries in the New Testament and then by showing how two of the most important twentieth-century theologians of the Word, Karl Barth and Rudolf Bultmann, interpreted this gospel in light of the preaching task. As we shall see, Bultmann's work continues to affect contemporary academic homiletics largely through his students, who further developed the hermeneutical program of demythologization. Their work, dubbed "the New Hermeneutic" in American circles, stands in both continuity and discontinuity with Bultmann. It forms the theological impetus for "the New Homiletic" that dominated North American homiletical theory from 1970 until the closing years of the last century. Barth's work continues in current homiletical theory through the hermeneutical proposals of Hans W. Frei (1922–1988) offered under the banner of postliberalism. Here, too, we find both continuities and discontinuities with Barth himself. For this reason, I advise students of homiletics to read Barth and Bultmann for themselves if they would wish to access and assess the profound ways their work continues to influence homiletical theory.

Granting all the differences between Bultmann and Barth regarding the interpretation of the gospel, both are united in the conviction that in its proclamation God is speaking, and is, therefore, the true

Preacher of his own Word. This is the key insight of a theological frame of reference oriented to the Word of God. Only with the acknowledgment, both formally and materially, that the living God has spoken and is speaking today, are preaching and homiletical theory faithful to "the gospel of God–with us."

3

ORATORS AND POETS

Rhetorical Homiletics

In a survey of speech education in America, John Hoshor reports that "the application of the principles of rhetoric to the art of preaching may be said to have been completed by the end of the [nineteenth] century."[1] Indeed, John A. Broadus (1827–1895) decisively defined homiletics for theological education when he wrote in 1870 that "homiletics may be called a branch of rhetoric, or a kindred art," and "we must regard homiletics as rhetoric applied to this particular kind of speaking," that is, preaching.[2]

Broadus' influential formulation of homiletics as a branch of rhetoric reflects the views of George Campbell (1719–1796) and Hugh Blair (1718–1800), whose "new rhetoric" was imported into North America from Scotland, with the advent of John Witherspoon's (1723–1794) presidency at the College in Princeton.[3] Beginning about 1768, and continuing until his death, Witherspoon lectured annually on rhetoric, or to use the preferred term of the time, "eloquence," devoting one lecture of the sixteen to that of the pulpit.[4] Since their posthumous publication in 1801, these "Lectures on Eloquence" have become recognized as "the first American rhetorical treatise."[5] For Witherspoon, Campbell, and Blair, "pulpit eloquence" is a particular instance of that "eloquence" also found in forensic oratory and deliberative discourse. Indeed, the judicial bar, the legislative

49

chamber, and the Christian pulpit are the three great modern arenas of eloquence. Each of these contexts shapes its speeches to its distinctive subjects and particular ends. Homiletics, therefore, is a "species" of rhetoric, eloquence adapted for use in the pulpit.[6] As with the old rhetoric, derived ultimately from Aristotle, Cicero, and Quintilian, and concerned with identifying the available means of persuasion, so likewise the new rhetoric of the Scottish Enlightenment concerned itself with the speaker, the audience, and the speech, together with its occasion and purpose. But as Nan Johnson has noted, what made this rhetoric "new," was its adoption of the faculty psychology of John Locke (1632–1704), its extension of rhetoric to all forms of discourse, including written, and its recognition of "taste," or innate sense of beauty, on style, standards of criticism, and moral formation.[7] Without exception, Campbell, Blair, and Witherspoon all reflected on the practice of preaching in light of these rhetorical canons. Indeed, beginning with Witherspoon, homiletics in America, has generally operated within a primarily rhetorical, rather than a theological, frame of reference.

In his magisterial *Philosophy of Rhetoric* (1776), George Campbell, paraphrasing Quintilian, writes, "The word *eloquence* in its greatest latitude denotes, 'That art or talent by which the discourse is adapted to its end.'"[8] Campbell further specifies the aims or ends of public speaking; namely, to "enlighten the understanding," to "please the imagination," to "move the passions," or to "influence the will."[9] What distinguishes pulpit eloquence from that of the courtroom or the legislative chamber is not these aims common to eloquence in general, but, rather, its subject for presentation.[10] The subject of a given sermon is derived from theology whose "doctrines of religion" furnish preaching with content, always shaped for the listeners without whom there is no discourse.[11] Therefore, pulpit eloquence, mindful of its audience, packages and delivers Christian doctrine.[12]

But to what end? Campbell declares, "The primary intention of preaching is the reformation of mankind."[13] The goal of preaching is to effect a "permanent" change in the listeners at the level of motivation, "to persuade them, for the love of God, to be wise, and just, and good."[14] Hugh Blair will later put it more succinctly, "The end of all preaching is, to persuade men to become good. Every sermon, therefore, should be a persuasive oration."[15] Since this is the case, ethos considerations are vital. "The preacher himself," Blair tells us, "in order to be successful, must be a good man."[16] Witherspoon, with more Evangelical piety than Blair's Moderatism would likely allow, tells his Princeton students "that one devoted to the service of the gospel should be *really*, *visibly*, and *eminently* holy."[17] Nothing less will do if preaching is persuasion on behalf of moral reformation.

Nevertheless, even in this confident Age of Reason–and Rhetoric, doubts did surface about preaching as eloquence. George Campbell himself admits that if the aim is to "persuade him that stole to steal no more, the sensualist to forego his pleasures, and the miser his hoards, the insolent and haughty to become meek and humble, the vindictive forgiving, the cruel and unfeeling merciful and humane," then the preacher "would need to be possessed of oratory superior to human."[18] In fact, achieving such repentance through preaching "seems to bid defiance to the strongest efforts of oratorical genius."[19] Campbell further observes, citing both the Crusades against Islam and conflicts among Christians themselves, that eloquence has too often and too easily stirred up the hatred and intolerance to which human depravity disposes us. In light of this sorry record, Campbell concedes that the positive role of eloquence in motivating goodness is "the almost impossibility."[20] Speaking as a theologically informed rhetorician, Campbell is forced to recognize that the rhetorical frame of reference in which he places preaching ultimately proves inadequate for achieving the intention of this form of discourse. This conclusion has not prevented contemporary homiletic theorists from offering fresh proposals for preaching within the framework of rhetoric.

One of the features of the contemporary academic scene is the widespread revival of interest in rhetoric.[21] Just as texts on rhetorical theory can be subjected to theological analysis and assessment, so theological texts can likewise be subjected to rhetorical analysis and assessment. Such rhetorical approaches are now quite commonplace. For example, thanks to George Kennedy, among others, rhetorical criticism is now a standard feature of biblical exegesis, complementing form criticism, redaction criticism, and literary criticism.[22] Even Karl Barth's writings have not escaped rhetorical analysis, as witnessed in the work of Stephen Webb, who identifies the tropes of irony and hyperbole as characteristic of Barth's early writings.[23]

In my judgment, the current turn to rhetoric is related to the advent of postmodernism, which stands opposed to the notion of indubitable, foundational truths known on universally accepted rational grounds. Without such grounds, the adjudication of competing knowledge claims, especially within or between diverse communities, becomes more and more "politicized." That is to say, in the absence of commonly shared values and beliefs, or in the absence of universally acceptable procedures for their acknowledgment or establishment, the adjudication of reality claims now proceeds along the same lines as matters of policy or polity regarding matters that could be otherwise. Hence, rhetoric, as the study of the means of persuasion, now takes on heightened academic importance over dialectics or "the search for truth" as such.

Since the original publication in 1971 of Fred Craddock's *As One without Authority*, American homiletical theory has increasingly attended to the role of the audience in the practice of preaching.[24] Recently, heeding David Buttrick's plea for homiletics "to make up and relate to rhetoric once again,"[25] Lucy Lind Hogan and Robert Reid have coauthored *Connecting with the Congregation: Rhetoric and the Art of Preaching*.[26] This "turn to rhetoric" in the pulpit can be seen, in the American context, as a "re-turn" to homiletics' native frame of reference.

The work of Hogan and Reid, on which I focus here, has numerous parallels in German homiletics, which until recently had largely privileged a theological frame of reference. Beginning in 1968, with a seminal essay by Manfred Josuttis,[27] followed by a spate of books from Gert Otto of the University of Mainz,[28] a growing body of scholarly work in Germany has called for a thoroughly rhetorical homiletics.[29] Otto heralds this new rhetorical paradigm, as freeing homiletics from theological tutelage:

> Preaching is a rhetorical task. Therefore, homiletics is treated in connection with rhetoric. Theological reflection, exegetical or historical or systematic, has its place then within the rhetorical conceptual framework; but, theology has neither priority nor superiority. For reflection on formulated homiletical questions, rhetoric is dominant, not theology.[30]

Otto explicitly rejects deriving rhetorical rules from the propositions of systematic or dialectical theology, and he blames this Barthian approach for the "practical ineffectiveness of modern homiletics."[31] The resulting crisis will only be remedied by taking renewed responsibility for preaching as an act of public speaking.

However high or low a theology may estimate preaching, it is undeniable that "*a sermon is a speech.*"[32] Whether it takes written form or not, a sermon is composed, its thoughts arranged, and it words chosen and delivered. Rhetoric reflects upon, directs, and is informed by these practices of public speech making, especially in connection with questions of audience and occasion. Preaching is both a rhetorical art and a rhetorical act. Rhetoric, therefore, is the basic frame of reference for homiletics. How could it be otherwise? As Otto observes, preaching must deal with "the same rhetorical, communication-theoretical, and psychological problems" as any other form of public address.[33] This explains why Hogan and Reid claim, "It is only when the student and preacher understand the basics of the art of effective communication that they can explore how it is that theology affects this practice."[34] In other words, rhetoric is the constant; theology is the variable.

For their part, Hogan and Reid define rhetoric as "the study of what is persuasive in human communication, whether intentional, or simply a consequence of the human condition."[35] Following Karlyn Kohrs Campbell, they also speak further of "a rhetorical act," for example, a sermon, as an "'intentional, created, polished attempt to overcome the obstacles in a given situation with a specific audience on a given issue to achieve a particular end.'"[36] What this latter-day Campbell calls a "rhetorical act," George Campbell long ago called "eloquence." Standing in this venerable tradition, Hogan and Reid present the classic rhetorical proofs, arrangement theory, and distinctions of style, all time-tested considerations that serve persuasive discourse and, thereby, pulpit eloquence.

Since the overarching purpose of a sermon is to "move and persuade people in the congregation,"[37] ethos considerations remain as paramount for Hogan and Reid as they were for Witherspoon, Campbell, and Blair. Admitting that listeners know their preachers' "frailties" well, Hogan and Reid assert that "Christian leaders who preach the gospel have always been called to strive for personal virtue because virtue matters in the proclamation of the gospel."[38] In this regard, they quote with favor Susan Hedahl's claim that "*Who* preaches is the most essential component for the receptivity of the Gospel."[39] The notion that God's Word might be on the lips of Graham Greene's licentious "whiskey priest" or Walker Percy's "stupid preachers" is far removed from this rhetorical framework where "virtue matters."[40]

If the task of preaching is broadly understood as persuasive, then what is the subject matter of preaching? Here, Hogan and Reid are evasive or vague. They do indicate that "early Christian homilies assumed that the subject matter of the Christian message was *revealed truth* (cf. 1 Cor. 2:1–5)," but, since "the subject matter of rhetoric is the *probable* and *plausible*," they do not themselves argue for "revealed truth" as the subject matter of preaching.[41] Again, Hogan and Reid claim that Martin Luther King Jr. (1929–1968) preached "God's Word"; that in King we hear "*eloquence* in service to the gospel"; that preachers "are the instruments upon which God plays" to bring "words of judgment…comfort and release"; that "human preachers can be the instruments of God's grace in the world"; and, that preaching is 'the proclamation of the good news," either in the sense of people "talking about what God has done for them," or "doing good deeds for others."[42] Other than further indicating that "God's Word," like human words, has "power,"[43] all of these terms, "God's Word," "gospel," "grace," "good news," suggesting a theological subject matter, are sprinkled here and there without definition or discussion of where the preacher might derive their content. Moreover, apart from a cryptic reference or two, Hogan and Reid do not discuss, with respect to the preaching event, whether the sermonic subject matter exercises agency. Sometimes, they seem to suggest that the subject matter is purely a malleable symbol awaiting rhetorical manipulation or construction.[44] These theological gaps do not seem to worry our authors, because the rules of rhetoric regulate the sermon–whatever its subject matter may turn out to be.

If Hogan and Reid are rather tight-lipped about what God may be up to in a sermon, they are enthusiastic about what rhetoric can enable the human preacher to accomplish. Indeed, with reference to Martin Luther King Jr., it was through "his careful attention to words and figures of speech, and by adaptation to his audience" that his pulpit became "a place from which to stand in order to move the world. Dr. King preached and the valleys began to be filled."[45] Preachers, we are told, "can learn to take control of the preaching intention implicit in the design of a sermon."[46] We are also assured that rhetoric can equip preachers "to facilitate an *Encounter* with God/Spirit/'the Lord'" should this "kerygmatic" option be desired.[47] Our authors further tell us "in the Kerygmatic approach that the preacher emphasizes the individual's ability to have an encounter with God in the context of a community of faith."[48] In other words, what is traditionally predicated of the Holy Spirit or the event of divine revelation can be accomplished by the preacher's own arsenal of weapons furnished and sharpened by rhetoric. It is the art of eloquence, not the Holy Spirit, that leads us to the eschaton.

Unlike George Campbell, who retained, even in the Enlightenment, enough of the doctrine of human depravity to acknowledge the limitations of rhetoric, one finds no such limitations in the homiletics of Lucy Hogan and Robert Reid. The individual has the ability to encounter God; the preacher has the power to make it happen; and, the rhetorical situation of preaching is that of "a good person offering good reasons to good people."[49] However we interpret these astonishing statements, with their echoes of American Civil Religion, they do reveal that a strictly rhetorical homiletics is never theologically neutral. In this case, it appears thoroughly and confidently Pelagian, with consequences for every doctrine of the Christian faith.[50]

As with George Campbell, so with Hogan and Reid, we again reach a point where the rhetorical frame of reference is simply inadequate to address or account for the theological subject matter at the heart of preaching. This does not mean that rhetoric cannot play a role as a partner in preaching; indeed, it is difficult to see how it could be otherwise, but it does mean that whatever role rhetoric plays must find its authorization in ways that honor the theological subject matter of preaching.

Remarkably, John Quincy Adams (1767–1848), lecturing at Harvard as the first Boylston Professor of Rhetoric and Oratory, sensed this very point when he confesses that rhetoric, with respect to the pulpit, "entirely fails us."[51] He continues,

> The eloquence of the pulpit is to the science of rhetoric what this western hemisphere is to that of geography. Aristotle and Quinctilian [sic] are as incompetent to mark its boundaries, as Pausanias or Strabo to tell us the latitude of…Cape Horn. In exploring this new region, like Columbus on his first voyage to this continent, we find our magnet has deserted us. Our needle no longer points to the pole.[52]

Though not a professional theologian, this Harvard rhetorician and future President of the United States perceives that something new enters history with the advent of Christian preaching—something that makes it so unlike other forms of public address that rhetoric proves unreliable as the primary frame of reference. Rhetoric "entirely fails us." It no longer provides definitive guidance, insofar as preaching witnesses to what Karl Barth would later call "a new world, the world of God."[53]

Theology and Rhetoric

The permanent contribution of Karl Barth for homiletical theory was to retrieve the true subject of preaching, namely, the subject matter of the Christian faith, the Word of God or God-with-us, in the act and event of self-revelation. Arguably paraphrasing the Second Helvetic Confession that "The Preaching of the Word of God Is the Word of God," Barth partly defines preaching, in the first instance, as "the Word of God which [God] himself speaks, claiming for the purpose the exposition of a biblical text in free human words."[54] The God of Christian preaching is the speaking God of the scriptures. We cannot preach as if this subject matter of our preaching were at our disposal or under our control. We do not create the Creator of the gospel, and the Word of God is not a commodity we peddle (cf. 2 Cor. 2:17). Rather, as Paul reminds the Corinthians, "We are ambassadors for Christ, *God making his appeal* through us" (2 Cor. 5:20, RSV). In this sense, Hedahl's claim is correct, "*Who* preaches is the most essential component for the receptivity of the Gospel"; but, the "Who" in question is not, as Hedahl supposes, Aristotle's pulpit orator; it is Christ Jesus, the Word of God. This Word alone is the subject matter of every sermon worthy of the name. Therefore, theology–not rhetoric–is the basic frame of reference by which homiletics finds its true orientation–or reorientation.

If we cannot preach as if the subject matter of a sermon were under our control, neither can we preach as if the subject matter were indifferent to our words of witness. Again, "*We are* ambassadors for Christ, God making his appeal *through us.*"[55] Rhetorical homiletics, however much it may seek to sideline or suspend the speaking God, correctly insists against all forms of pietism and spiritualism that whatever else a sermon is, it is at least a speech.[56] Its proponents render true service to the church when they call on preachers to take responsibility for their words in relation to their listeners. As preachers we do not invent the gospel of God, but we do invent our sermons. Rhetoric can teach us to speak more intentionally, more engagingly, and more responsibly. The same Second Helvetic Confession that identifies the Word of God with the preaching of the Word of God also requires "pious eloquence" for those seeking ordination to the ministry of this Word (5.150). Similarly, Barth defines preaching not only as "the Word of God which [God] himself speaks," but, continuing dialectically, as "the attempt enjoined upon the church to serve God's own Word, through one who is called thereto, by expounding a biblical text in free human words and making it relevant to contemporaries, as the announcement [*Ankündigung*] of what they have to hear from God himself."[57]

Having reaffirmed both the theological subject matter of preaching and the need for rhetorical responsibility in honoring it, have we not simply restated the impasse between two incommensurable frames of reference, namely, the theological and the rhetorical, albeit having done so dialectically and, to be sure, with an eye on the Chalcedonian Formula? We still need clarification about how these two frames of reference might be appropriately related.

In my judgment, Barth's own attempts to relate the two in his homiletical theory are incoherent. Let me offer two examples. First, recall that Barth rejects sermon introductions on the grounds that they mistakenly suggest a "point of contact" in the creature by which the divine Word enters. Here, Barth moves directly from dogmatics to formulate for homiletics a proscriptive guideline. In this case, the attempt falters largely on logical grounds. While sermon introductions could suggest this "analogy of being," it does not follow that they necessarily do so. Barth conflates the rhetorical "point of contact" between the preacher and the listeners, to which homiletics legitimately attends, with the "analogy of being" shared by the creature and the Creator, to which Barthian dogmatics is opposed. Having conflated two things that should have been kept distinct, Barth then rejects the former on the grounds of the latter. In this instance, all that dogmatics can rightfully say to a homiletics informed by rhetoric is that no sermon introduction, however eloquent, establishes revelation or has the power to introduce us to the living God. This could be a salutary word for homiletics to hear. But dogmatics, as such, has no right to demand, as Barth does, that homiletical theory should outlaw sermon introductions.

A second incoherence arises, again in regard to sermon introductions, when Barth advises that they are "distracting" and a "waste of time." He frankly admits that these are "practical" or "psychological" reasons for getting rid of them. As a former pastor, with years of preaching experience, Barth is certainly entitled to his opinions. Nevertheless, if the theological frame of reference is primary, then on what *theological* grounds can Barth unexpectedly move to a rhetorical frame of reference where the psychological needs and the cultural context of the listeners affect the very structure of the sermon? This incoherence in Barth's homiletical theory arises through his failure to furnish theological arguments authorizing rhetoric.

How does a theology of the Word of God authorize rhetorical judgments, made on rhetorical grounds, with respect to preaching? In pursuit of an answer, I offer the following thesis: *Preaching is more faithful to the Word of God when it is fitting or appropriate to its hearers' context.* One possible way to defend this thesis is by means of the concept of *concursus*, that is, the "concurring" or "accompanying" of divine and human action, traditionally associated with Lutheran and Reformed doctrines of providence.[58] As recently interpreted by Christopher Morse, *concursus* speaks of "the conforming of God's grace to the created integrity of its recipient"; that is, "God's providing is always custom made to fit the creaturely recipient so that the creature's own freedom is never abrogated but activated."[59] Grace is God coming all the way down to meet us, respecting and not violating, our creaturely context and condition. If this is the case, then God's grace is richly differentiated.

According to Barth's reading of the doctrine in his *Church Dogmatics*, God's "power...gives to each one that which is proper to it, that which God Himself has ordained should be proper to it. God…is not like a schoolmaster who gives the same lesson to the whole class, or an officer who moves his whole squadron in the same direction, or a bureaucrat who once an outlook or principle is embedded in his own little head rules his whole department in accordance with it."[60] By contrast, God accompanies the creature, honoring each one's dignity, integrity, and particularity.

This is the way it is with God-with-us in the economy of salvation. God accompanies us in those patterns of relationality by which God constitutes Godself as Father, Son, and Holy Spirit. As Barth explains,

> It is this God, who is not poor in Himself but rich, who works together with the creature. He does not do it uniformly or monotonously or without differentiation, for He is not uniform or monotonous or undifferentiated in Himself. If He were to do it in this way He would be doing violence to His own nature; He would not be God.[61]

God's grace is richly differentiated toward the creature because God is richly differentiated in his triune being.

This good news of God's own giving to each creature what is contextually fitting and appropriate to it, with full regard for its particularity, authorizes the church's own *concursus* in the ministry of this Word. Our own words of witness are to be fitting and appropriate to our listeners. As Gert Otto notes, the hearer "is not the 'addressee' whose name I simply write on the envelope, without a second thought about whom I am actually writing…What one, in the view of *these* hearers, in *this* situation, within *this* limitation, will *reach* and *effect*–e.g., encouragement or comfort, criticism or enlightenment or information, keener insight or highly voiced joy–is one of the most important questions that stands openly or secretly behind every [sermon] preparation."[62]

While the theological authorization of rhetoric is analogically inferred from the doctrine of *concursus*, and, therefore, indirect, it is sufficient for rhetoric to play its proper part in preaching.[63] This is not to say, in testing the language of the church for its fidelity to the Word of God, that Christian dogmatics or systematic theology can never utter a direct "No" by way of proscription or a direct "Yes" by way of prescription; but, it is to affirm that rhetorical considerations, requiring rhetorical judgments as to what is fitting and appropriate in relation to audience and occasion, are, in fact, entailed and authorized by the Word of God.[64]

Sermon: A Christmas Sermon on Peace

Martin Luther King Jr. first preached this sermon at the Ebenezer Baptist Church, Atlanta, Georgia, where he served as co-pastor. On Christmas Eve 1967, the Canadian Broadcasting Corporation aired it as part of the seventh annual Massey Lectures.[65]

It is a topical sermon on peace preached amid an escalating Vietnam War. Themes common to liberal theology, such as the brotherhood of mankind under one God and the universality of the moral law, find expression here. Clearly organized, the sermon comes complete with an introduction, three points, and an extended celebrative climax.

> Peace on Earth...
>
> This Christmas season finds us a rather bewildered human race. We have neither peace within nor peace without....And yet, my friends, the Christmas hope for peace and good will toward all men can no longer be dismissed as a kind of pious dream of some utopian....Wisdom born of experience should tell us that war is obsolete. There may have been a time when war served as a negative good by preventing the spread and growth of an evil force, but the very destructive power of modern weapons of warfare eliminates even the possibility that war may any longer serve as a negative good. And so, if we assume that life is worth living, if we assume that mankind has a right to survive, then we must find an alternative to war–and so let us this morning explore the conditions for peace. Let us this morning think anew on the meaning of that Christmas hope: "Peace on Earth, Good Will toward Men [cf. Lk 2:14, KJV]."[66]

King introduces his topic, namely, "the conditions for peace," and each of his three points develops one of those conditions. Given this approach, "the text" of Luke 2:14, wrenched out of its scriptural context and story, becomes a motto on which King's own points are hung.

The points are also stated clearly as transitions:

> Now let me suggest first that if we are to have peace on earth, our loyalties must become ecumenical rather than sectional.

> Now let me say, secondly, that if we are to have peace in the world, men and nations must embrace the nonviolent affirmation that ends and means must cohere.

Now let me say that the next thing we must be concerned about if we are to have peace on earth and good will toward men is the nonviolent affirmation of the sacredness of all human life.[67]

Each of these points advances an argument to persuade the listeners what they must think or do to enable world peace. Each point is illustrated by first person stories or by examples, drawn both from everyday experiences and historical material. (There is a digression on the three Greek words for love, namely, *eros*, *philia*, and *agape*, that does not seem integrally related to the third point under which it falls.)

King continually reminds his hearers what they *must* think or do: "Our loyalties must transcend our race, our tribe, our class, and our nation; and this means we must develop a world perspective";[68] "means and ends must cohere because the end is preexistent in the means, and ultimately destructive means cannot bring about constructive ends";[69] again, "Man is a child of God, made in His image, and therefore must be respected as such";[70] and, in a key exhortative sentence that I take as the beginning of the sermon's conclusion, rather than as a fourth point, King says, "If there is to be peace on earth and good will toward men, we must finally believe in the ultimate morality of the universe, and believe that all reality hinges on moral foundations."[71] Consonant with this last dogmatic claim, the role of Jesus Christ recedes to that of an exemplar, rather than a savior:

Christ came to show us the way. Men love darkness rather than light, and they crucified him, and there on Good Friday on the cross it was still dark, but then Easter came, and Easter is an eternal reminder of the fact that the truth-crushed earth will rise again. Easter justifies Carlyle in saying, "No lie can live forever." And so this is our faith, as we continue to hope for peace on earth and good will toward men: let us know that in the process we have cosmic companionship.[72]

The cross-resurrection kerygma is thereby demythologized in liberal fashion. It serves primarily as a "reminder" that truth will triumph in the end and, in that sense, manifests and confirms the moral law at the heart of the universe.

As King turns to the exhortative climax, he speaks descriptively, contrasting, the "nightmare" of murder, poverty, and war with the "dream" of human dignity, justice, and peace:

I have a dream that one day men will rise up and come to see that they are made to live together as brothers. I still have a dream this morning that one day every Negro in this country, every colored person in the world, will be judged on the basis of the content of his character rather than the color of his skin, and every man will respect the dignity and worth of human personality. I still have a dream that one day the idle industries of Appalachia will be revitalized, and the empty stomachs of Mississippi will be filled, and brotherhood will be more than a few words at the end of a prayer, but rather the first order of business on every legislative agenda. I still have a dream today that one day justice will roll down like water, and righteousness like a mighty stream [Am 5:24, cf. KJV, RSV]. I still have a dream today that in all of our state houses and city halls men will be elected to go there who will do justly and love mercy and walk humbly with their God [cf. Mic. 6:8, KJV]. I still have a dream today that one day war will come to an end, that men will beat their swords into plowshares and their spears into pruning hooks, that nations will no longer rise up against nations, neither will they study war anymore [cf. Isa 2:4; Mic 4:3, KJV]....I still have a dream today that one day every valley shall be exalted and every mountain and hill will be made low, the rough places will be made smooth and crooked places straight, and the glory of the Lord shall be revealed, and all flesh shall see it together [cf. Isa 40:4–5, KJV]....With this faith we will be able to speed up the day when there will be peace on earth and good will toward men [cf. Lk 2:14 KJV]. It will be a glorious day, the morning stars will sing together and the sons of God will shout for joy [cf. Job 38:7, KJV].[73]

Here the attestation of God's promises as correlative with human hope is accomplished by pairing the frank acknowledgment of the world as it now is with the world as God wills it to become. This is rhetorically performed through the reiteration of "I still have a dream" as a continuing refrain, together with the piling up of scriptural citations to great cumulative effect. As a result, the moralism inherent in King's earlier string of exhortative "musts" tends to be mitigated. For this reason, we leave King's sermon empowered and enabled and not simply challenged. The eschatological hope conveyed by King is not constricted or restricted to existential need, but is claimed for the purpose of advancing human dignity and equality in the local and global political and economic order.

Finally Comes the Poet

One of the important developments in North American homi‑ letics since World War II has been the emergence of poetics, in opposition to rhetoric, as the principal frame of reference for under‑ standing and guiding preaching. In place of the sermon as a species of a persuasive speech delivered by an accomplished orator, poetics understands the sermon as a plotted drama performed in the pulpit by a skillful narrative artist. Both rhetoric and poetics, as derived from Aristotle, aim in some way to "move" their audiences. Rhetoric directly adapts this aim to its audience and occasion, shaping the content and presentation of a discourse in light of its listeners' context to win them to the speaker's position, while poetics, focusing as it does on the formation and form of the artistic work itself, trusts in the dynamics of the plotted drama to do its therapeutic work of listener transformation. The distinctions, of course, are not hard and fast, but, with respect to homiletical theory, rhetoric often seeks to "take control" of the communication event, emphasizing the role and agency of the preacher, while poetics attends more to the power and agency of language and narrative. In North American homiletics, two poetic paradigms have undergirded popular theories of preaching; namely, the Aristotelian and the Heideggerian.

Aristotle's Poetics *and Homiletical Theory*

Writing at the end of the Second World War, a young preacher‑ scholar, W. Paul Ludwig, then pastor of Second Presbyterian Church, Washington, Pennsylvania, issued a call to reconceive the task and purpose of preaching from that of persuasive discourse, in line with Aristotle's *Rhetoric*, to that of dramatic performance as found in Aristotle's *Poetics*. Ludwig's essay was, in his own view, "unprecedented," not in bringing Aristotle's *Poetics* to bear on American letters in general–that had been done earlier by Bryant, Poe, Emerson, and Lowell–but in bringing it to bear specifically on preaching. In this new frame of reference, preachers are re-situated. They are no longer taken for orators; they are playwrights and actors. The purpose of preaching is no longer persuasion, but personal transformation or, to use Aristotle's term, "catharsis" often rendered as "purgation."[74]

Most broadly, "poetics" (Greek *poiesis*= to do or make) is a theory of aesthetics or artistic production, embracing all the forms of literature and drama. However, Aristotle's treatise of that title primarily focuses on a theory of tragedy. In his famous definition of tragedy, which Ludwig presses into the service of preaching, Aristotle writes:

> Tragedy, then, is an imitation [*mimesis*] of an action that is serious, complete, and of a certain magnitude; in language embellished with each kind of artistic ornament, the several kinds being found in separate parts of the play; in the form of action, not of narrative; through pity and fear effecting the proper purgation [*katharsis*] of these emotions.[75]

In recasting the task of preaching, Ludwig fastens first on two key aspects of Aristotle's definition, namely, "imitation" and "purgation," before taking up tragedy's two most important constituent elements, those of "plot" and "character."

In Ludwig's view, *mimesis* or imitation "means to Aristotle that life suggests or presents to the artist a certain phenomenon which the artist in turn represents in his own medium." In Greek tragedy, the media include not only language, but simultaneously rhythm, tune, and meter. Moreover, unlike the historian who tries to "show or tell what precisely occurred in a given event," the tragic playwright represents "what would probably or inevitably happen." That is to say, imitative art "seems to imply the existence of a set of moral standards and spiritual laws by which an ideal or tragic turn of events can be foretold." The task of the artist is to convey the working out of a *telos* "in terms that an audience can understand."[76]

Ludwig draws from Aristotle's theory of imitation several implications for preaching. First, as with tragedy, so with preaching, language is the primary artistic medium, but the media of melody and rhythm are also evident in the "prose cadence" of "great preaching." Second, the preacher, like the tragedian, artistically renders for specific audiences the unseen moral and causal laws "decreed from all eternity" that are operative "behind the scenes." When otherwise fragmentary or episodic moments of life are backlighted from this grander, transcendent viewpoint, "the permanent, catholic possibilities of human nature" are revealed. This means the historical or reportorial language of the modern pulpit, that only recounts past events or the news of the day, remains at a superficially mundane level. It may hold up a mirror to our chaotic culture, but it does not illumine human nature as such. Much preaching, therefore, lacks depth. For Ludwig, the preacher, like the poet, takes life situations and represents them in language and its related media within the perennial framework of the moral and spiritual laws that determine human destiny. In this way, the preacher, as much as the playwright of tragedy, leads us to an experience that transforms our experience.[77]

The function of preaching thus corresponds to the function of tragedy. Paraphrasing Aristotle's definition, Ludwig notes that tragedy arouses "the emotions of Pity and Fear in the audience in such a way as to effect a 'catharsis' or relief of these emotions." While catharsis or purging of the emotions had a role in ancient Orphic rites and Dionysian theology, Aristotle further develops the concept as a literary principle. In one sense, Ludwig writes, "We readily understand how the elements of a drama–suspense, impending disaster, tragic irony, tragic error–stir up emotions of Pity and Fear to which Aristotle refers." What is less clear in the *Poetics* is how Aristotle understands the relief of these emotions, and in search of an answer Ludwig turns to Aristotle's *Politics* where catharsis "appears to have largely a therapeutic and pathological sense–affecting man's soul as medicine heals the body." In this view of tragic performance as "therapeutic," Ludwig finds that "the latent pity and fear which we bring with us from the world of personal experience are allayed and an emotional cure achieved. Our apprehension of impending misfortune is transferred to an imaginative world where we can view our fears more or less objectively and shudder in sympathy for the hero in whom we see ourselves."[78]

Ludwig contends that this therapeutic goal of tragedy is also shared by preaching. Acknowledging that preaching can have other goals, further admitting that "there are many diseased souls in the pew which cannot be cured from the pulpit," Ludwig nevertheless boldly declares that "for most of our listeners 'the emptiness, the suffering, and the frustration' can be more than matched in the sermon." What is required of the preacher are not neat arguments fashioned for persuasion, but rather a literary and performance strategy that recognizes the emotional distress latent in the human heart. Given this poetic frame of reference for preaching, "Fear and pity are still paramount objects of our homiletical art." Moreover, as Aristotle indicates (14.1), these elements of pathos can be aroused simply by the plotted structure of a tragedy; they are not dependent on histrionic delivery or performance, what Aristotle terms "spectacular means." As such, the therapeutic purpose of tragedy is also transferable to preaching, and without the emotional excesses of overwrought revivalism. The preacher can convey "the peace of God so that the man who is surfeited with fear or with self-pity–who is afraid of himself and his weaknesses, and afraid of the universe and its brute strength–will find his fear drained off or sublimated in the catharsis of a service of worship....The might and majesty and abiding friendliness of God should be made so real that the personal, 'in-growing' features of pity and fear will be released and rechanneled into universal sympathy and social energy."[79]

By what literary strategy can preachers accomplish this therapeutic transformation in their listeners? Here, Ludwig highlights what Aristotle regards as the two most important of the six constituent elements of drama, namely, plot and character. By plot, Aristotle means "an imitation of an action that is complete, and whole, and of a certain magnitude. A whole is that which has a beginning, a middle, and an end."[80] In other words, "a standard plot, a ready-made plot" is neither a series of random happenings, nor a string of unrelated anecdotes, but an action or movement that unfolds in a necessary, causal sequence. For the preacher, the furnished plot is "the divine-human drama," and like a classic Greek tragedy it, too, unfolds in a sequence "of suspense or complication," followed by "the discovery or the reversal," the turning point that leads to the unraveling of the suspense in a "denouement." In Ludwig's judgment it is important that each "act" (or, in rhetorical terms, "point") of the sermon be subordinated to the overall "single idea." In other words, the "acts" are not episodic ends in themselves. They should each promote the development of the overall sermonic "plot." Like well-constructed dramas, sermons must not reach their denouement too early, lest all suspense be lost leaving "only dreariness if not rebellion" in the listeners. For this reason, "the reversal" should probably come "very near to the conclusion of the sermon." Hence, preachers are advised to write their conclusions first and then work backwards in constructing their plotted, that is, sequentially developed, points.[81]

As for "character," we find two senses in which that term can be understood with respect to tragic performance: the characters in the drama, the *dramatis personae*, and the characters in the audience. In Aristotle's theory of tragedy, character portrayal is subordinated to the plot. Hence, dramatic action is not about the moralistic exhibition of character on stage in the hope of strengthening the moral fiber of the listeners. On the contrary, in tragedy the plotted action is primary. We only need a sufficient knowledge of the portrayed characters to grasp the effect the plotted action has upon them. Still, sermons should borrow a leaf from plays and make more use of characterization to mitigate the unrelieved "theorizing, philosophizing, and moralizing" typical of the "most ineffective sermons."[82]

Tragic heroes must possess certain character traits. They must possess sufficient greatness and sufficient goodness if the tragic consequences suffered by them are to have the power to elicit both pity and fear and effect the purgation of these emotions in the listeners. In order for an audience to experience catharsis, the tragic hero must also be sufficiently similar to them in character–neither too good, nor too evil. For this reason, the tragic hero can neither be "the evil man who rises…from poverty to prosperity," nor "the perfectly good man who falls from prosperity to adversity."[83] Hence, Ludwig notes that Jesus Christ ill accords with Aristotle's description of the tragic hero. In contrast to Greek tragedy, "the pulpit's tragic hero is the perfectly good Man who suffered without deserving."[84] This distinction notwithstanding, Ludwig affirms that Jesus Christ "has stirred pity and fear, but beyond these–admiration for courage and obedience, and acceptance of the imperial mission of that chief episode in the total divine-human drama."[85] If Jesus Christ explodes the Aristotelian role of the tragic hero, he does so with the result of accomplishing more–but in any case not less–than the requisite awakening of pity and fear. With this christological qualification, Ludwig baptizes the entire Aristotelian apparatus for preaching.

Theology and Aristotelian Poetics

Within the poetical frame of reference furnished by Aristotle, preaching is understood as mimetic art, as therapeutic in purpose, as directed by and anchored in the inexorable laws of destiny, and as plotted action, even though Jesus Christ does not fit the character lineaments of Aristotle's tragic hero. What is completely absent is any sense that *God* is speaking through the mouth of the Christian herald in order to break the chains of causal necessity to deliver humanity from the slavery of sin and death. In the absence of this God, preaching becomes exclusively the property of the poet governed by the laws of poetics. The result is a theological reductionism that transfers the theological force of Christian claims about preaching to Aristotle's poetic strictures. The power of the gospel becomes the power of poetic performance. God disappears as a present Agent, and we are left with a drama about God and humanity. When all this is coupled with Ludwig's admission that the story of Jesus Christ is not a tragedy, we discover a sizable Achilles' heel in his proposal. Despite the burnished armor afforded preaching by Aristotelian poetics, in Ludwig's hands it remains vulnerable to theological criticism.

In general, the criticisms ventured here of Ludwig are also applicable to the proposal of Eugene L. Lowry to make Aristotle's poetics of plotted action, involving the pattern of complication, reversal, and denouement, essential for every sermon.[86] Unlike Ludwig, Lowry does not simply "baptize" Aristotle's *Poetics* for the pulpit; rather, he christens Aristotle's identification of the standard structure of a tragic plot.[87] These elements are taken up by Lowry as essential, or at least as the normative default pattern, for every sermon. The primacy of plot that Aristotle accords to dramatic action in a well-written tragedy, Lowry accords to the form of a well-prepared and well-presented sermon. He explicitly excludes "biblical, historical, doctrinal, or ethical content" as determinative of sermon form.[88] Such content, like Aristotle's "characters," must be subordinated to, or reformatted into, the contours of the plotted sequence or stages of "1) upsetting the equilibrium [Oops!], 2) analyzing the discrepancy [Ugh!], 3) disclosing the clue to resolution [Aha!], 4) experiencing the gospel [Whee!], and 5) anticipating the consequences [Yeah!]."[89] Again, Lowry insists,

> The homiletical view expressed in this writing assumes that ambiguity and its resolution is the basic form-ingredient to any sermon, whether life-situational, expository, doctrinal, etc. in content. There is always one major discrepancy, bind, or problem which is the issue. The central task of any sermon, therefore, is the resolution of that particular central ambiguity.[90]

In other words, with respect to sermonic form, poetics is the constant; theology is the variable. Whatever your theology, and whatever the particular subject or topic of one's sermon, it can be articulated in a sermonic form determined entirely by Aristotle's analysis of plotted action.[91]

Given this poetic frame of reference, we can see that Lowry would naturally oppose any competing sovereign role for rhetoric, such as found, for example, in Hogan and Reid, and, on the other hand, would concur with the view of Gert Otto in denying theology a determinative role in preaching, at least with respect to sermonic form. In this sense, both theology and rhetoric are homiletically subordinated to poetics, which alone provides the norm for form. This does not mean that a Lowry sermon does not possess theological content or attend to rhetorical considerations, but it does mean that neither theological content nor rhetorical considerations are determinative of sermonic structure. Within a poetic frame of reference, both theology and rhetoric are delimited by Aristotle's formula for plotted action.[92]

No doubt, Aristotle was fairly confident if playwrights followed his formula for plot development, based as it was on his observant analysis of the best Greek tragedies, that Hellenic audiences of his day would experience an emotional catharsis. Similarly, in his *Doing*

Time in the Pulpit, Lowry seems assured, perhaps unguardedly so, that following the steps of a properly sequenced homiletical plot leads ineluctably to an experience of the gospel: "When the sermon by its very form is narrative, this power turns words into events, preachers into poets, and God language into religious experience. *Narrative preaching can make it real.*"[93] Later, in *The Sermon: Dancing on the Edge of Mystery,* Lowry is emphatic that any change wrought by the Word in the listener cannot be produced by the homiletical employment of narrative techniques:

> Preaching I can do. I choose it; I prepare for it. Prayerfully I engage it, and I perform it. I do it. I will do it Sunday next. Proclaiming the Word is what I *hope* will happen next Sunday. I will attempt my preparation strategy in such a way as to maximize the chance for it. But proclaiming the Word? Nobody has the grip of control for it. You cannot capture it; you cannot possess it; you cannot package it; you cannot deliver it, and you cannot control the receipt of it. Sorry. Preaching the sermon is a task; proclaiming the Word is the hoped-for *goal.*[94]

While we have moved to firmer theological ground here in the claim that "proclamation," or "God's Word" in the proper sense, cannot be conjured up by the creature, we can still ask whether this claim is largely betrayed by a poetics that assigns to the creature the "strategy" to "maximize the chance" for revelation? If this were the case, then, preaching would truly be an exercise in wagering, with homiletics serving as the art and science of improving the odds on God. Switching metaphors from gambling to engineering, Lowry writes, "The bridge between sermonic task and achievement, the bridge between preaching and proclaiming is evocation"; but, in Lowry's view, this constructive task of evocation is undertaken by the preacher who is attentive to the inherent power of language.[95] In my judgment, a more faithful theological reading of revelation would regard preaching as epicletic, as *invocation,* rather than evocation, with any "bridge building" explicitly reserved to God's self-revelation, that is, in traditional language, the Holy Spirit (see Acts 4:24–31). Again, taking a metaphor from Jud Souers, Lowry further likens the preacher to a stagehand who pulls back the curtain to exhibit "the divine play–sometimes–perhaps–if I can get it open enough."[96] But can we really transfer this revelatory "unveiling" from the work of the Creator Spirit to the conditional "if" of the creature-preacher?

In *The Homiletical Plot*, Lowry emphatically affirms that the role of the preacher "excludes the producing of the end result," before qualifying this affirmation by declaring it is the "stage-setting" responsibility of the preacher "of doing those things which will place us in optimum position so that we may be changed by the power of the gospel."[97] So, again, we can ask whether the creature really has the power "to set the stage" for God's work or to "place us in optimum position." Can we really prepare our hearts or those of our listeners to receive the Word of God? In other words, can we transfer to the creature, or to creaturely language as such, what properly belongs to the work of the Holy Spirit–about which and about whom, and in accord with his poetic frame of reference, Lowry says relatively little?[98]

Heidegger and the Poetics of the Purely Spoken Word

More decisive for North American homiletics than the poetics of Aristotle has been that of Martin Heidegger (1889–1976) as mediated by the New Hermeneutic. Heidegger pursues the primordial question of why there is something rather than nothing by distinguishing between "beings" and "Being," that is between things that are and that by which they are.[99] There is thus between beings and Being a relationship, but also an "ontological difference." From Heidegger's viewpoint, there develops over time a taking of Being for granted, a "forgetfulness" or a losing sight of the wonder of Being, and a "fall" into metaphysics, that is, a turning from the question of Being (and non-Being) and a turning toward beings by way of categorizing, classifying, and ordering, so that the totality of beings becomes the "object" of thought by a thinking "subject." We now find ourselves in a situation where "few are experienced enough in the difference between an object of scholarship and a matter thought."[100] Thinking thus becomes one step removed from reality. Historically speaking, we find ourselves stuck between mythology and metaphysics: "We are too late for the gods and too early for Being."[101] We not only have a subject-object distinction that renders knowledge uncertain and problematic, but we have the knowing subject only acknowledging as real what can be "objectified" and thereby controlled, categorized, and classified. This explains why the whole history of Western philosophy, ordered by logical thought, is unable to treat the originating experience of philosophy, namely, wonder that there is Being instead of non-Being. We have exchanged the language of poetry for that of science and technology, "the essence of language" (Being) for the "language of essence" (logic and metaphysics).

Thus, the question of the meaning of Being (and non-Being) prompts us to "step back" behind logic and metaphysics in order to allow the "coming to light" of Being. The proper method of ontology, therefore, is descriptive or "phenomenological." Heidegger "does not ask the question about what something is; he asks about the how: how, in which way, something is. He asks about the mode of being, the *modus essendi.*"[102] Since it is human beings who discovered or discerned the "ontological difference" between Being and beings, thereby raising the question of the meaning of Being (and Non-being) and allowing Being to come to light, human existence is the place (*Da* = there) where Being (*Sein*) occurs, so that Heidegger can coin the term *Dasein* (or Being-there) for human existence. Heidegger's early magnum opus, *Being and Time*, is the phenomenological description of "the kind of being to whose own being the understanding of [B]eing essentially belongs."[103] In his later work, especially after the Second World War, Heidegger turns with greater focus on the role of language in the coming to light of Being. It is this linguistic, and more specifically, poetic, turn in Heidegger's thought that has most influenced the New Hermeneutic, and, with it, the New Homiletic.

In one sense, *Dasein* is necessary for *Sein*, in order for Being to emerge as itself, but in another sense *Dasein* exists for *Sein.*[104] Human being discerns *Sein*, because Being bestows itself on human being, opens itself to human being, and summons *Dasein* to wonder and to think in the presence of *Sein*. In this giving of Being to human being, Being actively takes the initiative and determines when and how human being may respond. Being (*Sein*) thus has priority over Being-there (*Dasein*). The response of human being to Being is the origin of language. True language is thus an instrument of Being, and the agency of Being is exercised through language so that language both constitutes human existence and comes to expression in human existence. "Language speaks. Man speaks in that he responds to language."[105] In turning from Being toward beings, however, humankind abandons true speech (*Rede*) for idle talk (*Gerede*). Where can we find, historically speaking, and amid all the "talk," true speech that witnesses to Being? For Heidegger, the answer lies preeminently with the poets.

In the 1950s, one of the most provocative attempts to appropriate Heidegger theologically came from Heinrich Ott, a young student who had for his mentors both Karl Barth and Rudolf Bultmann. Ott, whose theological career as Barth's successor in Basel was largely defined by his early encounter with the later Heidegger, maintains that propositional language of the "S is P" type, that is, language as the instrumental and informational tool typical of both scientific and everyday discourse, does not get at the "focal point" or "essence" of language.[106] Ott writes,

> Poetry (and Heidegger calls the poem "the purely spoken"…
> in which the very essence of language for him becomes
> perceivable) never speaks in the form of plain propositions,
> although when it is viewed in superficial, grammatical terms,
> there seem to be propositions. A poem, however, never
> simply informs about a particular, limited, or single state
> of affairs in the form of propositions, that is, "cognitive"
> propositions which must be correct or mistaken. "Essential
> thinking" does not follow the "informative" way. It does not
> make affirmations about limited, individual states of affairs,
> which can be subject to our control. Nor does it speak in the
> kind of propositions of the "S is P" type, although superficially
> it could appear that way. The grammatical appearance is
> deceiving. For Heidegger, rather, essential thinking is "the
> movement of showing."…Understanding means "following
> the movement of showing." We must, in the process of
> understanding, follow along the path. In so doing, it may be
> that we are really shown something, that something becomes
> clearer, and that we are guided toward a new vision of reality.
> But there is no guarantee that this will happen. Not everyone
> can understand every thought every time.[107]

As this commentary by Ott suggests, for Heidegger, historic texts of poetry are language-sites where Being has come to expression. Being is the *Sache* or ultimate subject matter of the *Sprache* or language of poetry. Thus, Heidegger understands language *essentially,* that is, as related to Being, as neither the expression of one's inner life or self-understanding, nor as a system of denotative words or signifiers conveying information. Rather, language is essentially the path toward, and event of, Being. To encounter this subject matter in and through language means inquiring beneath the textual surface and "reading between the lines." In ways reminiscent of Barth's discussion of scriptural exegesis, proper interpretation of poetic texts will accord with their subject matter, and this means following their linguistic path or "way of witness" and not simply excavating historical-critical information or submerging their subject matter in a torrent of "idle talk."[108] Because of the inextricable historical character of interpretation by finite beings, and the inexhaustible character of Being, the original events of responses to Being recorded in written texts can never be understood merely by their routine repetition. Through encountering these texts, contemporary interpreters, in and from new historical vantage points, can uncover or discern some aspect or dimension of Being unforeseen by the original author who is, after all, also a finite being. Thus, what true interpretation retrieves through a poetic text is more light from its inexhaustibly luminous subject matter, rather than some inferred or reconstructed "original intention" of its human author. It is this continuing retrieval, this allowing of Being to come further to light through language, that is properly meant by "hermeneutics."

Since Heidegger regards poetry as the form of language most open to the primordial and recurring call of Being and as the preeminent place for Being's self disclosure, it is tempting to speak of Heidegger's "poetics," and I do so in this ontological sense. On the other hand, erecting a poetics, in the sense of establishing rules for writing poetry or other literature, of practicing literary criticism of poems or other literature, or of uncovering formulaic patterns demonstrating how poems, tragedies, or narratives "work," is far, if not opposite, from Heidegger's intention. Heidegger is not Aristotle!

Theology and Heideggerian Poetics

One of the themes of the later Heidegger that Heinrich Ott deems significant for "practical church life" is Heidegger's emphasis on "the primal essence of language," which for Ott involves "language as it occurs in scripture and confession, in exegesis and dogmatics, in preaching and prayer, i.e., language as the medium of all the church's and theology's activity."[109] Under Heidegger's influence, Ott seeks a non-metaphysical theology, one that would step back from the enterprise in which an autonomous knowing mind posits God and then proceeds to think "about" God as an object of thought. In turning away from this understanding of theology, Ott boldly rejects theology as a second-order reflection on prayer, preaching, or scripture. "Rather theology should understand itself as an element of encounter, as encounter with what is to be thought, which shows itself, 'unveils' itself to thought and thus determines thought…When theology speaks of God, it does not speak 'about' God outside the encounter of faith; rather it speaks *out of* the encounter. Its talk about God is the encounter of faith explaining itself."[110] This means that theology is based on the experience of this encounter, that is, prayer as the human response in which God's Word comes to expression, and this encounter distinguishes theology's modes of inquiry and expression from those of logic and mathematics based solely on reason. Ott's proposal for reconceptualizing theology in its various fields as tied to a first-order encounter thus corresponds to Heidegger's attempt to overcome metaphysical language about Being with language arising from the encounter with Being. Likewise, Ott's invoking of prayer as the site of encounter of the Word of God is analogous to Heidegger's understanding of the role of poetry as the site or "clearing" for being's self-disclosure.

In Ott's judgment, "Theology is by its very nature the constant effort to eliminate empty talk from preaching, the incessant attempt to keep open or find ever new access to the subject matter via authentic understanding. This effort takes place, however, in a twofold direction: toward the understanding of the Biblical texts on the one hand and toward the understandability of the gospel in the present on the other."[111] How do we preachers and theologians "keep open" to the subject matter of the scriptures? Again, Heidegger proves instructive. As James M. Robinson notes,

> Rather than presenting a historical-critical exegesis of a poem, [Heidegger] enters into dialogue with the poem about the subject matter to which the poem admits him. Thus the poet's word is not an object of our study, but is an event calling up to us a subject matter that calls forth a response from us. The crucial issue is not whether the interpreter confines himself to exegesis to the exclusion of eisegesis, but rather whether he succeeds in entering into the movement of the poet's words, which are derived from the subject matter. The decisive issue is whether he hears the call of being to which the poet's words answered–whether he hears that call with sufficient clarity to be himself called upon to answer.[112]

In Ott's judgment, the preacher has a responsibility when confronting a text to look through the text to its subject matter, that is, the Word of God, that is calling for response, a response which also takes place in words that then become a present site for God's revelation. The text is to be taken in service to this subject matter and not as an end itself, whether as an aesthetic object or as a formulaic model. "For while we preach in each case on a particular text, it is of little importance to comment on the individual text as such. Rather, what counts is to preach, together with the text and taking up its call, the one and whole gospel."[113] Here we recall Karl Barth's strictures on scriptural exegesis, which subordinate historical-critical concerns to the subject matter of the text, namely the Word of God or Jesus Christ as God with us. Thanks to Ott, Barth's views on exegesis for preaching find supporting analogues in Heidegger's encounter with poetry as disclosive of Being and as responsive to the call of Being, thereby inviting and enabling the hearer's own response to this same call.

In an essay from 1961, Gerhard Ebeling, drawing upon other theologians of the New Hermeneutic, and, as an alternative to Ott, summarizes from his post-Bultmannian perspective how Heidegger relates to theology.[114] In general, philosophical speech is itself the word with which philosophy concerns itself on its path of comprehensive questioning. By contrast, theological speech concerns itself with the word of proclamation addressed to the conscience. Moreover, Ebeling insists against Ott that theology also has a regulative, or second-order function; it serves the word of proclamation by taking care over it.[115] In attempting to get behind the entire Western tradition of metaphysics to a renewed thinking of Being, Ebeling also finds it questionable whether Heidegger's thought still qualifies as "philosophy." Nevertheless, lest theologians infer from this that Heidegger is automatically an ally, Ebeling is quick to note that the call for thinking directed toward Being still remains rooted in the philosophical tradition–it does not involve itself with the proclaimed word of faith in the name of Jesus. On the other hand, Heidegger's project admittedly forces the question whether the language of theology remains bound to metaphysical thinking, and, if so, whether the experience of faith can really tolerate theology (in the second-order sense).[116]

Leaving aside these provocative questions, Ebeling, taking his bearings from the classic Lutheran distinction between the Word of God as law and gospel, that is, as command and grace or as condemnation and forgiveness, declares that Heidegger's thought cannot be equated with the gospel. Nevertheless, his thought can be equated with the law insofar as it illumines the human situation, e.g., as constituted by language ("the linguisticality of existence"), as determined by metaphysical thinking, or as forgetful of Being. Here emerges a further parallel with Lutheran theology, inasmuch as Luther, too, was suspicious of a metaphysical theology that obscured the reality and experience of faith arising from the Word of God. The parallel is also seen in Heidegger's inquiry into the difference between Being and beings that leads *Dasein* to the experience of powerlessness in the encounter with (the power of) Being. For Ebeling, we must not try to explain this "ontological difference" theologically, presumably as a way to ground faith in God. Rather, the "difference" with which theology should be concerned is that between God and the creature, that is, the power of the gospel amid the helplessness of the creature, a difference that comes to light and, indeed, takes place in the Word-event of God justifying sinners.[117]

Significantly, because Ott uses "analogy" to correlate Heideggerian and Barthian perspectives, while Ebeling employs the distinction of law and gospel to winnow his appropriations of Heidegger, we have no collapsing in either Ott or Ebeling of their theological frame of reference into the poetic, or the wholesale "baptizing" of Heidegger for theological purposes. Being is not identified as God; poetry is not, as such, taken as scripture; and the illuminating encounter by Being with beings is not held as synonymous with accepting the word of divine forgiveness uttered in the name of Jesus. Nevertheless, the poetic frame of reference furnishes both insights and analogues by which to reconceptualize the performative power of the proclaimed Word of God affirmed by faith.

While Ebeling also uncovers in Heidegger's thinking analogous patterns to those of a theology of the Word of God, he is more reserved than Ott about the permissible patterns of correspondence. The appropriation in Ebeling remains anthropological in the law-gospel Lutheran tradition of Bultmann rather than theological in the Reformed tradition of Barth. Nevertheless, the later Heidegger performs a kind of catalytic function for both of these mid-twentieth–century theologies of the Word, whose earlier battle cries were becoming hardened slogans. Heidegger provides them an indirect philosophic sanction to reconceive the linguistic character of existence and faith, the corruption of human words when divorced from their calling to speak the truth, the historicity of language and knowledge, the hermeneutical priority of the subject matter in the work of exegesis, and, not least, the eventfulness of language, of revelation, and of faith. This is not to say that Heidegger would have agreed with the way his work was finally appropriated by the post-Bultmannian New Hermeneutic school, or that Heidegger's own thought is not itself formatively shaped by Christian theology, or that Heidegger's "poetics" is not subject to quite varied interpretations. Granting all these caveats, the influence of Heidegger and his poetics as mediated into North American homiletical theory by the New Hermeneutic has been remarkable. That the mediation occurred through the post-Bultmannian New Hermeneutic of Gerhard Ebeling rather than the "post-Barthian" New Hermeneutic of Heinrich Ott probably served to reinforce, rather than challenge, the anthropological and soteriological character of American preaching.

4

FROM THE NEW HERMENEUTIC TO THE NEW HOMILETIC

"It was a fateful day," writes David James Randolph, "when the venerable John A. Broadus asserted, in the work that was to become the standard in its field for generations, that homiletics was a branch of rhetoric. American homiletics has not yet been completely reconstituted after this stroke which severed the head of preaching from theology and dropped it into the basket of rhetoric held by Aristotle."[1] What Randolph could not know at the time he wrote these lines, is that the appearance of his own volume, *The Renewal of Preaching*, from which this quote is taken, marked another fateful day for American homiletics. For in this volume, the theological insights of the German "New Hermeneutic" school were appropriated for North American homiletics in a way that would dominate the discipline for another thirty years.

Unlike the older rhetorical homiletics, the focus for the New Homiletic is no longer on what sermons *say*, but rather on what they *do*. This reorientation of preaching signals a move from the "exposition" of a text to its "execution," as performative dimensions of communication are given primacy over the cognitive. Reading Randolph today, one is struck with how many current homiletic commonplaces are seminally formulated here. It is Randolph who insists on the "eventfulness" of preaching; who further proposes that the literary forms of the Bible should determine the sermon's own structures; that "concretion" or experiential enfleshment is preferable to logical abstractions; that a well-told story need not simply illustrate a point, but can itself be the point; and, that indirect discourse often succeeds better in gaining a hearing than direct argumentative assaults. Randolph proposes these rules of art not on the basis of rhetoric, but on the Word-event theology of the New Hermeneutic.

Fred Craddock likewise signals the shifting of homiletical gears in his book *As One without Authority,* begun in 1968–1969 during a sabbatical year at Tübingen and its Institute for Hermeneutics. Craddock declares, "The starting point for the study of homiletics has been radically shifted. All considerations of structure unity, movement, use of text, etc., must wait upon the prior consideration of what words are and what they do," and, with an apparent allusion to Randolph, he finds in this new frame of reference "rich prospects for the renewal of preaching."[2] Drawing upon the insights of the New Hermeneutic, Craddock decries seminary courses in preaching taught by speech teachers aside from the rest of the curriculum, charging that "preaching so taught has its form defined not by the content of the Gospel nor the nature of Christian faith but by Greek rhetoric."[3] Rejecting that "the Gospel should always be impaled upon the frame of Aristotelian logic,"[4] Craddock argues for a "'theology of speaking,'" his euphemism for the New Hermeneutic, and he offers "the translation of this theology into a method of preaching."[5] Taking his cue from the then recent research and reflection on the parables of Jesus by Ernst Fuchs (1903–1983), Amos N. Wilder (1895–1993), and Robert Funk, behind which stand the meditations of the later Heidegger on poetry, Craddock holds that the method (and also the form) of a sermon is indivisible from its content: "The method is the message…*how* one preaches is to a large extent *what* one preaches."[6] One's method of preaching, therefore, no less than its content, "is fundamentally a theological consideration."[7] On such grounds as these, Craddock proposes his "inductive movement" method of preaching.

Standing behind the homiletical proposals of Randolph and Craddock is a common motive to rescue American preaching from its longstanding bondage to a rhetorical frame of reference. To accomplish this liberation, an updated theology of the Word, associated with the New Hermeneutic and informed by a Heideggerian ontology of language, is put into service.

This brings us to arguably the most important contribution of the New Hermeneutic to preaching: the concept of the "Word-event" (*Wortgeschehen*). In his 1965 Earl Lectures at Pacific School of Religion in Berkeley, California, Gerhard Ebeling, informed by Heidegger's reflections on language, notes that "the prevailing view of language is oriented towards the significatory function of words...based on the distinction between *signum* and *res*," that is, between the word as sign and what the word as sign signifies.[8] As we have seen, this denotative approach to language characterizes metaphysical, and Ebeling further adds, grammatical and cybernetic, thinking, and it assumes an understanding of language simply as a technical instrument. When so regarded, language becomes "cut off from that which is the constant source of its life–namely, the element of time."[9]

In developing this thesis, Ebeling observes that "the basic linguistic phenomenon is not the vocable as an isolated sign for an equally isolated thing." Of course, an uttered vocable can designate something, but, with the exception of exclamations, "when spoken it does not yet say anything." In other words, the basic unit of linguistic meaning is not the single word, but the sentence "which pieces together a subject in the medium of time." Moreover, "not only what is stated is temporal," so that I can speak in the past, present, or future tense, "but also the statement itself" is temporal, i.e., it takes place in time. It arises out of a situation, it comes into a situation, and it changes the situation by its own modifications "as address or promise, as instruction or conversation, as questioning or calling for help, as complaining or accusing, as cursing or praying."[10]

As "a temporal event" language "comes from the experience which has been given through time and which is based on the experience of time itself." We cannot speak without the language that has been handed down to us through time, and we cannot experience the world without language, insofar as we assign meaning to the world or experience it as meaningful. As Ebeling states,

> The necessity and power of human language is ultimately determined by the fact that the world is experienced as time. I do not merely in a factual sense have a past and a future like all temporal things, but I also *know* of this. It is solely through language that I can have a relation to past and future, that past and future are present to me, that I can go back behind my present and stretch out ahead of it. Indeed, I not only *can* do this, I *must* do it. Because I am knowingly

delivered over to time, I must take up my position towards past and future and answer for myself in relation to time. It is not the concept of signification, but far more profoundly the concept of answerability that points us to that which is fundamental in language.[11]

Here, we see Ebeling sketching out the first lines of an anthropology in terms of the linguisticality of existence. As Craddock later comments, "all the words we know are human words," and, what is more, to echo Ebeling, we only know this *through* human words.[12] By reflecting further on the nature of language, as inescapably placing the hearer into the sequence of time, language always presupposes answerability and, hence, human responsibility.

"Word" is thus understood, not simply as a vocable or even as a grammatical sentence, but rather as "the totality of statement," that is "word as an event, and thus word as inclusive of its relationship to historical contexts" or as embracing the situations in which it arises, into which it is spoken, and from which it is answered. Given this contextual understanding, actions can "speak" and "words" can act. Language does not merely point to or signify actions; language performs and elicits actions. For example, a word of pardon is not simply *about* a pardon, it pardons! In this way a word of pardon elicits a response, whether positive or negative, in the one to whom it is addressed. Thus, "it is the business of word to make present what is not at hand." As the case of pardon illustrates, only the word can call into the present a new future and a new freedom from the past. Indeed, our freedom and our future, in fact our humanity itself, are completely dependent upon and constituted by the gift of language. Likewise, if "God" is to have any meaning, it will have to be in terms of the human situation as grounded in the temporality of language, in other words, as "Word-event," the term Ebeling comes to employ for the proclamation of the Word of God.[13]

From the Christ-Event to the Word-Event

We can speak of the "post-Bultmannian" character of the New Hermeneutic, not simply because it chronologically *follows* Bultmann and was largely led by two of his students, Ernst Fuchs and Gerhard Ebeling, but because the New Hermeneutic *passes through* Bultmann.[14] His conclusions, some of them problematic from the standpoint of traditional Christian theology, furnish the New Hermeneutic with its starting points for reflection. The theological appeal of the later Heidegger's reflections on language comes by way of providing an account of the performative character of language furnishing a necessary and further step in the process of demythologization rooted in, but going beyond, Bultmann's own positions.

As we have seen, Bultmann explains the performative power of the Christian kerygma by embracing the formula, "Jesus has risen into the kerygma." Similarly in his treatment of the Fourth Gospel, Bultmann translates the myth of the Incarnation as the contemporary enfleshment of God's address to us in human speech (cf. Jn. 1:14). In this way, the cross-resurrection and the Incarnation are no longer regarded as mythical-historical events of the past on the basis of which Christian witness becomes efficacious by virtue of its verbal reiteration of this event. Rather, for Bultmann, the efficacy of Christian witness *is* itself the resurrection or revelation of Jesus Christ.

Yet, in this transposition wrought by demythologization, Bultmann arguably still appeals to a miraculous, supernatural act by Christ who makes the ordinary language of witness extraordinarily efficacious.[15] For example, Bultmann claims the kerygma as the exclusive locus for the presence of Christ: "Christ, the Crucified and Risen One, encounters us in the word of proclamation–nowhere else," and "in the preached word, and only in it, is the Risen One encountered."[16] Again, Bultmann also identifies the contemporaneity of Jesus Christ with Christian preaching: "Christianity proclaims an event, or rather in the proclamation, the event that is called Jesus Christ takes place continually, the revelation of God in a human word."[17] Moreover, Bultmann further asserts the agency of Jesus Christ with respect to contemporary church proclamation: "Jesus Christ is the eschatological event not as an established fact of past time but as repeatedly present, as addressing you and me here and now in preaching."[18] These formulations, among many others that could be cited, raise the question whether Bultmann's understanding of preaching as the event of Christ's resurrection or revelation is tantamount to "word magic." If Bultmann is opposed to supernatural interventionism, should this not extend more consistently to his account of the language of Christian proclamation? In other words, to use the traditional language of dogmatics, in his project of translating the first form of the Word of God, that is, the Christ-myth, into the third form of the Word of God, that is, the contemporary Christ-event, Bultmann does not entirely succeed with his own intention of a non-mythological restatement of the kerygma. There is still a mythological remainder that fails the plausibility test of a modern world picture; namely, an appeal to a supernatural act of God and an alleged contemporary speaking by a risen Christ.

By contrast, the New Hermeneutic, informed by a Heideggerian theory of language or poetics, is able to account for the performative power of the Christian gospel without lapsing into the objectivized, denotative language of myth (or, for that matter, science) and without appealing to a supernatural act of God. As we have seen, performative power is inherent in language itself, since language has the natural capacity or agency to render present what is otherwise absent, to reveal what is otherwise hidden, and to set going a new future. Given the linguisticality and temporality of existence, God can only be confessed as present to faith through the event of language. Thus, Bultmann's demythologizing is taken one step further. The explanation for the transforming power of the proclaimed Word of God lies not in miracles of any sort, resulting in a contemporary Christ-event, but rather in the "Word-event" in which the God, who came to expression in the teaching and preaching of the historical Jesus, again comes to expression in our teaching and preaching.

In light of the primitive Christian kerygma, Bultmann finds no saving significance in Jesus Christ apart or in abstraction from his eschatological destiny as the crucified Lord. True, Bultmann held and to some degree demonstrated that we can through form criticism recover the message of the historical Jesus.[19] Nevertheless, for Bultmann, that message only had saving significance for Jesus' contemporaries. It does not and cannot have that significance for us. That would be to know Christ "according to the flesh" and on this side of the cross, "we know him no longer in that way" (2 Cor. 5:16). By contrast, for the New Hermeneutic, this reading of Paul would bind the church to a timeless Christ-symbol that denies and defies the historicity of existence, a historicity which Jesus, as fully human, shares with us, and in which the Word of God always resounds.

For this reason, the claim that the historical Jesus is the basis of faith, must first begin with Jesus as the witness to faith by retrieving his preaching and teaching from the Synoptic Gospels. In so doing, what is discovered is that "the rule of God is undoubtedly the core" of Jesus' message. In Ebeling's view, "the emphasis does not lie on a spectacular apocalyptic happening, but on the nearness of God himself." This nearness is not to be heard as foreboding but as hopeful, for "what is peculiar and unique in Jesus' proclamation of the rule of God is that his call to repentance is wonderfully transformed into a call to joy. The message of Jesus does not aim at instilling fear, but at giving courage." Since God is about to arrive on the scene, Jesus can exhort his hearers to take heart. Moreover, in Ebeling's account, Jesus authoritatively taught ("You have heard that it was said...But I say unto you ...") that the will of God lies not in casuistic, meticulous keeping of the law but in obedient freedom to love one's neighbor. Ebeling further translates Jesus' call to discipleship as a call to faith, that is, to a way of life that is not determined by anxiety but by the rule of God who is near.[20]

Thus, to follow Jesus in the way of faith is to trust the God of the future by entrusting the future to God now. Entering on to this path means living here and now in freedom from anxiety and in freedom for love of one's neighbor. This is the message of Jesus and, in Ebeling's view, it is also the experience of faith arising from Jesus' proclamation, and, therefore, the normative criterion for testing the faithfulness of contemporary preaching. If we want to know about faith in God as a way of life, we can discover its illustration, or better, instantiation, in the figure or story of Jesus, together with the parables that formed a large part of his preaching. Both the parables and figure of Jesus, on New Hermeneutic grounds, are interrelated. Since language cannot be divorced from the situation in which it is uttered, Jesus' message, particularly as expressed in his parables, illumines his way of life, just as his way of life illumines his parables. Before turning to the figure of Jesus in the thought of the New Hermeneutic, we pause over his parables, for "it is his parables which are typical of Jesus."[21]

Here emerges in the New Hermeneutic a distinct parallel with Heidegger's reflections on language. Just as poetry for Heidegger is the place one will find "pure speech" as opposed to "idle talk," so the parable–as a form of poetic speech–functions in the New Hermeneutic as the purest form of the kerygma of Jesus. As Being comes to speech in poetry, so in the parable "Jesus intends to 'bring God to speech.'"[22] Fuchs comments:

> Jesus does not put his own words into other people's mouths. They themselves have to be able to say what they have understood. That is why he speaks to them in parables which simply portray the new situation. Between the present which they share with Jesus and the future in which God shall accomplish his rule, they find themselves as between a tiny beginning and a magnificent end: that is the intention of the parables of the mustard seed and the leaven (Mt 13:31–32 and parallels; 13:33 and parallel). But all of them, together with Jesus, move within this occurrence, when they understand and have faith; even though in relation to the rule of God, their faith itself appears like a grain of mustard seed (Mt 17: 20 and parallel). That is the decisive achievement of the parables of Jesus: whoever understands and goes this way moves already in a new context, in being before God.[23]

Note here that the parables are not understood in an "S is P" sense, as denotative signifiers of "this" equals "that," or "this" stands for "God's Kingdom." Rather, as an extended simile, what is portrayed by the parables of Jesus is a *new situation* that cannot simply be contained within the typical or customary patterns of life, even though Jesus employs ordinary language and draws on familiar characters and allusions. This new situation portrayed by the parables calls its hearers not to catechetical recitations (*fides quae*, "the faith which") but to everyday responses of faith as open trust in the coming rule of God (*fides qua*, "the faith by which"). Faith's openness to the future as a present stance is also iterated and instantiated in the life of Jesus and his followers. The eventfulness of faith is not simply in coming to understand the new situation in which the coming rule of God places us now, thereby altering our self-understanding and to which the parables witness, but faith's eventfulness also lies in its character as a way of daily living "shared with Jesus" and unfolding before the coming rule of God. The word of Jesus "not only calls forth faith but also accompanies it."[24] Here is the basis for Craddock's subsequent assertion that "the subject matter is not the nature of God but the hearer's situation in the light of God."[25] The hearer and the hearer's situation are thus a constitutive part of parabolic proclamation.

Thus, the coming God, who is already rendered near by the parabolic word of Jesus, in so drawing near through language, creates a new situation on earth in which the figure of Jesus moves. In this sense, the life of Jesus interprets his parables just as they illumine and interpret his life–and that of his would-be followers. "Jesus' preaching is exactly like his conduct, his whole appearance: it is quite simply *the announcement of the time itself,* the *new* time of the kingdom of God....But in distinction from the Baptist, Jesus announces the new time not because it is coming but because it is here."[26] His preaching and teaching cannot be fully understood apart from his healing of the sick, his encouragement to others, his table-fellowship with sinners, and, most of all, his holding fast to faith even when charged and crucified for blasphemy and sedition. Only on the cross, did the witness of Jesus to faith come to an end, "My God, My God, why have you forsaken me?" (Mk. 15:34). Yet even in this cry of dereliction, Jesus witnessed to faith in the God who, as "my God," remains near.[27]

The question thus arises how Jesus, the witness to faith, became the basis of faith, or, to use the language of the Book of Hebrews, how "the pioneer" became the "perfecter of our faith" (12:2). The traditional answer, of course, is that Jesus was raised from the dead. But how is this to be understood, as it were, in good faith and without a *sacrificium intellectus?*[28] The New Hermeneutic formulates its answer by beginning where Bultmann ends, namely in the recognition that the proclamation of the resurrection is not the announcement of an objective historical event that happened to the crucified Jesus. Such an event, so regarded, is clearly mythological as Bultmann correctly recognized. Nevertheless, the New Hermeneutic rejects Bultmann's solution of sharply separating the "Christ of Faith" from the "Jesus of History," which Bultmann held by virtue of the resurrection as the eschatological event annulling any alleged saving significance of the historical Jesus. In a post-Bultmannian move, Fuchs retains the historical Jesus as the basis of faith on the one hand, while on the other hand demythologizing even more radically than Bultmann the contemporary experience of faith. For the New Hermeneutic, any claim for the presence of the risen Christ in proclamation, indeed, even of Christ as the ultimate proclaimer of the proclamation, is further demythologized as the continuing retrieval and interpretation by Christian proclamation of the performative speech of the historical Jesus. "Faith in the risen Christ therefore means the faith the historical Jesus was God's word to us, and that word was present, and is to be believed as present, in the very death of Jesus on the cross....The victory of the resurrection consists, therefore, concretely, in the victory of the words of Jesus over the death of Jesus on the cross."[29]

The "language of God has in Jesus' cross become precisely the language of Jesus' cross." The language-history of Jesus or the Word-event of Jesus of Nazareth thus continues today as the language of Jesus' cross is re-released in the sermon. Since in his teaching and preaching "Jesus opposed the self-assertion of men who feel compelled to ground and justify their existence for and to themselves," his contrasting "passive obedience," to use traditional dogmatic language, becomes in the New Hermeneutic "the final act of that opposition." We who hear the "word of the cross" (1 Cor. 1:18, RSV) are forced to the decision whether we will let the crucifixion of Jesus judge our own inauthentic existence, as determined by our compulsive self-preservative moves in the face of death, and therefore, in so condemning us, simultaneously free us for the new life of faith, hope, and love. In Jesus, this freedom for God, and from self-assertion, led him to the cross. What had, up to then, been only a human possibility, the actualization of authentic existence, became a historical reality. The word of the cross thus poses to us the same decision for our existence that was posed to the historical Jesus. Will we live for ourselves or for God? Jesus, too, had to decide for faith. Jesus, too, had to decide for a selfhood free from self-assertion–even if it led to death. That death could not overcome the Word-event, which came to expression in Jesus, means that it can yet come to expression for us and in us. Jesus is thus not only the witness to faith, he is the basis for our own faith, or in the words of Hebrews, "the pioneer and perfecter of our faith" (2:12).[30]

The mid-century theological transition from Bultmannian to post-Bultmannian theology, which was also a generational transition, can thus be summarized by the slogan, "From the Christ-event to the Word-event." The cross-resurrection kerygma of Jesus Christ calling for faith, which stood at the heart of Bultmann's understanding of the gospel, now gives way to the "Jesus kerygma," that is, the teaching and preaching of "the historical Jesus" as the witness to faith and the basis of faith today. Hand in hand with this transposition, the New Hermeneutic launches a new, second quest for the historical Jesus. Unlike the first, liberal quest of the late nineteenth-century and the third quest of the late-twentieth century spawned by the "Jesus seminar," that of the New Hermeneutic is motivated more by a kerygmatic than a biographical interest. What is at stake is the retrieval of the Word-event that came to expression in Jesus. This retrieval, which entails both the message and figure of Jesus, is the first step in interpreting his word so that it might again be interpreted by Christian proclamation for our contemporary situation. In conjunction with this new focus on the historical Jesus, and informed by Heidegger's poetics, there also arises a new emphasis on the parables of Jesus as providing the primary models for preaching the Word of God, both its method and its message.

From Scripture to Sermon

With the historical Jesus and his kerygma serving as an authorizing and a winnowing norm for Christian preaching, the homiletical task becomes understood as interpreting the Word of God that came to expression or "eventuated" in Jesus in order that this same Word may again come to expression today. By definition, therefore, preaching is a hermeneutic enterprise, and theological hermeneutics arguably arises out of the preaching task. Just as the preacher cannot be concerned with the dispassionate exposition of texts but must continually press the "So what?" question on behalf of the hearers, so the New Hermeneutic no longer understands its task simply as the interpretation of texts, but more broadly as the interpretation of existence by means of texts. To cite Ebeling's formulation,

> *The primary phenomenon in the realm of understanding is not understanding OF language, but understanding THROUGH*

language. The word is not really the object of understanding, and thus the thing that poses the problem of understanding, the solution of which requires exposition and therefore also hermeneutics as the theory of understanding. Rather, the word is what opens up and mediates understanding, i.e. brings something to understanding. *The word itself has a hermeneutic function.*[31]

That is to say, in accord with Heidegger's theory of language or poetics, what is obscure and needs clarification is not ultimately the word itself, but the situation in which the word arises and to which it is spoken. And this clarification can occur only by means of the word.

Given the linguisticality of existence, whereby we understand existence, language, and the subject matter of language only through the event of language itself, authentic existence never takes place apart from words. Language and existence, word and faith always go together. Words are not just "words." "It is 'word,'" writes Ebeling, "that unites God and man." Ebeling continues, "Salvation is to be expected solely from God and that salvation is to be expected solely from words and is therefore at one and the same time a wholly divine and a wholly human thing." So human words are the medium of divine revelation and human salvation. In this sense, faith truly comes only from what is heard (cf. Rom 10:17).[32]

Given this perspective, it is hardly surprising that the New Hermeneutic is keenly interested in preaching. Ebeling writes, "Whatever precise theological definition may be given to the *concept of the Word of God,* at all events it points us to something that happens to the movement which leads from the text of holy scripture to the sermon ('sermon' of course taken in the pregnant sense of proclamation in general)."[33] In other words, the situation of proclamation is correlative with the theological concept of the Word of God, and as such the Word of God is properly understood from the start as an event, as a movement *from* scriptural text *to* sermon, and always presupposing the hearers of its message.

The movement from scripture to sermon points to the fact that the scriptures of both Testaments aim to serve proclamation. This is not to say that every text of scripture is appropriate as a text for a sermon, or that it is texts as such that are actually proclaimed. What is proclaimed is the subject matter of the scriptural texts, that is, the Word of God revealed or opened up through texts, those linguistic artifacts of previous proclamation. So the movement from text to sermon is "a transition from scripture to the spoken word." Thus the hermeneutical task is ultimately the homiletical task of "making what is written into spoken word or…in letting the text become God's Word again…by interpreting the text as word." This does not mean expositing the text as past proclamation, distancing its claims as if the preacher were a historian or a cultural archaeologist enamored of "Bibleland." Rather, what is called for is executing the text in the present, verbally carrying forward its subject matter, the Word illuminating our situation before the God who is near. In this way, preaching becomes a hermeneutic aid to our hearers. The aim of preaching is not to force words down people's throats or to put them into people's mouths, rather it is to invite the hearers to interpret their existence, summoning them to answer for their existence, in the light of God's ever-present future, just as Jesus once did for the hearers of his parables.[34]

The New Homiletic follows the New Hermeneutic in understanding the Word of God primarily and preeminently as the Word-event, always presupposing both speaker and listener, and occurring in the movement from text to sermon. As Craddock puts it, "The Word of God, if it is to be located, is to be located in movement, in conversation, in communication between Scripture and church."[35] If that is the case, then what form should the sermon take as it emerges from this movement? Obviously, the form cannot simply be taken from the controlling canons of rhetoric without regard either for the poetics of the biblical text or the dynamics of the Word of God. What is required is an alternative sermonic form shaped "by the content of the Gospel," or "the nature of the Christian faith," or the poetics found in the biblical canon, especially the parables of Jesus.[36]

Closer inspection of Craddock's proposal finds him nevertheless oscillating between two very different approaches inherent in it. On the one hand, Craddock calls for the sermon to follow the scriptural text in reiteration of its thoughts, spirit, and sometimes, at least, even its form so that there should be "an attempt to make the form and spirit of the message congenial with the form and spirit of the text…Let doxologies be shared doxologically, narratives narratively, polemics polemically, poems, poetically, and parables parabolically."[37] On the other hand asks Craddock, "Why not on Sunday morning retrace the inductive trip he [the preacher] took earlier and see if his hearers come to that same conclusion?"[38] Elaborating further, Craddock envisions this Sunday journey as an act of recreating for the congregation the following: the preacher's "experience and insight" as he or she engaged the text, his or her "own process of discovering," his or her "inductive experience of coming to an understanding of the message of the text," and his or her "experience of arriving at a conclusion."[39] In other words, if the first version of Craddock's proposal really makes the poetic frame of reference central relying on the transposition of textual dynamics into sermonic dynamics, the second and more daring version of Craddock's proposal takes up Ebeling's thesis about the Word of God and appropriates it directly for homiletical method. Since the Word of God is located in the movement from text to sermon, why not bring the listeners of the sermon directly into an encounter with this very movement by inviting them into the preacher's journey from text to sermon? *The sermon, therefore, is not so much an exposition of the text as it is a public repetition or reenactment of the preacher's own inductive attempt to understand the text.*

Obviously, the transposition of textual dynamics into sermonic dynamics and the sharing of the preacher's experience of understanding the text are not necessarily the same thing.[40] In the latter case, where the exposition of the preacher's own experience is central, in contrast to the "poetic" version of Craddock's proposal, any number of sermonic forms are imaginable in relation to specific biblical forms, including, one presumes, testimony, or even a recounting of one's stream of consciousness, since the point is to repeat or reenact the preacher's own discoveries about the text. Moreover, exegetical discoveries about doxologies, for example, will not necessarily be shared in a "doxological" form, since it is the process rather than the product of discovery that is key. In fact, the process of sharing one's inductive discoveries seems inherently biased toward a narrative form. Craddock's proposal implies a marked incoherence, although we can see both a poetic and a theological frame of reference clearly in operation, even as they tug in different homiletic directions.

Do we have in the history of preaching any examples of preachers either repeating or "recreating" their own inductive attempts to understand a scriptural text? Augustine's *Confessions* come to mind, but these ruminations were not preached in the pulpit. As Eric O. Springsted has observed, "In the hundreds of pages of his [Augustine's] sermons on the Psalms or the Gospel of John, we garner fewer personal facts about their author than we would in an average sermon of a Protestant minister given to illustrating Scripture from his or her own personal experience."[41] The testimonies of eighteenth and nineteenth-century women also come to mind.[42] In public address, they openly struggled with interpretation of scriptural passages that appeared inimical to the ordination of women. Did such discourses proceed inductively in the manner Craddock prescribes? Possibly. Certainly, the parables of Jesus do not have Jesus sharing his puzzlements and discoveries about scriptural texts, but the oration Luke has Paul delivering before King Agrippa may come closer to Craddock's vision of a sermon creating a journey of understanding through which the listener is invited to believe (Acts 26). Without sufficient historical precedents and analogues, Craddock's preaching method may appear utterly his own. This judgment is ventured not only by the effectiveness of Craddock's own preaching, but by the frequent failure of others who attempt to imitate him, with Barbara Brown Taylor perhaps serving as a happy exception.

Given Craddock's sharp attacks on rhetoric, the reader of *As One without Authority* may be most surprised to discover how very anchored to the rhetorical frame of reference Craddock's homiletic finally remains. The cardinal rhetorical rule that Craddock reiterates is that there must be for every sermon "singleness of theme," "the restraint of a single idea," "the point," "this one idea," the "point in one simple sentence," "the central idea," "this one governing theme," "a controlling thesis," and "a single germinal idea."[43] In fact, he can even describe the sermon as "the careful unfolding of an idea."[44] From where does this idea come? Most often, but not always, Craddock indicates it is taken from the text, and he even cites a narrative like John 9, the healing of the blind man, to announce that "the point of the story" should become the "governing consideration" for the material in the sermon, because "no preacher has the right to look for points until he has the point."[45] Craddock is quite insistent that having an overall governing theme to every sermon is not inimical to sermonic movement: "The more confined the topic fixed in mind, the greater the freedom of mental range in pursuing and developing that topic."[46]

A century earlier, one of the most influential textbooks of rhetorical homiletics ever written suggested, in ways far less insistent than Craddock, that while there was frequently no need for an explicit statement of the subject, "what is technically called the Proposition," such was most often helpful. Propositions could function not only to bestow unity on a sermon by way of sermonic focus, but they could also be stated in a more open-ended or "modest" fashion so as "to propose an inquiry rather than a process of proof." Having suggested this inductive approach to preaching, the writer went on to affirm that "an effective discourse" needs both "a plan" and "movement" or "progress," and he complimented "the Greek and Roman orators" on how often their speeches had "no clearly marked divisions" disrupting such movement.[47]

As is evident from this summary taken from John A. Broadus, despite Craddock's frequent attacks on rhetoric, his New Homiletic remains at key places firmly anchored within the old rhetorical frame of reference. Indeed, "what he had blocked at the front door–an idea centered approach to preaching–he welcomed through the back door."[48] For Craddock, the purpose of exegesis is to extract from the scriptural text the governing theme or idea which then becomes available as the governing theme or idea of the sermon. As Thomas Long points out, what makes Craddock's "approach innovative is that these ideas do not come alone but always clothed in the garments of the inductive sleuthing process by which those ideas were discovered in the first place."[49] Craddock, like the Greek and Roman orators mentioned by Broadus, does not want to divide the sermon into further points, and in that sense he does depart from the homiletical models favored by the medieval Schoolmen, the early-modern Puritans, and the more recent "three-point" preachers. Craddock's strict insistence upon the invariable formula of a single governing idea directing the sermon, insofar as that idea is distilled from a scriptural text, would appear to stand in tension with the perspectives of the New Hermeneutic. Does the encounter with the subject matter of a scriptural text, made possible through the dynamics of the textual form itself, really require reduction to a single denotative sentence in order to be rereleased in proclamation? This is precisely what the New Hermeneutic says the parables of Jesus do not do.

Thus, we find in Craddock all three frames of reference, theology, rhetoric, and poetics, but without any clear sense as to which is primary and which are subordinate to it. The poetic frame of reference is evident inasmuch as the dynamics of the biblical word, and possibly even the form of the biblical word, are to be reiterated, repeated, or recapitulated in the sermon. The theological frame of reference is evident insofar as Ebeling's location of the Word of God in the movement from text to sermon is taken as authorizing the "re-creation" in the sermon of the preacher's own experience of inductively discovering meaning in the text. Nevertheless, and despite his polemics against rhetoric, it is still this framework that is most dominant in Craddock. This may be indicated in that Craddock defines preaching only from "below" as a human task, and not also from "above" as something God is doing, and by the virtual absence of references to the Holy Spirit.[50] Moreover, his insistence that every sermon have a governing theme or thesis, reducible, to a single sentence, and that such provides guidance or structure for the unfolding movement of the sermon likewise indicates we are in the presence of a rhetorical homiletics.

Sermon: "Faith and Fear"; Text: Matthew 14:22–33

Fred Craddock, as a retired professor of preaching at Candler School of Theology, Emory University, preached this sermon at Cherry Log (Georgia) Christian Church, where he was then pastor. The text, taken from the Revised Common Lectionary, suggests that the sermon was probably preached in early August of 1999.

The sermon begins not with the text, which includes the story of Jesus walking on water toward a boat of terrified disciples amid a storm, but with Craddock sharing how, as a former professor of preaching, he had students read sermons from a variety of preachers. Only at the end of the long introduction, comprising about a fifth of the sermon, do we come to this key transition:

> There was one sermon that I had them read every year. It was the sermon that we have just read as our text this morning. The students were a little surprised when I called this a sermon, because they thought this is a text of scripture, this is what you use to get a sermon. It is not a sermon itself. But yes, it is a sermon. Matthew took an experience that the disciples had with Jesus–and by the way, some ancient writers thought possibly it was a bad dream that Simon Peter had had and that he had woken up screaming and saying, "It's a ghost!"–but Matthew took this experience with Jesus and made it into a sermon.[51]

In these brief sentences, Craddock accomplishes several things. First, he points to the fact that scripture is essentially kerygmatic material, that is, written and recalled for the purposes of proclamation. By reference to ancient interpreters of the text, he also indicates that textual meaning is not obvious or univocal, but a matter for interpretation. He also reminds the congregation of his career as a professor and thereby establishes his ethos as a teacher, and thereby his authority. In so doing, he transposes the congregation into a preaching class as they now join their teacher on a journey of textual understanding. His language is conversational, even folksy, written for the ear, and frequently employing the rhetorical device of anachronism as when Jesus tells his disciples, "Get out of my face...I need some time with God."[52]

Craddock notices the unusual detail that Jesus compelled his disciples to get into the boat while he dismissed the crowds before retiring to pray. After briefly suggesting possible motivations, Craddock sketches the scene. Using his students' jokes about "walking on water" as a point of departure, and thereby acknowledging our own incredulity, Craddock offers his interpretation of the text:

> When the students got through with all this cuteness, we went back to the point. And the point is this: *Only God can walk on the waves.* That is what the Bible says. In Job, in Isaiah, in Habakkuk, in the Psalms, it is God who walks on the storm, God who makes a path in the sea. Why? To show a miracle? To say, "Hey, look, I'm walking on water"? No, don't be shallow. In ancient times the sea was the place of evil. The evil monster was there; the Leviathan was there. The enemy of all that we know as good and right is there in the water. In the Bible, the water is the abode of all the forces that are against us. And God walks on the sea. In other words, there is no power, no storm, no wind, no force in the world that God cannot conquer, no evil over which God is not superior, nothing that can destroy your life because God loves and cares for you.
>
> Jesus' walking on the water is not to be understood as a miracle. Look at it, listen to it. Jesus comes in the storm on the sea and says, "Take heart, I am." These words are translated, "It is I" or "I am he," but what Jesus actually says is, "I am." "I am"–that's the name for God.[53]

Consistent with his homiletical theory, Craddock states here with clarity and emphasis the sermonic theme, or governing idea: "there is no power...no evil over which God is not superior, nothing that can destroy your life because God loves and cares for you." Notice that the statement is not simply about God, but about God in relation to the hearers. What is different from traditional propositional statements governing a sermon is that Craddock has withheld giving his until reaching the midpoint of the sermon. It now comes as an "aha" moment, as an answer, inductively reached, against taking the text in a supernaturalist way.

Craddock also reads this passage through other scriptural texts in order to bring to the surface its latent apocalyptic character as focusing on God's dominion over the power of evil. Not only does he provide a broad intratextual context for interpretation, but he goes deeply into the text by proposing a more accurate English translation that heightens the christological significance of the action by identifying Jesus as God. Such precise dogmatic assertions are very rare in a

Craddock sermon. But even here, he simply reports his exegetical findings and leaves it for the listener to absorb and evaluate the claim. Craddock is not interested in the deity of Jesus Christ apart from its existential implications for his listeners.

Having himself raised and heightened the apocalyptic overtones of the text (e.g., Peter's lack of faith here is connected with Jesus' subsequent rebuke, "Get behind me, Satan"), Craddock concludes his sermon by an explicit act of demythologization. The cosmological imagery now attached to the text through intratextual reading itself undergoes a translation into the language of existence:

> A lot of people say to me, "Well those stories in the Bible, I don't know. I believed all that when I was a kid…" Of course I'm not a child anymore. I don't believe there are demons in the water. Nobody who jumps off the high dive into the water says, "Look out for the demons!" We don't believe that anymore.
>
> Then where are the demons if they are not in the water? I know where they are. I know where the fears are. You don't believe in demons? Why the fear? You know what jealousy is don't you? It is fear of the loss of love. Why are people greedy and just get as much as they can? It is a fear, a fear of insecurity. Why do children cheat at school? A fear of failure. Why does anybody tell a lie? A fear of punishment. Fear, fear, fear.…I don't believe there are demons in the water, I tell you folks, I wish they were in the water, but that's not where they are….
>
> In the boat–and we are all in the boat–we can give pep talks to each other. "We'll make it. Some of you bail, we're going to make it." We can start whistling and singing. But the plain fact is that without trust in God, we are not going to make the shore. But if we trust in God, "we are more than conquerors through him who loves us…, and neither death nor life, nor angels, nor rulers, nor things present, nor things to come, nor powers, nor height, nor depth nor anything else in all creation will be able to separate us from the love of God in Christ Jesus our Lord" [Rom 8:37–39].[54]

In this concluding section, the earlier christological affirmations become soteriologically correlated with the anthropological situation, so that faith in Jesus or "trust in God" becomes the antidote for those deep human fears out of which flow our many sins. Demons do not really refer to personified minions of Satan, but are symbolic of the deep fears that hold us back from vulnerable lives of love. While we may question Craddock's placement of a conditional "if" before the concluding doxology of Romans 8, it does leave his hearers with an implied decision about where they will place their trust: either in God or in themselves.

The New Hermeneutic:
Feminist Appropriation and Critique

In 1989, Rebecca S. Chopp's book, *The Power to Speak: Feminism, Language, God,* marked the first sustained attempt by a feminist theologian to appropriate and rehabilitate the dogmatic concept, "Word of God." Precisely at a time when such theologies had gone into eclipse with the advent of political and liberation theologies, Chopp's second-generation feminist work moves beyond the early rejectionist phase of feminism by proclaiming a new vision of God and humanity from within Christianity. Only in this way can the tradition itself be redeemed, or to use Chopp's term "emancipated." Rather than withdrawing from the Christian tradition, Chopp claims the power to speak in and to that tradition, specifically, in its Protestant strand that centers on the Word.

Chopp's connection to the New Hermeneutic is not simply that of historical or chronological succession. There are material connections as well. In many instances, the conclusions of Fuchs and Ebeling form Chopp's premises. For example, Chopp accepts the linguisticality of existence, or as she might prefer to say, the linguisticality of subjectivity. Again, so far as I can tell, as in the New Hermeneutic, by "the Word" Chopp does not mean the incarnate, crucified, and risen Jesus Christ. So for Chopp, the traditional first form of the Word of God plays no role at all. If one is to speak of a word or logos underlying our words, for Chopp it would be to speak of the primordial "perfectly open sign," an oracular term that Chopp does not specifically define, but which seems to suggest a pure and uncorrupted word by which all empirical words are measured.[55] It is this word that empowered the emancipatory rhetoric of Jesus; it is this word that all emancipatory rhetoric partially actualizes or approximates. Thus, as with the New Hermeneutic, so with Chopp, the traditional third form of the Word of God, refers not to the Christ-event taking place here and now in the proclaimed word (pace Bultmann), but as demythologized it is now further reinterpreted as an *emancipatory* language-event.

Finally, Chopp shares with the New Hermeneutic a return to the Jesus of the gospels in place of the kerygmatic Christ of faith.

For Chopp, too, the importance of Jesus lies neither in his atoning work nor in his eschatological destiny and kerygmatic presence, but rather in his *message*. Chopp finds the message of Jesus prototypically distilled in the gospel of Luke, especially chapter four. While Chopp's liberationist Jesus is different from the existentialist Jesus of the New Hermeneutic, her appropriation of Luke stands on this side of the Synoptic turn taken by the New Hermeneutic. For Chopp it is not the cross-resurrection kerygma of Paul or the Incarnation of the divine Logos which comprise the gospel message. Rather, it is the Jesus kerygma that provides the contemporary church with its prototype for contemporary proclamation. By appropriating the New Hermeneutic, Chopp brings an often estranged feminist theology back into conversation and, hence, relation with the last great Protestant theology of the Word. Nevertheless, despite strong formal and material continuities with the New Hermeneutic, Chopp's work is more than an extension of this theological tradition. Chopp's feminist liberation perspectives challenge the New Hermeneutic at key points, indicating her project as one of critical appropriation.

The early 1970s witnessed the rise of political theology in Europe, represented by Jürgen Moltmann and Dorothee Sölle (1929–2003), and various liberation theologies in the Western Hemisphere represented by such figures a Gustavo Gutiérrez and James H. Cone, among others. What was common to all these movements was a new awareness that human beings, and the words they use, are shaped in large measure by their social location and historical context. In his book, *Theology of Hope*, whose appearance in 1964 marked the end of the New Hermeneutic's hegemony in German theology, Moltmann, taking aim at Bultmann asked, "Is any self-understanding of man conceivable at all which is not determined by his relation to the world, to history, to society?"[56] He answers his own rhetorical question by declaring, "Always man's self understanding is socially, materially, and historically mediated."[57]

For Chopp, this means that while our subjectivity is inextricably linguistic, the language we employ is a social, material, and historical product that determines the possibilities that are available to our self-understanding or subjectivity. As she observes, "We experience the world according to categories given to us by language. What it is to be a woman or a man varies in different cultures and at different times and places, but these definitions are prior to the individual, indeed, they allow the individual to become a man or woman in the acceptable modes of that culture."[58] We gain our subjectivity, we come to understand ourselves, only through social constructions of reality, or dominant discourses, into which we are born: "The gaining of subjectivity occurs simultaneously with the guaranteeing of the social-symbolic order."[59]

But "such discourses can change, be displaced, or be transformed, and the change of discourse allows different forms of subjectivity to appear."[60] This is what Christian preaching does. The preaching of Jesus shows the possibility of new discourses emerging, discourses which have the power to overturn or to subvert reigning social constructions of reality. When these dominant discourses are subverted and over-thrown, our subjectivity, our self-understanding, is emancipated and thereby transformed. In this way, Chopp understands that the language-event or the Word-event of Christian proclamation calls into question an oppressive status quo and in this way emancipates those in its bondage to this dominant power. Thus, we have in Chopp not only a transposition of salvation from existentialist to liberationist categories, but we also have a reconceptualization of the New Hermeneutic's Word-event. No Word-event exists apart from the radically historical and social texture of our language and its use, *and no authentic Word-event exists apart from its power of emancipation and social change.* Thus, for Chopp, using language is always a "political activity," and, insofar as that activity is on behalf of emancipation, and, hence, "saving," it cannot be confined to either the church or to its witness.

Again, in line with liberation theology, Chopp proposes a "hermeneutics of marginality." That is to say, all theological claims, all God-talk, including claims and talk about the Word of God, must emerge from the ranks and communities of the oppressed themselves. This is the theological correlate of the claims for self-determination that emerged in the social movements of the 1960s. Beginning with the Black Power Movement in the late 60s, this emphasis on self-determination has continued up until our own time. We have only to note the so-called genitive "theologies of" the American Indian Movement, the Women's Liberation Movement, the Gay, Lesbian, Bisexual, and Transgendered movements, and the efforts of the physically disabled (or "differently abled") to secure equal accessibility to the goods of civil society. All these consciousness-raising movements for liberation and self-determination have set themselves against the dominant social constructions of racism, sexism, heterosexism, and handicappism, which are all seen as deeply etched in American society. To the degree that these movements have produced theologians, these theologians have generally argued that they are responsible primarily, if not exclusively, to their respective

oppressed communities. Only the oppressed can truly speak to and
for the oppressed.

This point was tellingly made in the Broadway play of some
seasons ago, *Children of a Lesser God.* Phyllis Frelich played the part
of Sarah Norman. Like the character Sarah in the play, actress Phyllis
Frelich is also hearing impaired. In the play, she made a memorable
statement when with her hands she signed these words to her do-
gooder, therapist husband: "No one will ever speak for me again."
That is one of the key themes of liberation theology. Chopp claims
to speak out of the experience of marginalization that women have
suffered often in the name of Christianity. She also claims to read
the scriptures from the standpoint of this situation of marginality.
The community, then, for which Chopp claims to speak is that of
"women-church," but in Chopp's definition this really includes all
women, whether in, half-in, or out of the institutional church, who
are seeking emancipation for women.[61]

The hermeneutics of marginalization is designed to interpret
subjectivity in its social construction and to proclaim the liberating
Word for those on the margins or in marginalized communities. The
aim of this hermeneutics of marginalization is the deconstruction
of present dominant discourses for the purposes of emancipating
oppressed communities. If the Lutheran theologian thinks of salvation
in terms of how I can be forgiven my sins and justified in the sight of
God, the liberationist theologian thinks of salvation in terms of the
emancipation of the oppressed. As is common among liberationist
soteriologies, the focus here is not on sinners needing justification,
but on victims needing emancipation. Again, the question of the
Enlightenment, over which Bultmann took such pains, "How can
I believe in a gospel rendered mythological by the modern world
picture?" or, "How can I believe in the face of doubt occasioned by
scientific findings?" is not the problematic of liberation theology. The
question for Chopp is not what word to say to sinners or to doubters,
but rather what word to say to victims, to the least and to the last, who
survive on the margins. For Chopp, there can be no word authentically
related to its character as a perfectly open sign apart from a human
word that emancipates women from injustice and oppression.

Chopp further correlates the language of emancipatory proclamation, not with discrete individuals–as in the case of Bultmann and the
New Hermeneutic–but in the power of this proclamation to create true
community, in other words what is traditionally termed "the church."
Here, Chopp picks up a key Reformation theme for reinterpretation.
The Greek word *ekklesia,* translated as "church," never refers to a
building in the New Testament. As someone has said, "The church

is what you have left the day after the building has burned down." In the New Testament, the *ekklesia* is composed of those "called out" from the world, those who are thereby assembled, gathered, and elected by the proclaimed Word of God (cf. Acts 2). Thus, the church is essentially an event, constituted by the proclamation of the Word, and only, secondarily, an institution (cf. Acts 6).

Today, in Chopp's judgment, another model of the institutional church operates in wide segments of bourgeois Christianity. This current "ecclesiology" is characterized by therapeutic, indeed, psycho-therapeutic, understandings of salvation, on the one hand, and by entrepreneurial and managerial styles of leadership and organization. If you think Chopp is far off the mark in her analysis, read the advertisements in church magazines aimed at pastors. The intertwining rhetorics of therapy and business management increasingly indicate the ethos of the institutional church. Chopp suggests we are ripe, if not overdue, for a reformation of our reigning models of the church, and, she further suggests, as in the sixteenth century, it will come only through renewed attention to the proclamation of the Word.

In this sense, Chopp stands in continuity with the ecclesiology of the Reformers. Over against dominant institutional models of the church, the Reformers stressed the church as event, as the creation of the Word of God. This *koinonia* or communion of those called from death to life, from conformity to the world to conformity with Christ's cruciform life, this community happens whenever and wherever the Word of God is proclaimed in sermon and sacrament. In other words, from the standpoint of the Reformation, all that is necessary for there to be a church is the proclamation of the gospel. Without the gospel proclaimed, one may have an institution or a business called "church," but it will not be a "true" church, even if it boasts a perfect apostolic pedigree, or, more to the point today, even if it is a packed Sunday crowd managed by relaxed, confident entrepreneurs.

In Chopp's reinterpretation of the church-creating power of the Word, emancipatory proclamation creates the community of emancipatory transformation, which then, in turn, takes responsibility for emancipatory proclamation with the example and message of Jesus as its prototype. Salvation is not located in a Christ-event, whether in the past, or in the present; rather, salvation is located in a community-forming event that is simultaneously the language-event of emancipation. This Word-event which creates a new community of freedom, for Chopp, is confined neither to the institutional church nor to the sermon. To borrow Peter C. Hodgson's words from another context, it happens "wherever and whenever a free, truthful, and salvific word comes to speech."[62]

True, Chopp shares with Bultmann and the New Hermeneutic a common conviction; namely, that the hearers of the Word or the Church of the Word are essential in and for the event of the Word. For Bultmann there is no kerygmatic communication, and, for Chopp, no language of emancipatory transformation apart from the concrete situation of the hearer (Chopp would insist on "hearers") awaiting proclamation. Nevertheless, Chopp understands the hearers' situation or, if you will, sin, differently. For Bultmann, human beings, driven by anxiety in the face of death, are driven, willingly or unwillingly, knowingly or unknowingly, by a quest for authentic existence. This quest is really the question of God, and it is this question the gospel answers. In the cross of Christ, all our false securities, as the inauthentic responses to anxiety, are crucified, and in the proclamation of the cross we are set free from them, from the past, and from the world in order to enter into eschatological existence of love for the neighbor.

By contrast, Chopp sees the situation confronting proclamation as that of human beings entrapped and entwined in corporate and social structures of oppression or marginalized by such structures. That is precisely for her the situation that confronted Jesus as he announced his own ministry of the Word to the marginalized in the synagogue at Nazareth. Thus, Jesus becomes an example, for our own ministry of the Word. Jesus is a strategic prototype for contemporary feminist theologians in calling into being new communities marked by freedom from injustice and freedom for justice. Thus, if soteriology for Bultmann and the New Hermeneutic is articulated in the language of existentialist self-understanding, for Chopp it is more adequately expressed in the Marxist or liberationist language of social transformation.

Chopp's attempt to bring a broader liberationist vision to the positions of the New Hermeneutic is reminiscent of the earlier attempt of Dorothee Sölle to open Bultmann's constricted existentialism to Marxist social analysis. Whether Chopp's proposal engenders new ecclesial and liturgical forms, as did Sölle's–if relatively briefly–only time will tell. In my judgment, Chopp's work represents the final development of the New Hermeneutic school, a significant attempt at a critical correction. What is less clear is whether it marks a sustainable new departure for homiletics.

The New Hermeneutic and Homiletics:
Concluding Theological Assessment

Arguably, the greatest contribution of the New Hermeneutic school to homiletics was in its insistence that preaching is not simply

a matter of signifying the Word of God, but rather it is part
in the event of the Word of God. In this sense, the New Her
stands in formal continuity with Bullinger's dictum, "The preaching
the Word of God is the Word of God." Rather than simply reiterate this
dogmatic claim (as does Karl Barth's *Church Dogmatics,* for example), or
to interpret it within the framework of signifying, denotative language
(as Bullinger himself does as heir to the classical rhetorical tradition),
the New Hermeneutic attempts to correlate this Reformation claim
with the anthropological principle of the linguisticality of existence
and with analogues derived from the relation between language and
Being, e.g., that Being is the true subject matter of language. In this
way, the eventfulness of God's Word as decisive for existence, and not
simply as a cognitive datum, is brought to the fore. Preachers must
welcome with gratitude the theologians and homiletical theorists of
the New Hermeneutic for their insistence that words do not simply
speak, they act.

As taken up by the New Homiletic, this perspective on the
performative power of language leads to the following key emphases
in homiletics, among many others that could be noted:

First, preaching is not primarily the exposition of information
about God (i.e., the Word of God) as an idea or topic, rather it enacts
or performs the Word of God, or, perhaps to formulate the matter
more faithfully by closer attention to the Heideggerian analogues,
it participates in the continuing enactment and performance of the
Word of God. For this reason, poetics, which is concerned with the
dynamics of the Word of God as found in scripture, provides more
helpful insights and models for preaching than does rhetoric in
which the power of the communication event rests primarily with
the speaker rather than through the properties of language illumined
by its subject matter.

Second, the New Homiletic takes seriously the task of scriptural
exegesis as the site of previous Word-events in which God came to
expression. In this context, the term "exegesis" is only worthy of the
name, if it is, in Thomas G. Long's formulation, "biblical exegesis
for preaching."[63] As Randolph puts it, "Preaching carries forward the
intentionality of the biblical text by following the arc of action called for
by the biblical word to its point of intersection with the contemporary
congregation."[64] As the record of past language-events that eventuated
in salvation, the Bible does not record them for the purpose of
dispassionate record keeping. They were recorded so that what came
to expression in these words might again come to expression through
them. The scriptures have preaching as their primary context. If

exegesis does not proceed on the basis of this intentionality, it simply misses the point. This is not to dismiss the historical-critical method, which after all helped to uncover the kerygmatic content and context of scripture, it is only to say that this method and its results cannot themselves be the *goal* of exegesis. Such an approach, however erudite, misses the point–the preaching point.

Third, the New Homiletic takes seriously the tendency of theological language to degenerate over time into pious shibboleths, clichés, and bromides. The habitual use of theological language in the liturgy and preaching of the church, while preserving the linguistic storehouse which future reflection requires, inevitably risks linguistic diminishment through reflexive overuse and through changing historical circumstances distancing words from their originating contexts. As Paul Tillich observes amid the stuffy, churchy atmosphere following World War II, "There are few words more strange to most of us than 'sin' and 'grace.' They are strange, just because they are so well-known."[65] Similarly, Ebeling confesses "my heart beats more and more for those for whom the great traditional formulae of Christian doctrine are stones instead of bread."[66] Fred Craddock, too, declares, "There is no intrinsic value in simply repeating the confessional language of other people, even if their words are in the Scriptures."[67] As Ebeling notes, "even pious talk of God which does not prove itself real talk of God" is "godless."[68] For the New Homiletic, therefore, preaching can never be a matter of chanting code words, pastoral platitudes, or rhetorical mantras. Such habitual "preacher talk" is not true preaching, but "idle talk." That is to say, the proclamation of the gospel can easily slide into propaganda, self-promotion, and the rhetoric of "public relations" as its words get increasingly lost from their true subject matter. For this reason, "in speaking of God a decision is made about God. Either God is spoken of in such a way that he loses his divinity, or God is spoken of in such a way that he really comes to expression as God."[69]

Fourth, the New Homiletic also urged preachers to take up with seriousness the hermeneutic responsibility to serve the Word of God, through renewed listening to the scriptures, through renewed attention to their performative power, through deeper theological reflection, and through spending more time in sermon preparation, all in order to participate more faithfully in and with the Word as the eventful happening it is, rather than as the "godless" habit our indifference would wish to it to become.

More controversially, in response to Rudolf Bultmann's separation between the Jesus of history and the Christ of faith, the New

Hermeneutic insists that both "Christ" and "faith" find their content, context, and criteria in the inseparable work and word of Jesus, as that work and word are retrieved and reconstructed from the Synoptic Gospels by the historical-critical method. As a result, the parables of Jesus are given primary weight and attention as models of how the Word of God eventuated in his life and ministry. Again, the resulting soteriological Christology is explicated with reference to the anthropological principle of the linguisticality of existence and with analogues derived from the relation between language and Being.

In my judgment, the attempt to make the teaching, preaching, and faith of the historical Jesus foundational for the contemporary faith of the church, with the corollary that the parables of Jesus are the norm for contemporary Christian preaching, stands matters on their head. The primitive Christian kerygma was neither the proclamation of the preaching of Jesus nor simply a presentation of Jesus through his sayings as found, for example, in the *Gospel of Thomas*. The Christian message or kerygma, which generally appears to have been proclaimed in a variety of non-parabolic forms and genres, declared that salvation had happened and was happening not on account of Jesus' preaching and teaching, but on account of his destiny as the crucified and risen Lord. This is borne out by the Pauline kerygmatic summaries, such as Romans 4:24, Peter's Pentecost sermon (Acts 2:14–42), and even Jesus' discourse on the road to Emmaus (Lk. 24:13–35). However, mythologically formulated, e.g., in terms of Jewish apocalyptic, the significance of the canonical gospels is that they subsequently narrate the kerygma as a story about Jesus. Jesus is presented as the crucified Messiah who is vindicated by God in being raised from the dead. To understand why he was crucified and raised, we are referred to the faith-based narratives of the Gospels, not to a hypothetically constructed "historical Jesus" standing under or behind the text.

Because of the legendary and fragmentary character of the Gospels taken as historical sources, determining Jesus' self-understanding or faith through historical reconstruction is a highly speculative process. (The Gospels, incidentally, never speak of "the faith of Jesus.") After reviewing nearly a dozen books on the subject of "New Studies of Jesus," John Riches gleans in six points about all we can say historically about Jesus: (1) A man called Jesus of Nazareth existed "who was a prominent religious figure"; (2) "He was baptized by and an associate of John the Baptist"; (3) "He called disciples (probably 12), performed works of healing and exorcism, taught his disciples and a wider audience and engaged in controversy with Jewish teachers of the

Law"; (4) He associated with tax collectors and sinners and this caused offence to some of the Jewish devout"; (5) "He performed some kind of prophetic action in the Temple"; (6) and, "He was crucified by the Romans at the instigation of some of the Jewish leaders."[70]

If we accept and wrench these "historical facts" out of the biblical narrative, and only correlate them with what form criticism deems the authentic parables of Jesus, then any identity for this Jesus must be hung on some other story line than the kerygmatic one furnished by the Gospels. The alternative story line, strung between Nazareth and Golgotha by the imagination of the historian, inevitably means that the historical Jesus begins to look and sound rather like the historian who creates him. Moreover, the Jesus about whom historians can agree is soteriologically and even culturally beside the point. Those accounts of Jesus that place his significance into the apostolic horizon of his eschatological destiny have been ponderable through two millennia. It is because of this horizon and this destiny that the figure of Jesus and his parables are remembered and through which they should be interpreted. His eschatological destiny is not simply a way of saying that Jesus' words are prolonged beyond his death, it is also a way of saying that they must be interpreted eschatologically or retrospectively in light of his death and resurrection. In this sense, the Christ kerygma interprets the Jesus kerygma; the former cannot be replaced by or reduced to the latter.

While the aim of the New Hermeneutic to overcome the gap between the Christ of Faith and the Jesus of History is laudable, the end result is to shrink considerably the saving significance of Jesus Christ, attenuating its cosmic implications to that of individual existence, transferring–rather than doubling up–the predicates of salvation from God to language, from the Christ-event to the Word-event, and, in the judgment of some, substituting the work of hermeneutics for the gift of the Holy Spirit. For these reasons, it is hardly surprising that there would be theological and homiletical responses from many sides of the theological compass; not only from political and liberation theologies, but from the Barthian camp as well. To that final chapter in our story we now turn.

5

PREACHING AS PROMISSORY NARRATION

So pervasive has been the reconfiguration of theology as hermeneutics in the thought of Rudolf Bultmann, or as inextricably bound to poetics or a theory of language in the view of the New Hermeneutic, that subsequent theological opposition to these developments has itself come to be framed in the language of hermeneutics and poetics, or, more specifically, narratology, which as "a subdivision of poetics…is concerned with the formal properties of a special kind of discourse or text, viz., narrative."[1] To turn to the matter at hand, in the work of Hans W. Frei, mediated as a postliberal homiletic by Charles Campbell, Barthian theology is presented largely through Erich Auerbach's (1892–1957) theory of "realistic narrative." Although the theological frame of reference is not absent from the earlier work of Frei, the narratological frame of reference is primary, probably in the interest of apologetics, since literary criticism was the common currency of academic discourse at Yale, where Frei taught, and was rapidly replacing the history of religions as the lingua franca of biblical studies. In this way, the poet finally comes even for Karl Barth! In Frei's later (posthumously published) work, a cultural linguistic theory of religion and doctrine becomes more dominant, under the influence of George Lindbeck, but this actually results in reinforcing Frei's longstanding narratological convictions.

Postliberalism

It may be helpful to begin our discussion by identifying some distinguishing features of postliberalism. As we find it emerging in the 1970s and 1980s at Yale Divinity School, there is a concern for the preparatory, formal questions of theological and hermeneutical method, rather than for the material task of dogmatic production or systematic theological reconstruction. No major dogmatics or systematic theology has yet emerged from the Yale School, but it has produced methodological studies and taxonomies that have had a major heuristic influence in theology. In this regard, especially noteworthy are George Lindbeck's *The Nature of Doctrine: Religion and Theology in a Postliberal Age* (1984),[2] together with Frei's *The Eclipse of Biblical Narrative: A Study in Eighteenth and Nineteenth Century Hermeneutics* (1974)[3] and *The Identity of Jesus Christ: The Hermeneutical Bases of Dogmatic Theology* (1975).[4] While the practice and problems of preaching have not been the originating forces behind postliberalism, Charles Campbell transposes Frei's perspectives on narrative christology into homiletical theory in his book, *Preaching Jesus: New Directions for Homiletics in Hans Frei's Postliberal Theology* (1997).[5]

Second, postliberalism of the Yale stripe is consciously antifoundationalist in its understanding of theological claims. Foundationalism is the effort, following René Descartes (1596–1650), to ground all knowledge claims in some fundamental certitude that cannot by self-contradiction be doubted. Foundational theologies often embrace the apologetic strategy of attempting to ground or correlate their particular claims, for example, those about Jesus Christ, in some broader claims that can be accepted universally and apart from faith. For example, Augustine's claim that God is the only satisfying answer of human longing can be correlated with the claim that human beings universally and restlessly seek for the Good, which through revelation is confessed as God. Again, the New Hermeneutic attempts to show that the theological concept of the Word of God is coherent within the ontological framework of the linguisticality of existence. In other words, by grounding or correlating the specific claims of the Christian faith in a wider, more broadly based or universally accepted understanding of reality–whether Platonic or Heideggerian or whatever–theologians have attempted to show that particular Christian claims correspond to reality, to the truth, established or known on grounds other than faith. This apologetic strategy is rejected by postliberalism for several reasons, not the least of which is the assumption or contention that all knowledge is derived from malleable modes or ways of knowing that are historically and culturally specific and contingent. Thus, epistemic claims made within these contexts are not, by definition, sufficient to sustain the claim of universal certitude.

Third, postliberalism operates with a cultural-linguistic paradigm of religion and a regulative or rule theory of doctrine. Lindbeck argues that "religions resemble languages together with their correlative forms of life and are thus similar to cultures (insofar as these are understood semiotically as reality and value systems–that is as idioms for the construing of reality and the living of life)."[6] Within this cultural-linguistic definition of religion, which is indebted to Ludwig Wittgenstein's (1889–1951) theory of language, Lindbeck then situates his definition of doctrine. "The function of church doctrines that becomes most prominent in this perspective is their use, not as expressive symbols or as truth claims, but as communally authoritative rules of discourse, attitude, and action."[7] In other words, Christian God-talk takes place in concrete communities. If you want to know what Christians mean by the term "God," you must enter into their language game. You must go to their churches, and attend to their rituals, liturgies, hymns, prayers, and other practices. In short, you must immerse yourself like any good anthropologist into the Christian way of life. Only then will you know what Christians mean when they say, "God." What you cannot do is to assume a priori that when Christians say, "God" they mean the same thing as Jews mean when they say, "God," or Muslims mean when they say, "Allah." What words mean is determined by their function within their specific, communal forms of life. Religions are, if you will, different idioms for construing reality; they are first-order explanatory frameworks.

Moreover, Lindbeck asserts that "there is no higher neutral standpoint from which to adjudicate their competing perceptions of what is factual."[8] Why? Because even in science, which prizes rational objectivity so highly, we are now aware that "all observation terms and all observation sentences are theory-laden," and, hence, culturally and historically conditioned.[9] Human concepts, whether scientific or theological, are relative to particular, concrete forms of life. There is no court of appeal to truth outside of a specific communal language game. In this sense, truth is radically relative to particular construals of reality, and postliberalism rejects the Enlightenment notion of universal truths whose rational demonstrability is independent of cultural particularity.

Within this framework, then, "doctrine functions in a regulatory way to recommend and exclude certain ranges of…propositional utterances or symbolizing activities."[10] For Lindbeck, that is all that doctrines do. So when Christians make propositional statements, for example, "Jesus is Lord," and symbolize this in a confirmation ritual or proclaim it in a sermon, the task of theology is to ask whether this proposition coheres with the Christian language game. If it does, then it is true for the Christian community. "True," in this case, means "valid" within a specific context of religious practice.

Fourth, this cultural-linguistic stance of postliberalism suggests that the historical Jesus, the Jesus reconstructed by the historian from Christianity's literary remains–both canonical and otherwise–is thus a product of a very different language game than that of the church. These "lives" of Jesus often narrate more about their authors than they do about Jesus. As we have seen, once Jesus is wrenched out of the biblical narrative, a new one has to be constructed on which to hang the very few facts about Jesus that qualify as "historical." The new narrative that is constructed from Nazareth to Golgotha is derived from the historian's imagination and inevitably reflects his or her biases and values. The Jesus that results is not the one to whom the church offers its worship, praises, prayers, or confesses in its creeds. He is rather the construct of a rather particular academic language game of a certain kind of historiography. If we want to know who Jesus is for Christians, then we must attend to their scriptures, creeds, and liturgical practices, and that is quite another language game than that "played" by academic historiography.

Moreover, postliberalism argues that the Jesus of the Bible does have a "history-like" identity so that when Christians confess, "Jesus is Lord," the name Jesus has content or meaning on the basis of the Gospels. Where postliberalism diverges from the New Hermeneutic in this regard is in its refusal to require that its predications of Jesus be restricted either to historical reconstructions lying behind the narratives of the canonical Gospels, or to those portions of the canonical Gospels deemed historically trustworthy. This strategy proves fatal for christology because the identity of Jesus Christ, insofar as it is saving, is only found as narrated in the ecclesiastically received redaction of the Gospels. The saving Jesus is the principal character in this story and not an academic construct standing behind it. If we will attend to this story, then we will be given a clear identity description of our crucified and risen Lord, and how he can be said to be present to us today as our Savior. The task of theology is to "unpack" and interpret this particular, concrete story in order to help the church enact it, ritualize it, and preach it with assurance.

Postliberal Poetics

Frei's remarkable experiment in theology attempted a Barthian theology of the Word of God, in opposition to Bultmann and post-Bultmannian developments, through the language of hermeneutics and poetics, or, more specifically narratology. This is accomplished by Frei's dual appropriation of Erich Auerbach's narratology, as well as the formalist theories of literature associated with the New Criticism.

Frei derived from Auerbach's *Mimesis* (1953) the notion of "realistic narrative," a fictional genre of literature. Its characteristics include depicting a common public world, both spatially and temporally; following chronological sequence; closely interacting characters and incidents, thereby rendering distinct, unsubstitutable individuals; effecting the sublime through the vernacular of ordinary, everyday events and language; and yielding a natural or literal meaning ("history-like") between the story and its referent(s). For example, the story of Abraham's sacrificing Isaac is nothing more or less than the story of Abraham's sacrificing Isaac. This story has a self-referential integrity; it does not symbolize or stand for something else, as in a myth. In other words, the stories in the Bible, and in fact, from Frei's perspective, the Bible taken as one cumulative story (through the intratextual connective tissue of typologies), create an imaginative, but recognizable, world that summons us to fit ourselves into it. These features of literary realism emerge in the West under the influence of the biblical tradition and artistically culminate in the realistic novels of nineteenth-century France.[11]

Although it arises from the criticism of poetry, the perspectives of the New Criticism, which reigned in American letters during the 1940s and 1950s, also influenced Frei.[12] For the New Critics, a poem is a self-contained or self-referential object. Eschewing interpretations based on reader response, authorial intentions, or parallels in the text and its historical contexts (including the author's biography), New Critics perform close readings of poetry in the confidence that meaning lies *within* the poem and the interaction of its words, literary devices, and structured patterns of language. The privileging of the organically united form and content of an "autonomous" text over its contexts coincides nicely with dogmatic views of scripture as self-referential.[13]

In his interpretation of Frei's work, and in contrast to Mark Ellingsen's earlier effort to relate Frei to homiletics (one warmly endorsed by Lindbeck), Charles Campbell works hard to distance Frei from both the narratology of Auerbach and the poetics of the New Criticism, even though Frei himself acknowledges their influence on the two books he authored during his lifetime. Campbell argues on the basis of Frei's posthumous publications that there was a subsequent conversion to his colleague George Lindbeck's cultural-linguistic theory of religion and doctrine as holding the real hermeneutical clue to scriptural interpretation.[14]

Nevertheless, as Campbell also acknowledges, the turn in Frei's thinking from formalist poetics to cultural-linguistic hermeneutics in no way causes Frei to abandon his earlier narratological conviction of the Gospels as "realistic narratives." In fact, I would argue that Lindbeck's theory seems only to have reinforced this conviction because it enables Frei to claim that the church has always read the Gospels as realistic narratives.[15] In this way, Frei's turning point is not a turning *from* but a renewed turning *toward* realistic narrative, albeit now on the conservative grounds of their ecclesial reception–rather than on shifting judgments of narratological theory alone.

Thus, a particular narrative theology emerges simultaneously within postliberalism in the 1970s at Yale, particularly in the work of Frei, as a way to overcome the impasse between the irrelevant Jesus of History who, stripped of his destiny as deity, does not belong to the Christian language game, and to the anonymous Christ of Faith, who shorn of human identity, and reduced to a naked "X," also lies outside the bounds of Christian discourse. Neither of these approaches is soteriologically valid. Neither approach, whether Bultmannian or post-Bultmannian, honors the Lord to whom Christians through the ages have offered thanksgiving and praise and recalled in sermon and sacrament "in accordance with the scriptures."

From Myth to Narrative

As with the theologians of the New Hermeneutic school, Frei, too, is troubled with Bultmann's account of the presence of Jesus Christ in the proclamation of the gospel. The assumptions behind form criticism, and the practice itself, eliminate the Gospels as legitimate sources for retrieving or reconstructing either the inner intentions or the outer career of the historical Jesus. Moreover, Jesus' eschatological destiny as the annulment of Christ "according to the flesh" (2 Cor. 5:16) means that Jesus' personality contributes nothing to his divine election or to the possibility or reality of his contemporaneity. Thus Bultmann concludes that Jesus' presence to us as the Christ, as the kerygmatic eschatological salvation event, requires only *that* he lived and precludes any saving significance in *how* he lived or in *what* he was like–even if such information were more readily available to the historian. The problem, of course, is that shorn of his identity as Jesus of Nazareth the *Christus praesens,* the Christ who is present today, logically risks becoming a naked "X," a "mythological cipher," a "spectre" or a "ghost."[16] If the concept of personal presence requires a "who" in order to make any sense at all, then how can Bultmann speak of the presence of Jesus Christ in Christian preaching without also speaking concretely of his identity and, hence, personality?

As we have seen, the response of the New Hermeneutic to this untenable situation was to relaunch a quest for the historical Jesus so that there could once again be content to the term "Jesus Christ," greater than that furnished by the believer's own transition into authentic or eschatological existence. Frei, recognizing the difficulty in Bultmann's position, nevertheless remains in solidarity with him in refusing to join in a renewed quest for the historical Jesus hidden behind the text of the Gospels. Rather than the dubious attempt to reconstruct the self-understanding of Jesus from the text analyzed as a source, Frei proceeds to derive the identity of Jesus Christ from the final or canonical form of the text. Jesus is taken for the chief character of the Gospel story; the incidents of the story reveal the intentions of this character; these intentions enable the reader in turn to construe and construct his identity. Once this character identity is established, Frei will infer from it a claim for the contemporary presence of Jesus Christ. In other words, the narratological canons and identity descriptions employed by Frei replace historical criticism and reconstruction in order to establish dogmatic claims.

Whereas Bultmann gives priority to Paul and John because they, among the canonical writers, most completely grasped the eschatological reality of the saving event known as Jesus Christ, Frei bases his christology on what he terms "the Gospel narrative."[17] Nevertheless, this major shift in orientation should not obscure the fact that, with respect to the Synoptics, both Bultmann and Frei understand Jesus Christ as the "chief character" in a soteriological narrative.[18] Frei parts company with Bultmann in rejecting the category of myth as appropriate for either the story line or the chief character of the Gospels. If Bultmann pictures the Synoptics as sharing a common Christ myth, on which all sorts of materials and genres have been strung, including the occasional novelistic motif, Frei imagines the obverse: the Synoptics share a common novelistic story, into which a mythical motif is occasionally slipped.[19] Frei finds the real analogue for "the Gospel narrative" in the modern novel and thereby attempts, in ways reminiscent of Barth, "to distinguish the Gospel *story* of the Savior from a common savior *myth* of the period."[20]

This distinction between myth and narrative becomes crucial for Frei's argument. The distinction is not that a narrative is a story and a myth is something else. Rather, the distinction lies in the Gospel story being a peculiar kind of narrative, what Frei, following Auerbach, terms a "realistic narrative." That is to say, the Gospel narrative is more akin to "history-writing and the traditional novel" than to myth in at least three respects; "its depiction of a common public world…, in the close interaction of character and incident, and in the non-symbolic quality of the relation between the story and what the story is about." Frei's contention that the Gospels are more appropriately approached through the genre of "realistic narrative" than through "myth" leads him to rechristen Bultmann's mythical Christ as the "storied" Jesus. As a character in a story, Jesus achieves his identity in the same way Madame Bovary attains hers, namely, through the techniques of realistic rendering.[21]

Behind this shift from myth to realistic narrative stands not only the narratology of Auerbach, but also the theology of Barth. Auerbach's category of "realistic narrative" is appropriated by Frei to give legitimation to Barth's dogmatic judgment that the consecutive historical narration of the Bible is neither myth, in the ancient sense, nor history, in the modern sense, but rather, "saga" or "legend."

To focus for a moment on the resurrection, where the issue of literary genre is most joined, Barth agrees with Bultmann that the resurrection, by definition, is not, and cannot be a "historical event," if by that term one means "the outline of an event as it can be seen in its 'How' independently of the standpoint of the onlooker, as it can be presented in this way, as it can be proved in itself and in its general and more specific context and in relation to the analogies of other events, as it can be established as having certainly taken place."[22] On the other hand, the resurrection, for Barth, is recorded in the New Testament as "an event which took place in space and time," "which really happened," "which though it cannot be grasped historically [i.e. by means of scientific historiography] is still actual and objective in time and space."[23] "Jesus Himself did rise again and appear to His disciples. This is the content of the Easter history, the Easter time, the Christian faith and Christian proclamation, both then and at all times."[24] The resurrection accounts, while not "scientifically" speaking "historical," cannot be characterized as "mythological." They do not "speak of the non-spatial and timeless being of certain general truths, orders and relationships" in the "poetical form of a narrative," so that their "true content" can be separated "from their poetic form as narratives…by an idealized, symbolical and allegorical interpretation of the form."[25]

Thus, for Barth, the resurrection account, as a consecutive narrative, is neither "scientific" history nor prescientific mythology, nor a combination thereof, but rather it belongs to a genre apart, namely, "biblical saga."[26] The Gospels as saga may be said to narrate a non-historical or pre-historical history. To use Frei's term they are "history-like" accounts whose verisimilitude is wrought by realistic narrative depiction. For this reason, the real analogue for "the Gospel narrative" is not the cult-myths of the Graeco-Roman world, but, rather, the modern, nineteenth-century novel.[27]

Before attempting to show how the Gospel narrative renders the identity of Jesus Christ, Frei first proposes a working definition of human identity. It is "the specific uniqueness of a person...quite apart from both comparison and contrast to others," or "the self-referral, or ascription to him, of his physical and personal states, properties, characteristics, and actions."[28] For Frei's purposes, an identity description only presupposes (1) "that to which changing actions, states, and properties are ascribed or referred is nothing more than they themselves under a certain focus, the focus of self-referral. And when the actions, states, and properties change, their change is the self's change"; and (2) that no set of changing states, properties, and in particular, set of actions, exhausts the self in such a way that it cannot also provide the bond of continuity between these distinctive acts, states, and properties which it is." Leaving aside the question of how successfully the substituted term "self" avoids the metaphysical complications (or enrichment) of "soul," Frei is saying that descriptions of human identity must consider both continuing *change* and abiding *continuity*.[29]

Accordingly, an identity description that captures a person at any given time, in the interplay between inner self and external circumstances, Frei terms an "intention-action" description. Such a description answers the question "What is he or she like?" by focusing on an external action emerging from an inner intention and thereby constituting a person's "unsubstitutable identity." On the other hand, an identity description that captures "the person himself in his on-going self-continuity" Frei terms a "self-manifestation description." Such a description answers the question "Who is she or he?" by focusing on the self's expression through the public media of its own words and body. Without exhausting the elusiveness or diminishing the uniqueness of the self, these media fitly represent it and are the self as subject. Through language and embodiment, therefore, the identity of a person becomes manifestly describable.[30]

Frei uses these two kinds of formal identity descriptions, one involving "intention-action" and the other "subject manifestation," to highlight the identity of Jesus Christ as rendered by the Gospel narrative. Frei contends that "a good storyteller" is able to describe both the changes in, and the persistence of, a person's character as it acts–and is acted upon–over a period of time.[31] To see how this is so, we turn now to Frei's own reading of the Gospels. The point is to see how they render the identity of their chief character–without which he cannot be present here and now as Christ the Savior.

Despite his likening of the Gospels to traditional novels, Frei can find only two places in the entire Synoptic narrative where the "inner intention" of Jesus is made clear, namely the temptation scene, and, more importantly, the prayer scene in Gethsemane. Each of these two scenes portrays Jesus' intention as only a novelist can, that is, from "the inside," an intention Frei characterizes as "obedience" to God on behalf of human salvation. Just as Jesus' obedience depicted in the temptation scene is immediately enacted in his preaching at the Nazareth synagogue (Lk. 4:16–30), so his obedience to God depicted in the Gethsemane scene ("Yet not what I will, but what thou wilt," Mk. 14:36, RSV), is subsequently enacted in giving up his life on behalf of humankind. Therefore, in his passion and death, Jesus enacts his inner intention, thereby constituting his identity as "the man completely obedient to God."[32]

Following Jesus' surrender of his will in Gethsemane, the narrative increasingly transfers the power to initiate action from Jesus to his opponents, and above all to God, whose own power to redeem Jesus from death brings the resurrection. Yet "in the resurrection, where the initiative of God is finally and decisively climaxed and he [God] alone is and can be active, the sole identity to mark the presence of that activity is Jesus." Precisely in the resurrection, "when God's supplantation of him is complete," the event is so hidden by the narrative from direct view that the identity of Jesus as God's act and presence becomes manifest only at the very point where death denies to Jesus the power to enact his obedience. For this reason, another kind of formal identity description, "the subject (or self-) manifestation" pattern, must also be invoked.[33]

This second kind of identity description stresses "the continuity of a person's identity throughout the transitions brought about by his acts and life's events." Here the aim is not to focus narrowly on "a specific sequence of events" by which a person's intention is enacted, but on "the whole scope or stretch of a person's life." Hence, in Jesus' case, a self-manifestation description "involves the full scope of the Gospel story." Frei argues that, taken as a composite, the Synoptics exhibit three distinct narrative stages, marking step-by-step, and every more fully, the identity of Jesus.[34]

In stage one the narrative depicts Jesus from birth to baptism. In a variety of forms (prose, liturgical, and poetic), Jesus is identified in a stylized, representative way "wholly in terms of the identity of the people of Israel." Jesus is not an individual but the summing up of the story of Israel, as parallels and references to the Exodus and Exile indicate. At his baptism Jesus begins to emerge "as an individual in his own right." Yet even in this second stage of narrative depiction, Jesus does retain something of the symbolic quality he has in stage one, in that he represents the imminent Kingdom of God (as, e.g., in Lk. 4 and 17:19–23).[35]

Only with Jesus' "announcement to his disciples that he and they would now go to Jerusalem" do we reach the third, and most important, stage of Jesus' developing identity. In Frei's view, this is the "part of the story most clearly history-like." By "history-like," Frei means "that it describes an individual and a series of events in connection with him that, whether fictional or real, are what they are in their own right." Hence, in this third stage, Jesus does not simply symbolize some reality, say that of the Kingdom of God, but becomes the center and focus of the narrated pattern of events. Through these events he acquires an unsubstitutable identity, and, through him alone, these events acquire an unsubstitutable significance. The earlier connection between Jesus and the Kingdom of God becomes loosened, as the Passion story focuses on Jesus "in his unadorned singularity." Then, in the resurrection appearances, notably that of the Emmaus Road (Lk. 24:13–31), Jesus himself reappropriates as his own such stylized or mythological titles as "the Christ." He defines them, much more than they him. Thus, the identity of Jesus Christ is manifested preeminently in stage three as the narrative sharpens its focus on him. Who is Jesus? Described by his "self-manifestation" in the narrative, he is "the unsubstitutable Jesus of Nazareth who, as that one man, is the Christ and the presence of God."[36]

Frei's method of reading the four Gospels as a single Gospel narrative must give us pause. One of the virtues of form and redaction criticism as practiced by Bultmann and the New Hermeneutic, is that it allows the distinctive voices of the multiple witnesses to faith to come to expression in contemporary preaching. The more one reads Frei's account of the identity of Jesus Christ as depicted by the Gospel narrative, the more apparent it becomes that this term refers to no work of literature whatsoever but only to a literary-critical construct imposed on the Synoptic Gospels by Frei's imagination. What he presents is a postmodern "harmony of the Gospels," which, like its older siblings, whether liberal or conservative, still picks and chooses from the three Synoptic accounts whatever it needs to construct Jesus' character, or in Frei's words, "Jesus' inner life," albeit "within the story."[37] A close reading of Frei indicates that in practice his "Gospel narrative" is essentially the Lucan narrative, since throughout *The Identity of Jesus Christ*, Frei follows Luke(-Acts), supplemented as needed by Matthew, Mark, and even John. What is absent is any theological, hermeneutical, or narratological discussion of why Luke should be given preeminence over the other Gospels, or why they should be employed not as distinctive witnesses but as harmonized "sources" for a "life of Jesus," albeit, "within the story."[38]

In this way, and with his two formal principles of identity description, namely, "intention-action" and "subject-manifestation," Frei extracts or, better, constructs, from "the Gospel narrative" the identity of Jesus Christ. More correctly, he succeeds in extracting or constructing the identity of Jesus Christ as the "storied" and "history-like" chief character in the Gospels. Having accomplished this task, he now proceeds in his argument to show how knowing the identity of Jesus Christ "is identical with having him present or being in his presence,"[39] for to know *who* Jesus is, "in connection with what took place is to know *that* he is."[40] Whereas Bultmann argued on form-critical grounds that the Gospels "peculiarly intertwine" the Christ of myth with historical traditions about Jesus of Nazareth, Frei argues that "the Gospel narrative" fictionally renders an identity description of the chief character of the story entailing the claim that he factually existed as a historical person and now factually exists as the Risen One.

Frei summarizes his position by employing the literary device of speaking in the name of the Synoptic writers:

> "Our argument is that to grasp what this identity, Jesus of Nazareth (which has been made directly accessible to us), is is to believe that he has been, in fact, raised from the dead. Someone may reply that in that case the most perfectly depicted character and most nearly lifelike fictional identity ought always in fact to have lived a factual historical life. We answer that the argument holds good only in this one and absolutely unique case, where the described entity (who or what he is, i.e., Jesus Christ, the presence of God) is totally identical with his factual existence. He is the resurrection and the life. How can he be conceived as not resurrected?"[41]

Thus, Frei infers the factuality of both the historical Jesus and the Risen Lord on the basis of the fictional, but "history-like" identity descriptions of the "storied" Jesus.

Preaching Jesus[42]

According to Campbell, Frei's legacy for preaching, as enlarged by Lindbeck, brings to the forefront five normative criteria for "preaching Jesus." First and foremost, preaching must be a telling or expositing of the Jesus story, including its logic or figurations, which are found throughout scripture. In this way, preaching renders the Savior's unsubstitutable identity and presence. Second, preaching must not assist listeners "to find their stories in the Bible, but rather... make the story of the Bible their story."[43] As Charles Hardwick puts it, instead of listeners "responding to a sermon by saying, "Look, there's a story in the Bible just like what I experience every day!" the sermon should move them to exclaim, "Uh oh, I might be a modern-day Pharisee!"[44] Third, "the function of preaching is not that of locating individual human needs and then offering God as an answer or solution to them...Rather, the sermon moves from the identity of Jesus Christ to the 'upbuilding' of the church."[45] Indeed, the church physically embodies the saving pattern of the earthly Jesus through its habitual homiletical and liturgical retellings of the story of Jesus. Fourth, becoming a Christian is not anything as "sublime" as an existential encounter or experience, or a revelatory or eschatological event. Rather, it is a mundane, everyday matter of internalizing or appropriating the language and practices of Zion. "Sermons become a means through which the Christian community enters more deeply into its own distinctive speech, so that Christian ideas, beliefs, and experience become possible." The language of faith takes precedence over the experience or life of faith.[46] The sermon must not attempt any "translation" of the gospel into the idioms, culture, or situation of the listener. Postliberal preaching becomes largely catechetical and ethical; the goal is socialization into the church understood as a contrast-society, an interpretive community of character set over against the world around it. Fifth, (and this is Campbell's own contribution independent of Frei or Lindbeck), preaching must be an act of nonviolent resistance to the "principalities and powers" of evil in continuity with the teaching and preaching of Jesus himself, thereby constituting the church as a community of nonviolent resistance.[47]

Postliberalism: A Theological Assessment

Frei's argument is an impressive tour de force as he deftly moves from a description of formal narrative properties to normative theological and historical claims. What emerges is actually a christological version of Anselm's ontological proof for the existence of God. Anselm (1033–1109), it will be recalled, had argued that God is that than which nothing greater can be conceived. If God existed only in our thought, and not in reality or independently of our thought, then God would not be God, that is, nothing greater than that which can be conceived. Therefore, precisely as that than which nothing greater can be conceived, only God necessarily has real existence. To distill this argument into the narratological account of Frei, just as God's presence is entailed by God's identity, so the presence of Jesus Christ is entailed by his identity as the Risen One. If Frei's premise that knowing the identity of Jesus Christ "is identical with having him present or being in his presence,"[48] for to know *who* Jesus is, "in connection with what took place [in the narrative] is to know *that* he is,[49] then narrative presence would be equivalent to "real presence." Frei's christological deployment of Anselm's argument assumes with Anselm that we can move from an existent in our thought to that same existent in reality, but, in Frei's case, the existent in our thought is, after all, a literary character.[50]

Why does Frei's attempt to move from the narrative identity to the presence of Jesus Christ fail? Why, at the end of the road, can we not claim that knowing the narrative identity of Jesus Christ "is identical with having him present or being in his presence"–at least as the saving Subject or acting Agent of our salvation? The answer is that a story, even a "realistic narrative," does not necessarily function as a "performative utterance" by a "self-involving" agent. Admittedly, a narrative can render character identities, as good storytellers know, and, arguably, a "realistic narrative" may do this better than a "myth." Indeed, a narrative can depict the identities of putative subjects and agents; but a narrative as a narrative, unlike a promise as a promise, for example, does not render self-involving agency, which is what the claim for Christ's presence in proclamation entails. Short of this kind of 'self-involving" presence, a narratively rendered presence of Jesus Christ can only be, at best, the presence of information, of an "entity," or of a literary character. In this case, Bultmann's point is well taken that "I am not at all helped by reading touching stories of how Jesus forgave the sinful woman or Zacchaeus."[51] Help comes only when, in faith, I hear through such a narrative a *promise* from Jesus Christ.

As Philipp Melanchthon (1497–1560) observed at the time of the Reformation, "Faith does not mean merely knowing the story of Christ, for even the devils confess that the Son of God appeared and arose from the dead, and in Judas there was a knowledge of Christ. *True faith* is truly to retain all the words which God has given to us, including the promise of grace....The symbol [i.e. the Apostles' Creed as the sum of the gospel] includes not only the story but also the promises and the fruit of the promise."[52] In my judgment, Frei's exclusive focus on the "story" of the gospel, without attention to the promise of the gospel to which faith is correlative, leads to the failure of his narratologically informed proposal to account adequately for how faith finds itself addressed by Jesus Christ, or of Jesus Christ as the presently acting Subject of the proclaimed Word of God.

Frei's contention that knowing the narrative identity of Jesus is "identical with having him present or being in his presence" takes "the Gospel narrative," as narrative, as the primary, if not, exclusive meaning and locus of the Word of God. The result, to borrow Barth's language, is to collapse the first and third forms of the Word, namely the incarnate Logos and the Logos proclaimed, into the second, the scriptural witness to the Logos, now redefined essentially as "realistic narrative." Once this hermeneutical move is made, there remains no logical need, or basis, for preaching as interpretive witness; narrative recitation will suffice, and the cantor can replace the preacher, the lectern the pulpit. If "the Gospel narrative" as such brings Jesus to life, why would anyone bother to preach on it? Why not just read or recite it? Why muck things up with preaching or precede scriptural exposition with a prayer for illumination? If narrative presence is all we can have of Jesus Christ, then preaching cannot be understood as Paul and John understand it, namely, as direct address from Jesus Christ himself in and through his heralds' proclamation (2 Cor. 5:18–6:2) or the paracletic Word of the church (Jn. 14:26; 16:12–15).[53]

Charles Campbell attempts to refute my argument that Frei's proposal logically undercuts any need for preaching other than narrative recitation, by simply noting that Frei's work offers resources for "moving beyond mere rote recitation" and by observing that "Frei's own sermons did not take an explicitly narrative form."[54] But this response simply underscores my point. The very practice of preaching as interpretive discourse, known from the earliest days of the church and of the synagogue before it, belies the view that the Gospel narrative, as narrative, sovereignly renders the presence of Jesus Christ. If it did, preaching as an interpretive act would simply be unnecessary. Therefore the persistence of preaching as an interpretive act, especially in the sermons of Frei, as reported by Campbell, shows the inadequacy of postliberal homiletical theory. If I may appeal to the *sensus communis*, Frei's application of narratological theory simply does not account for what the church has always done in preaching. More needs to happen in preaching than repeating the Gospel narrative, or absorbing our world into that of Gospel narrative, as Frei's homiletical practice demonstrates.[55]

Some seven years after the original serial publication of *The Identity of Jesus Christ,* Frei attempts to break out of the biblical narrative world into which he had painted himself. He urges the supplementing of his original two categories of formal identity description with "the formal analytical devices which sociologists of knowledge and Marxist literary critics use to identify the relation between individual personhood and the contextual social structures."[56] Here, at last, we have a tacit admission that there is a real world addressed *by* the text that is not identical with the real world *of* the text and that the real world originally addressed *by* the text has itself an influence on the real world *of* the text. For this reason, preaching can never be simply the reiteration of the biblical world by means of recital alone. Preachers cannot remain in "Bibleland," but must in the power of the Holy Spirit risk taking account of the world *in* which the Christian message is proclaimed and *to* which it is addressed. The preaching office itself and every invocation of the Spirit in the liturgy of the Word make this hermeneutical point as nothing else can. The Word of God attested in scripture wills to go forth into ever-new situations and therefore the arduous task of interpretation simply cannot be laid aside.

Nevertheless, the poetic frame of reference has provided two important insights with which a theology of preaching can make common cause. Preaching can only welcome the New Hermeneutic's insistence that words do not simply speak, they act. This insight calls us to the further possibility that the Word of God may freely employ a whole class of performative utterances, of which "promises" are theologically among the most significant for preaching. Second, preaching can profit from the insistence of postliberalism that biblical narrative provides meaningful identity descriptions of Jesus Christ. Drawing on insights from both the New Hermeneutic and postliberal schools, the proclaimed gospel may be more appropriately thought of as promissory narration or as a narrated promise. In this way, a theological frame of reference insisting on the agency of God in preaching can draw from a poetic frame of reference without losing its own distinctive calling.

Preaching and the Promises of God

If we attend to the scriptures and to the liturgical traditions of the church, we discover that promises about the future are embedded and enacted in them. In these promises, God is repeatedly identified as the one who makes them (e.g., Acts 13:32; Rom. 4:21; Gal. 3:8); and, those to whom the promises are made are directly or indirectly invited to believe them, so that saving faith and God's promises are correlative (Acts 2:37–39).

Think for a moment of Abraham and Sarah. When we first encounter them in the Book of Genesis, they strike us as rather unpromising. They are old, well past their prime, and death is near. What is more, they are childless. While they have possessions, they have no hope of posterity. They cannot generate new life. But into that situation, God's promise for the future met them: "Now the Lord said to Abram, 'Go from your country and your kindred and your father's house to the land that I will show you. And I will make of you a great nation, and I will bless you, and make your name great, so that you will be a blessing. I will bless those who bless you, and the one who curses you I will curse; and in you all the families of the earth shall be blessed" (Gen. 12:1–4). Commenting on this passage centuries later, the Book of Hebrews says, "By faith Abraham obeyed when he was called to set out for a place that he was to receive as an inheritance; and he set out, not knowing where he was going….By faith Sarah herself, though barren, received power to conceive, even when she was too old, since she considered him faithful who had promised" (Heb. 11:8, 11).

Reflecting on such biblical testimony, and informed by the work of Walther Zimmerli (1907–1983), Jürgen Moltmann describes a promise as follows:

> A promise is a declaration which announces the coming of a reality that does not yet exist….The promise binds man to the future and gives him a sense for history….If the word is a word of promise, then that means that this word has not yet found a reality congruous with it, but that on the contrary it stands in contradiction to the reality open to experience now and heretofore….The word of promise therefore always creates an interval of tension between the uttering and the redeeming of the promise. In so doing it provides man with a peculiar area of freedom to obey and disobey, to be hopeful or resigned….[T]he promise is not regarded abstractly apart from the God who promises, but its fulfillment is entrusted directly to God in his freedom and faithfulness…[57]

Moltmann's characterizations indicate that a promise is indeed a "speech act." A promise, we are told, "initiates" and "determines" history; a promise "binds" its hearers to the future; and a promise "gives" its receivers a sense of history (and destiny and hope) by "creating an interval of tension" between its uttering and its redeeming. The performative power that Moltmann assigns to promise is clearly one of agency.

We might say, then, that Christian preaching and the life of faith are occurring in the interval created by the promise of God to reconcile the world to Godself. While the turn of the ages has occurred in the cross-resurrection of Jesus Christ, and the church has been established as its bridgehead, and the Holy Spirit has been given as the "guarantee" of God's final victory (2 Cor. 1:22, 5:5), and the eschatological "goods" of God's rule (justification, sanctification, reconciliation, etc.) are now all on the scene, nevertheless all has "not yet" happened. As Ernst Käsemann points out with reference to the future tenses of Romans 6, only Christ–not the Christian–has been raised from death.[58] And so "we walk by faith, and not by sight" (2 Cor. 5:7) in the interval between the first and final advents Jesus Christ. And like Abraham and Sarah, we, too, "look forward to the city that has foundations, whose architect and builder is God" (cf. Heb 11:10). In this interval, can more be said for preaching, not only as an act of proclaiming God's promised salvation, but as the linguistic medium for God's own promise making?

In his 1979 study of *The Logic of Promise in Moltmann's Theology*, Christopher Morse brought into the conversation with systematic theology Anglo-American analytic philosophy represented by J. L. Austin (1911–1960), Donald D. Evans, and John R. Searle, in order to better understand and deploy "promissory narration" with respect to theological claims.[59] From Austin's pioneering work arises the term "performative utterances," which is language used not simply to describe the action we are doing, but the actual doing of it. For example, when we promise to "to take you to be my wife or husband, to have and to hold from this day forward...until we are parted by death," we are not simply informing a hearer that a promise has been made. Rather the speaking *is* the promising. A promise, therefore, does not refer to a commitment; it *is* the commitment itself.

That is, a promise not only announces or informs as to a future state of affairs but does so in such a way as to constitute a new state of affairs in the present. Moreover, promises do not refer or report about independently existing states of affairs, they institute them. The marriage vow, for example, institutes a new reality: the marriage. Subsequently, Austin was led to conclude that all speaking involves the performance of acts, so that the term "Word event" or "speech act" is in a way redundant. The issue for Austin is what *type* of acts our speaking involves. He went on to distinguish the locutionary (the act of saying something), the illocutionary (the act the speaker performs *in* saying something), and perlocutionary (the act which occurs *by* saying something). Austin further analyzes illocutionary utterances into five subtypes, one of which he terms "commissives," typical of promises. "They commit you to doing something, but also include declarations of announcements of intentions." So, a commissive utterance is "an assuming of an obligation or the declaring of an intention." When Jesus says, "I am with you always, to the end of the age" (Mt. 28:20) or the Lord says to Paul, "My grace is sufficient for you, for my power is made perfect in weakness" (2 Cor. 12:9) we have examples of commissive speech.

By uncovering the conventions by which everyday language works, Donald Evans holds that modern linguistic philosophy can help us understand how God's Word, as human speech, can be said to exert a power on us in the present. In analytic terms, faith may be said to be a "correlative performative," that is a response to the commissive force of God's promise. The logic of commissives is that they entail the self-involvement both of the one assuming an obligation or announcing an intention, and of those for whom an obligation is assumed or to whom an intention is announced.[60]

We have already noted Bultmann's description of the proclaimed kerygma as "personal address [*Anrede*], demand [*Forderung*], and promise [*Verheissung*]; it is the very act of divine grace."[61] Such language proceeds analogically on the model of the personal communion between one human being and another.[62] Specifically, Bultmann construes the presence of Christ as analogous to the encounter of an Addresser with Addressee when and where the former says to the latter, "I love you."[63] The statement "I love you," on Bultmann's grounds, is an "existential" statement in that it does not simply convey information but a self-involving declaration. In saying, "I love you," the speaker does not discourse about love but *enacts* love concretely. This word of love *is* the love of which it speaks. While the theme of the kerygma as promise is not developed by Bultmann, his discussions of existential language do suggest its connections with promise-making as illumined by analytic philosophy.

In fact, it is Morse's elaboration of the theological implications of promissory language that illumine its connections with "existential" language. That God's Word is spoken in and through ordinary language means that the logical force of such language, uncovered by linguistic analysis, is appropriated and not violated by God. Second, promissory language always entails the "self-involvement" of a promisor. To hear the Word of God as a promise entails God as the promising Subject. This agency, as promissory, is not an impersonal causal mechanism, but personal, or existential. God is actively committed to others in the present for the future. As a promisor, God includes both a who and a what, that is both self-involvement and commitments that have content. In this regard, however, while a promise entails a self-involving promisor, it cannot reveal the content of the promisor's character or commitments. For this reason, we do need scriptural narrative to identify the God who makes promises. The kind of relation established between God the promisor and the believer is of the order of a "correlative performative." That is knowledge of God is not theoretical but personal. "Faith is present whenever the proclamation of the gospel is heard as God's first person, present indicative promise to us."[64] When the kerygma is heard as a promise of Christ death and resurrection on behalf of our salvation, then it is heard as a promise from Christ himself (Rom. 10:17; 2 Cor. 5:20, 13:3). Thus the presence of a promise, entails the "real presence" of the promisor.

In preaching, of course, a human being proclaims the promise or Word of God speaking "on behalf of" the Word of God or Jesus Christ (cf. 2 Cor. 5:20). But this no more vitiates the promise as God's than when an ambassador, speaking for a head of state, conveys official greetings or pronouncements. If the American ambassador promises, in the name of the United States government, several billion dollars to his or her host country, such a promise is no less valid than if made in person by the President of the United States. Such "double agency" is a common feature of everyday language, and it is characteristic of preaching as Paul's descriptions of the preacher as herald (Rom. 10:13–17) or ambassador (2 Cor. 5:20) indicate. Who speaks as God's deputy is not simply determined by self-appointment, and for that reason the church continues to seek appropriate criteria for faithful ministerial service as part of its continuing call to "test the spirits to see whether they are from God" (see 1 Jn. 4:1–6). Nevertheless, as Morse notes, "The self-involvement which is evidenced in proclamation insofar as it becomes for faith a commissive speech-act is never dependent upon or equatable with the involvement or lack of involvement of any human speaker."[65] If Jonathan Edwards preached staring at the bell rope, and Paul Tillich preached looking down at his manuscript in heavily German-accented English, this rhetorical "distance" did not disqualify their preaching from being a means of grace to many.

While speech-act theory can in no way "prove" that scripture is the Word of God or that "the preaching of the Word of God is the Word of God," to recall Bullinger's dictum, it can help us to make sense of this claim. With respect to preaching of the gospel as "promissory narration" (Morse) or as "narrated promise" (Thiemann), we are offered a corrective to postliberalism insofar as narrative alone cannot account for the self-involving agency of God as the ultimate Subject of sermonic discourse, or of faith as a "correlative performative" from the side of the hearer. On the other hand, Bultmann's understanding of the proclamation of the kerygma as the event of God's promise of grace, while indicating the self-involving agency of the Word of God or Jesus Christ, and the self-involving response of the hearer, gives inadequate attention to the identity of Jesus Christ, which, as Frei has shown, can be inferred from "the Gospel narrative." Preaching as promissory narration, therefore, is an attempt at mutual correction of these theological proposals in a way that is more faithful to the gospel.

In my judgment, while the sermon should always speak God's Word of promise, in accordance with a theological frame of reference, the narrative rendering of Jesus Christ in his unsubstitutable particularity is not always required of the sermon. In fact, comparative studies of the sermons of Frei, Campbell, and Walter Brueggemann show this to be the case even with their preaching.[66] An examination by Charles Hardwick of Frei's untitled sermon on John 15:1–8 finds Frei far removed from providing an account of Christ's unsubstitutable identity. "In fact," notes Hardwick, "the events of Jesus' life, death, and resurrection are so absent from this sermon that Jesus verges on becoming the mythic figure Frei decries throughout *Identity*."[67] However embarrassing such findings may prove for postliberal homiletics, we should not find them surprising. Narrative rendering goes on in the larger liturgical context of the church, which is also a context of active proclamation and includes the reading of scripture, the singing of hymns, the reciting of creeds, and the services of baptism and the Lord's Supper. Provided that the story of Jesus is told and enacted with regularity in the worship of the congregation, the sermon need not carry this responsibility every Sunday. What preaching cannot abandon any Sunday is its exposition and declaration of the promises of God, promises which are also embedded in the liturgical forms of the church.

Sermon: "Believing Without Seeing"; John 21:29

Fleming Rutledge, a priest of the Episcopal Diocese of New York, delivered this sermon on the Second Sunday of Easter in 1996 at All Saints' Chapel, Sewanee, Tennessee.[68]

This is an occasional sermon, that is, it is really an Easter sermon (made possible on the Sunday after Easter by a liturgical tradition of the fifty days of Eastertide stretching beyond Easter Day). The occasion of Easter, therefore, rather than the specific text from the Risen Lord, "Blessed are they who do not see and yet believe," is the departure point for a lengthy introduction, actually three introductions, that take up nearly half the sermon. What this lengthy introduction accomplishes is to enflesh *this* world of *Newsweek* cover stories, of various traditional and secular forms of Easter greetings, and in a vignette of Rutledge's first Easter in New York to capture the silence and indifference of a deserted Manhattan early on Easter morning in contrast to the preparations already under way for its celebration in the parish church. It is *this* world into which the story will be retold.

In the second movement of the sermon, Rutledge, continuing in everyday, ordinary language retells the story of Easter from the standpoint of Thomas:

> On the evening of the day of Resurrection of our Lord Jesus Christ, the disciple Thomas had a lot more to feel depressed about than a few empty sidewalks. He had not seen anything to convince him that Jesus had truly risen from the dead.... When the disciples were gathered together in that room where the risen Lord first appeared to them all, Thomas was not with them; he was so angry and bitter and broken up that he could not, or would not, seek fellowship–very much like many of us, don't you think, when we are mad at God or mad at the world and we stay away from the Lord's Supper? Thomas stayed away, and he missed it!–he missed the visit of the Lord who had risen from the dead.

> The next day, the other disciples went to Thomas and they said, "Thomas! He is risen!" Try to imagine this, not as a seasonal greeting or even as a piece of startling new information, but as the transmission of the most genuinely earth-shaking message that the world has ever heard....

> Thomas' response is consistent with his personality. He says, "I don't believe it, and unless I see the print of the nails, and place my finger in the mark of the nails, and place my hand in his side, I *never will* believe it." We have all known people like Thomas, perhaps we are like Thomas ourselves, creating our own conditions for faith. I won't believe unless God gives me a sign, whether it be a sunburst on Lower Broadway or a direct appearance of Jesus himself. We want to create our

own conditions for faith. Sometimes the conditions we set are conditions we believe *will never be met....*

Thomas, however, is not completely hardened by any means. Like many of us who stay away from worship for a while, hope against hope draws us back....Once again Jesus appears in the room...Once again the Lord bestows them his promised peace, and then he turns directly to Thomas, singling him out. Imagine that!...If I had been Thomas I would have been completely overwhelmed, so overpowered by unexpected graciousness and maybe also fearsomeness that I would forget all about my impertinent demand to touch his wounds.

Jesus doesn't let Thomas forget it, though....In his boundless graciousness, Jesus actually grants to Thomas the signs which he so presumptuously had demanded. It is a perfect example of the way grace goes before the knowledge of sin; Jesus' willingness to meet Thomas's conditions exposes the disciple's effrontery far more effectively than any rebuke would have done. Jesus does not meet him halfway; Jesus meets him all the way and from beyond all the way....

The words that Thomas speaks–*My Lord and my God*–are the supreme titles given to Jesus in the Bible....The fourth gospel has come full circle; the proclamation of the Prologue, "The Word was with God and the Word was God," reaches its true destination on the lips of Thomas a mere human being who would now be entrusted with carrying that proclamation to the world.[69]

In this retelling, we see "postliberal" approaches. The story is retold using the sturdy theological and liturgical language of the tradition ("the day of Resurrection of our Lord Jesus Christ," "the Lord's Supper," "grace goes before the knowledge of sin," "*My Lord and my God,*" and "The Word was with God and the Word was God.") The preacher makes no attempt either to translate or didactically belabor these terms for an Easter congregation, perhaps consisting of many nominal Christians or occasional churchgoers. The terms are simply given in the retelling of the story, so that the story interprets them to the degree that they are interpreted. Nevertheless, the preacher incorporates her listeners into the story by suggesting we may either know people like Thomas or be like him ourselves. More importantly, the story is retold not to highlight Thomas and his failings ("a mere human being" to be sure), the typical anthropological move, but, equally and even more, to ascribe to Jesus Christ his true identity as a *gracious and personal* Lord and God, indeed as one who is, whether I know it or not, or believe it or not, nevertheless, "my Lord" and "my God."

The sermon concludes in a dramatic way, as the preacher, still using the language of the scriptures, ventures to proclaim the Easter faith to her congregation by performing it as the promise to which our own faith is correlative. Here the preacher is not talking "about" Jesus Christ, but as Christ's herald and ambassador makes bold to pronounce his blessing and promise to the congregation before her, and by extension to you who are reading these words as well:

> This morning I have nothing to show you in the way of proofs—no legal arguments, no signs, no stigmata, no miraculous relics. Magical proofs have I none, but what I have I give you: what I have is no less than what the first apostles had, what the Christian church has had from the beginning—the gift of faith. The church was not built on seeing with the eyes, but on the "bond of trust between those who live in the presence of Christ today and those who first carried the Easter message 2000 years ago."
>
> And so this morning, through the word of this merely human witness, the risen Lord looks at you this very day—looks past Thomas and the other disciples through the walls of All Saints' Chapel and across eternity and says, "Blessed are they who have not seen, yet believe."
>
> Alleluia! Amen.[70]

CONCLUSION: PREACHING AND THEOLOGY

In our journey of theological understanding, at least three issues have recurred with regularity. They are the question of agency, the question of the meaning of the gospel, and the question of whether proposals in theology can meet the test of "preachability."

Who's in Charge Here?

One of the basic questions with which every preacher must grapple is who is the ultimate agent of Christian preaching. From the standpoint of Bullinger, Barth, and Bultmann, the primary Agent or Subject of the Christian sermon is God, or more specifically the Word of God understood as Jesus Christ. For the New Hermeneutic, informed by Heideggerian poetics, that agency is accorded to language itself, particularly to the language of scripture moving into the present as the Word-event occasioned by the sermon. Similarly, postliberalism accords to "the Gospel narrative" the power to render the reality and presence of Jesus Christ. Finally, rhetorical homiletics sees the preacher, armed with the weapons of rhetoric and the virtues of high moral character, as the decisive actor in the moment of preaching.

In my judgment, there is truth in all of these positions. Insofar as a sermon is a speech, the canons of rhetoric are not dismissible. Likewise, insofar as a sermon is rooted in the linguistic artifacts of scripture, the insights of poetics as to the agency and power of language are pertinent. Can preachers be less attentive to the scriptural witness than literary critics to their chosen texts? Nevertheless, the claim of the Reformation, as it listened again to the scriptural tradition, is that God both commissions the church to proclaim his Word, and in this

129

proclamation God is again heard and confessed by faith "today" as the one who speaks saving promises. Given the resulting distinction, therefore, between rhetorical and poetical power and effectiveness on the one hand, and the "power of God for salvation" on the other (Rom. 1:16), any inherent claim of the former as equivalent to the latter crosses the line into idolatry. Why, then, should preachers work at their craft, not only theologically but rhetorically and poetically, if, in fact, God is the real Preacher of every true sermon?

In my studies, I have found the answers given to this question by Alexandre Vinet (1797–1847) to be among the most satisfying. In light of the fact that God has commissioned preaching in the church (2 Cor. 5:18–20), once it is conceded that God calls upon the human creature to speak the gospel in his or her *own* words, "this itself is sanctioning the study and the practice of an art, which is nothing but the rational and thoughtful use of all the natural means that are at the preacher's command."[1] In other words, if God has elected to convert humanity by means of humanity or determined that "man is the medium" through which "truth shall come to man," then who are we to despise the human role accorded by God as intrinsic to divine revelation?[2] "If God uses means, we surely may use them; our faculties are not more unworthy of us than we are of God; and if it is certain that God consents to make man his instrument, let us employ the whole of the instrument, that is to say, the whole of man in God's service."[3] While we cannot attribute revelation or salvation to the creature and creaturely language as such, nevertheless these means must not be despised, since in the Incarnation, in the human witness of scripture, and in the human witness of subsequent Christian proclamation, God has, in each instance, made use of these very means to speak forth his Word.

Preaching, therefore, honors language and its use. Preachers need never apologize for being wordsmiths or even narrative artists. These linguistic and artistic means, however, are powerless in themselves to force God onto the scene, but since oral witness to salvation through Jesus Christ is ordained by God, at least two responses are appropriate on the part of the preacher. First, preaching can only be undertaken as prayer. Our words do not control or constitute the new creation. They are witnesses to the living God, but they are not God. Whatever power is intrinsic to language and its forms cannot be identified as such with the power of the gospel. All sermon preparation therefore must be a prayer for the Holy Spirit to take our ordinary words, however eloquent or inarticulate, and make them the bread of life. Here the sermon, on analogy with the Lord's Supper, is always a matter of epiclesis or invocation, at least where preaching is acknowledged as means of grace. Second, and again on analogy with the Lord's Supper as "Eucharist," the sermon is an act of worship on the part of the preacher, an oblation of thanksgiving and praise on behalf of the gathered assembly of Christians.[4] In this sense, sermons should call forth the preacher's best efforts, knowing that all our works are called to give glory to God alone. For these reasons, we cannot appeal to divine agency as excluding or denigrating human agency, even as we confess boldly that "we have this treasure in clay jars, so that it may be made clear that this extraordinary power belongs to God and does not come from us" (2 Cor. 4:7). *Come Creator Spirit!*

What's the Message?

I sometimes ask my students, "What is the gospel?" This is a question that should be pressed on every theological student, and to leave seminary unable to give some answer, however halting, would be unworthy of our calling. Nevertheless, simply to repeat verbatim the answer of 1 Corinthians 15:3–5, while better than nothing, might not be worthy of our calling either! As we saw, the Christian message or gospel is in fact summarized in this text with respect to the death and resurrection of Christ Jesus with respect to salvation. Here the emphasis is on the gospel as a particular transmission of tradition. As we also learned, the gospel can also be articulated, as in Paul's letter to the Galatians, as God's invasive incursion into the world to redeem or rescue those under the oppressive bondage of sin and death. Here the emphasis is on the gospel as God's act. Taken together, we discover that double agency common to revelation: God's act in the event of the cross and resurrection of Jesus Christ and the human witness to that event in the form of proclamation and tradition.

The question arises, however, whether preaching is simply the reiteration of the cross-resurrection kerygma every Sunday. What we discovered attending to the prophets of the primitive Christian community is that while the cross-resurrection kerygma is always the basic criterion for faithfulness to the gospel, its proclamation into concrete situations also means that *we can never know in advance of its proclamation precisely what form or what content it will take.* We know it should accord with the rule of faith and love, and we know that it should not be anti-Christ. Yet even within these scripturally sanctioned norms, we should expect great diversity and great freedom within the proclamation of the Christian message as ever new situations, not envisioned by the first witnesses to the gospel, are taken into account in the interpretation rendered by the preacher.

Thus, the contextual factor in preaching is not only unavoidable and inescapable, it is the very means through which the Word of God continues to go forth into ever new situations. As I argued on the basis of the doctrine of *concursus,* if God's grace comes to the creature in such a way as to respect the creature's created integrity, and, hence, context and condition, then the church's witness to this grace can do no less. Nevertheless, the exhaustive awareness of context, even if it were achievable, cannot secure the event of revelation. Great caution must be observed to think that we know a culture or a context very well, perhaps, especially, if it is our own. (This is why cross-cultural dialogue is so important for both theology and preaching.) If my own biography, motives, and desires are largely hidden from my conscious understanding, how much more veiled from my view are those of my hearers? Again, we attend to our listeners and to their varied contexts in the awareness that only the Holy Spirit can connect our words to their needs. Only the Holy Spirit can make our words finally fit situations that, in candor, often prove stubbornly inaccessible to preachers. *Come Creator Spirit!*

Will It Preach?

In this book, we have admittedly focused more on how a theological frame of reference clarifies the practice and content of preaching than we have on how preaching clarifies the task and content of theology. Nevertheless, we have noted that the practice of preaching itself, together with the preaching office, stand as a barrier to both fundamentalist and postliberal construals of scripture either as self-interpreting or as standing in one-to-one correspondence with revelation. The very fact that the church requires preaching, and offers prayers of illumination and invocation in the context of preaching, indicates the inadequacy of simply reading or chanting the scriptures in worship apart from their explicit interpretation into the concrete situation of the hearers.

Insofar as preaching is regarded as a liturgical practice of the church, appeals to preaching may, in certain cases, serve simultaneously as appeals to the public worship or prayer of the church, that is, the *lex orandi* or "law of prayer."[5] While this, of course, is not an exclusive criterion for the establishment of Christian teaching, it is certainly an essential one. For example, Christopher Morse notes that Calvin taught double predestination in his *Institutes,* but, like Augustine before him, urged that it should only be preached so "that no one is ever viewed as rejected" or deprived of hope. This shows a Christian doctrine, well supported on various grounds, meeting "resistance in the proclamation of the gospel in Christian worship."[6] Similarly, a few years ago, a Presbyterian theologian delivered a strikingly anti-Roman Catholic sermon at Nassau Presbyterian Church in Princeton. The negative reaction of the congregation dictated that this sermon could not be aired on the radio the following week as was ordinarily the custom. It wouldn't preach. Again, when the late Channing E. Phillips, the Minister of Planning and Coordination at the Riverside Church in New York City, declared in his sermon "On Human Sexuality," on May 9, 1985, that "deviation from the parable of the heterosexual relationship ordained by marriage is contrary to God's will–is sin," a protest demonstration broke out in the congregation even before a benediction could be pronounced.[7] Phillips' sermon was not heard by many in the assembly as Christian teaching.

In citing these examples, I am not trying to adjudicate here the dogmatic claims for double predestination, for anti-Romanist Protestantism, or for normative heterosexuality. To evaluate properly these positions, one would need to engage an entire panoply of theological criteria. What one can say is that whenever Christian teaching meets resistance within the liturgical assembly, whether at the Schlosskirche in Bonn in 1933 or at the Riverside Church in 1985, it tags with urgency a matter for further theological reflection en route to adjudication. If over time, Christian doctrines won't preach, or cannot be received by the company of the faithful as part of the gospel, then they are likely–and rightly–to fade away. Conversely, if over time specific theological proposals are heard from the pulpit as congruent with the gospel, for example, the abolition of slavery or the ordination of women, then preaching contributes mightily to new understandings of the Christian message. In due season, such can even become normative doctrines. Nevertheless, because group spirit is not simply equivalent to the Holy Spirit, a point borne by the travails of church history, here, too, we must proceed both boldly and cautiously at the same time. Here, too, the preacher, no less than the theologian, must begin and end with invocation: *Come Creator Spirit!*

NOTES

Preface

[1]Barth's characterization of Billy Graham's preaching in Switzerland in 1960. See Eberhard Busch, *Karl Barth: His Life from Letters and Autobiographical Texts,* trans. John Bowden (Philadelphia: Fortress Press, 1976), 446.

Introduction: Frames of Reference

[1]Fred B. Craddock, *As One without Authority,* 3d ed. (Nashville: Abingdon Press, 1979), 112.

[2]James Forbes, *The Holy Spirit and Preaching* (Nashville: Abingdon Press, 1989), 53.

[3]André Resner Jr., *Preacher and Cross: Person and Message in Theology and Rhetoric* (Grand Rapids: William B. Eerdmans, 1999), esp. 135–41.

[4]"Titles/Frame of Reference," *Crash,* DVD, directed by Paul Haggis (2005; DEJ Productions, 2005).

[5]Robert Disalle, "Space and Time: Inertial Frames," *The Stanford Encyclopedia of Philosophy* (Fall 1999 Edition), ed. Edward N. Zaltaj, available at http://plato.stanford.edu/entries/spacetime-iframes/.

[6]See W. Caspari, "Homiletik," in *Realencyclopaedie für protestantishce Theologie und Kirche,* 3d ed., vol. 8 (Leipzig: J. C. Hinrich, 1900), 295–96 for the history of the term *Homiletik,* coined between 1672 and 1677. Behind this term is the Greek *homilia* (cf. Lk. 24:14; Acts 24:26) meaning conversation, discourse, or communication. One advantage of "homiletics" is its relative neutrality as to which frame of reference is guiding the reflection on preaching. Other terms have been proposed that make the theological frame of reference decisive, such as *Keryktik* (or, we might say today, "kergymatics") proposed by Rudolf Stier (1800–1862) and *Martyretik* advocated by Theodore Christlieb (1833–1889). Neither proved successful in replacing "homiletics" as the usual term for academic reflection on preaching.

[7]"Let rhetoric be [defined as] an ability, in each [particular] case, to see the available means of persuasion." Aristotle, *On Rhetoric: A Theory of Civic Discourse,* ed. and trans. George A. Kennedy (New York: Oxford University Press, 1991), 36 [2.1].

[8]Gert Otto, *Rhetorische Predigtlehre: Ein Grundriss* (Mainz: Matthias-Grünewald-Verlag; Leipzig: Evangelische Verlagsanstalt, 1999), 7.

[9]Thomas H. Troeger, "A Poetics of the Pulpit for Post-Modern Times," in *Intersections: Post-Critical Studies in Preaching,* ed. Richard L. Eslinger (Grand Rapids: William B. Eerdmans, 1994), 43. Italics omitted.

[10]For the concise overview of early meanings of "theology" from which I have drawn here, see Jacques Fantino, *La théologie d'Irénée: Lecture des Écritures en répose à l'exégè gnostique: Une approche trinitaire* (Paris: Les Éditions du Cerf, 1994), 8, n.2.

[11]See Paul Rorem, *Biblical and Liturgical Symbols within the Pseudo-Dionysian Synthesis,* Studies and Texts 71 (Toronto: Pontifical Institute of Medieval Studies, 1984), 17–22.

[12]See Geoffrey Wainwright, *Doxology: The Praise of God in Worship, Doctrine, and Life* (London: Epworth Press, 1980), 468, n.31, citing the Alexandrian liturgy of St. Mark and the Byzantine liturgy of St. Basil. The Greek texts indicate the plural usage "never-ending theologies" in each instance. See *Liturgies Eastern and Western,* ed. F. E. Brightman, vol. 1 *Eastern Liturgies* (Oxford: Clarendon Press, 1896), 131 and 323.

[13]Wainwright, *Doxology,* 21.

[14]Thus the Pseudo-Areopagite can use the term "theology" to refer to his own words about God "based upon, and an interpretation of, the biblical 'God-word.'" Rorem, *Pseudo-Dionysian Synthesis,* 18.

[15]See Karl Barth, *The Göttingen Dogmatics: Instruction in the Christian Religion,* vol. 1, ed. Hannelotte Reiffen, trans. Geoffrey W. Bromiley (Grand Rapids: William B. Eerdmans, 1991), esp. Par. 2, "Preaching as the Starting Point and Goal of Dogmatics," 23–41.

[16]"Wherever we see the Word of God purely preached and heard, and the sacraments administered according to Christ's institution, there, it is not to be doubted, a church of God exists." John Calvin, *Institutes of the Christian Religion,* ed. John T. McNeill and trans. Ford Lewis Battles, Library of Christian Classics, 2 vols. (Philadelphia: The Westminster Press, 1960), 2:1023 (1.4.9) drawing upon Article 7 of the Augsburg Confession. For the latter, see Philip Schaff, *The Creeds of Christendom* (New York: n.p, 1877), 3:11–12.

[17]See the provocative, but castigating, statements of William H. Willimon, *Proclamation and Theology* (Nashville: Abingdon Press, 2005), esp. 2–4.

Chapter 1: Preaching as the Word of God

[1]Gardner C. Taylor, *How Shall They Preach* (Elgin, Ill.: Progressive Baptist Publishing House, 1977), 24.

[2]"The Second Helvetic Confession," in *The Constitution of the Presbyterian Church (U.S.A.),* pt. 1, *Book of Confessions* (Louisville: Office of the General Assembly, 1994). For the Latin text, see Philip Schaff, *The Creeds of Christendom* (New York: n.p., 1877), 3:233–306, which unfortunately eliminates the marginalia; for the German text, see Walter Hildebrandt and Rudolf Zimmermann, eds., *Das zweite helvitische Bekenntnis* (Zürich: Zwingli Verlag, 1966). For background, see Arthur C. Cochrane, Introduction, in *Reformed Confessions of the Sixteenth Century,* (London: SCM, 1966), 220–33; Edward A. Dowey, "Der theologische Aufbau des Zweiten Helvetischen Bekenntnisses" and "Das Wort Gottes als Schrift und Predigt im *Zweiten Helvetischen Bekenntnis,*" in *Glauben und Bekennen: Vierhundert Jahre Confessio Helvetica Posterior; Beiträge zu ihrer Geschichte und Theologie,* vol. 1, *Zur Geschichte des Bekenntnisses,* ed. Joachim Staedtke (Zürich: Zwingli Verlag, 1966), 205–50; and Philip Schaff, "The Second Helvetic Confession," in *The Creeds of Christendom,* 1:390–420. Translations from Dowey are those given in his unpublished papers, "The Theological Structure of the Second Helvetic Confession" and "The Word of God as Scripture and Preaching." My citations of the Confession use the text and numeration of the PC(USA) *Book of Confessions.*

[3]See Pope Paul VI's second encyclical, *Mysterium Fidei* (1965), "In still another way, He [Christ] is present in the preaching of his Church, since the Gospel she proclaims is the word of God, and it is only in the name of Christ, the Incarnate Word of God, and by his authority and with his help that it is preached…" (par. 36). For a helpful survey of these and other conciliar and papal documents, see Stephen V. DeLeers, "'Written Text Becomes Living Word': Official Roman Catholic Teaching on the Homily, 1963–93," Papers of the Annual Meeting, Academy of Homiletics, Santa Fe, New Mexico, 1996, 1–10, where references to the above document will be found.

[4]Gerhard Ebeling, "Discussion Theses for a Course of Introductory Lectures on the Study of Theology," in Ebeling, *Word and Faith,* trans. James W. Leitch (London: SCM Press, Ltd., 1963), 424.

[5]Gerhard Ebeling, *God and Word,* trans. James W. Leitch (Philadelphia: Fortress Press, 1967), 8.

[6]Rebecca S. Chopp, *The Power to Speak: Feminism, Language, God* (New York: Crossroad, 1989), 5.

[7]Ibid. Italics added.

[8]Ebeling, "Discussion Theses," in *Word and Faith,* 424.

[9]See Richard Lischer, *A Theology of Preaching: The Dynamics of the Gospel,* rev. ed. (Durham, N.C.; Labyrinth Press, 1992), 9.

[10]Christopher Morse, *Not Every Spirit: A Dogmatics of Christian Disbelief* (Valley Forge, Pa.: Trinity Press International, 1994), 87.

[11] Ibid., 92.

[12] Ibid.

[13] See, e.g., *Dei Verbum*, "Dogmatic Constitution on Divine Revelation," 1965, pars. 21 and 24 in Austin P. Flannery, ed., *Documents of Vatican II* (Grand Rapids: William B. Eerdmans, 1975), 750–65.

[14] "Feminist theology must create a new textual base, a new canon…Feminist theology cannot be done from the existing base of the Christian Bible." Rosemary Radford Ruether, ed., *Womanguides: Readings toward a Feminist Theology* (Boston: Beacon Press, 1985), ix. In a new Preface to a second edition of this book, Ruether prefers "touchstones" to "canon" to designate the new "working collection of stories." She restricts the term "canon" to the principle guiding the selection of these "stories" rather than to the "working collection" itself. See *Womanguides*, xi–xiv.

[15] Robert W. Funk, *Honest to Jesus: Jesus for a New Millenium* (San Francisco: Harper, 1996), esp. 314.

[16] "For the Word of God is the will of God. Instead of Mark's 'who does the will of God' (3:35), Luke has (8:21) 'who hear the word of God and do it.' That is true exegesis. Man encounters the will of God in God's Word, and to accept this will is the only way to understand it." Rudolf Bultmann, "The Concept of the Word of God in the New Testament [1933]," in Rudolf Bultmann, *Faith and Understanding*, ed. with an Introduction by Robert W. Funk, trans. Louise Pettibone Smith (Philadelphia: Fortress Press, 1987), 291.

[17] See ibid., 298, n. 38, and noting also Acts 20:32, Jas. 1:18, 21; and 1 Pet. 1:23.

[18] David J. Lose, *Confessing Jesus Christ: Preaching in a Postmodern World* (Grand Rapids: William B. Eerdmans, 2003), 157.

[19] See Rudolf Bultmann, "New Testament and Mythology: The Problem of Demythologizing the New Testament Proclamation [1941]," in Rudolf Bultmann, *New Testament and Mythology and Other Basic Writings*, ed. and trans. Schubert M. Ogden (Philadelphia: Fortress, Press, 1984), 1–43.

[20] Cf. "The Second Helvetic Confession," 5.007. With greater strictness, Article 5 of the Lutheran Augsburg Confession rejects any role for the internal Word apart from the external Word. For parallel Latin and English texts of the Augsburg Confession see Schaff, *Creeds of Christendom*, 3:1–73.

[21] Morse, *Not Every Spirit*, 97.

[22] "Can the event of the Word of God be served at all by scientific methods? Must the hermeneutic approach as such not at once have a destructive effect on the concept of the Word of God, as also on the corresponding concept of the Holy Spirit?" Gerhard Ebeling, "Word of God and Hermeneutics," in *Word and Faith*, 314. That *Ebeling* poses this question is noteworthy.

[23] This question was taken seriously by the older homiletics, not least because pious students were pressing it on their professors! See, e.g., Robert L. Dabney (1829–1898), *Sacred Rhetoric; or, A Course of Lectures on Preaching* (Richmond: Presbyterian Committee of Publication, 1870), now reprinted as *Evangelical Eloquence: A Course of Lectures on Preaching* (Edinburgh: Banner of Truth Trust, 1999), 13; and, Alexandre Vinet, *Homiletics; or The Theory of Preaching*, 2nd ed., trans. and ed. Thomas H. Skinner (New York: Ivison and Finney, 1854), 35–37.

[24] See Charles Hodge, *Systematic Theology*, 3 vols. (London: Thomas Nelson and Sons, 1880), 1:1–17.

[25] Morse, *Not Every Spirit*, 106.

[26] The terminology of the threefold form of the one Word of God is taken from Karl Barth. In his *Church Dogmatics,* his discussion of the Word of God follows the sequence of the *ordo salutis,* that is, as preached, written, and revealed. In his earlier *Göttingen Dogmatics,* the sequence of discussion is reversed as revelation, holy scripture, and Christian preaching. For our purposes, the first form of the Word will refer to revelation, the second to scripture, and the third to preaching. Cf. Barth, *The Göttingen Dogmatics: Instruction in the Christian Religion,* vol. 1, ed. Hannelotte Reiffen, trans. Geoffrey W. Bromiley (Grand Rapids: William B. Eerdmans, 1991), 43–313, and Barth, *Church Dogmatics,* vol. 1., pt. 1, *The Doctrine of*

the Word of God, ed. G. W. Bromiley and T. F. Torrance (Edinburgh: T. & T. Clark, 1975), 88–124.

[27]Dowey, "Wort Gottes als Schrift und Predigt," 235–36.

[28]Ibid., 238.

[29]See ibid.

[30]In addition to the four texts discussed here, see also 5.059 on Mt. 11:28; 5.098 on 2 Cor. 5:18ff.; 5.134 on Jn. 10:5, 27, 28; and 5.143. Significantly, Bullinger cites (5.003) 2 Tim. 3:16, the often used proof text for inspiration, only "in support of the multiple uses of Scripture." Dowey, "Wort Gottes als Schrift und Predigt," 236, n. 3.

[31]Dowey, "Der theologische Aufbau," 214.

[32]Ibid., 230–31.

[33]William H. Willimon, *Proclamation and Theology,* (Nashville: Abingdon Press, 2005), 95.

[34]See Dowey, "Wort Gottes als Schrift und Predigt," 240–41. Cf. Dietrich Bonhoeffer (1906–1945): "The decisive arguments for the church come from Scripture...Evangelical pastors are answerable to the Scripture. They must be able to establish scriptural evidence for their thinking." *Worldly Preaching: Lectures on Homiletics,* ed. and trans. Clyde E. Fant (New York: Crossroad, 1991), 117.

[35]For a formative treatment of the rule of love and the rule of faith in relation to preaching, see Saint Augustine, *On Christian Teaching,* trans., ed., with an introduction by R. P. H. Green (Oxford: Oxford University Press, 1997), 17, 68–70, and 155.

[36]Dowey, "Wort Gottes als Schrift und Predigt," 242–43.

[37]Fred B. Craddock, *As One without Authority,* 3d ed. (Nashville: Abingdon Press, 1979), 120.

Chapter 2: The Gospel of God with Us

[1]See Hughes Oliphant Old, *The Reading and Preaching of the Scriptures in the Worship of the Christian Church,* vol. 1, *The Biblical Period* (Grand Rapids: William B. Eerdmans, 1998), 19–110; Ronald E. Osborn, *A History of Christian Preaching,* vol. 1, *Folly of God: The Rise of Christian Preaching* (St. Louis: Chalice Press, 1999), 77–180; and O. C. Edwards Jr., *A History of Preaching* (Nashville: Abingdon Press, 2004), 8–11.

[2]In light of 1 Cor. 15:1–8, it is disconcerting to find a preacher announcing that "in regard to the gospel, there is no 'handing down' or 'handing over'; there is simply 'the sharing of.'" See Fred B. Craddock, *The Cherry Log Sermons,* with a foreword by Barbara Brown Taylor (Louisville: Westminster John Knox Press, 2001), 53.

[3]See Gerhard Kittel and Gerhard Friedrich, eds., *Theological Dictionary of the New Testament* (Grand Rapids: William B. Eerdmans, 1985), s.v. "keryx [etc.]."

[4]Rudolf Bultmann, *Theologie des Neuen Testaments,* 9th ed., ed. Otto Merk (Tübingen: J. C. B. Mohr [Paul Siebeck], 1984), 308; hereafter cited as *TdNT.*

[5]That "gospel" and "kerygma" are synonymous is shown in that both are "the object of faith (*pistis*). For "gospel" see 1 Cor. 15:2 and Phil. 1:27; for "kerygma" see 1 Cor. 1:21; 2:4–5; 15:11, 14.

[6]Rudolf Bultmann, *Theology of the New Testament,* 2 vols., trans. Kendrick Grobel (New York: Charles Scribner's Sons, 1951–1955), 1:319; hereafter cited as *TNT.* Cf. *TdNT,* 319. See also *TNT,* 1:302, cf. *TdNT,* 301, where the proclaimed word is characterized as "anredenden, fordernden und verheissenden." Bultmann's exegetical case for kerygma as *Anrede* is based on the New Testament's occasional substitution of both *kerygma* and *keryssein* with terms associated with exhortation, e.g. *martyrein* ("testify," 1 Cor. 15:15; cf. Gal. 5:3); *martyrion* (testimony," 1 Cor. 1:6; 2:1); *parakalein* ("summon," 2 Cor. 5:20; 6:1); and *paraklesis* ("appeal," cf. 1 Thess. 2:3 with 1 Cor. 2:4). See Bultmann, "Church and Teaching in the New Testament [1929]" in *Faith and Understanding,* ed. Robt. W. Funk, trans. Louise Pettibone Smith (Philadelphia: Fortress Press, 1987), 1:219, n. 28.

[7]Bultmann, *TdNT,* 308. According to Bultmann, "Paul calls all missionaries 'apostles' (1 Cor. 9:5; Rom. 16:7; 2 Cor. 11:5, 13; 12:11f.) And the same usage is still found in Acts 14:4, 14, and Did. 11:4–6." *TNT,* 1:60.

[8]See Thomas G. Long, *The Witness of Preaching* (Louisville: Westminster/ John Knox Press, 1989), 24–30. Noting its strengths, Long still finds herald model insufficiently attuned to the rhetorical and contextual factors of preaching.

[9]Thomas W. Gillespie, *The First Theologians: A Study in Early Christian Prophecy* (Grand Rapids: William B. Eerdmans, 1994), 5.

[10]Ibid., 149.

[11]Ibid., 197.

[12]Ibid., 199–235. The kerygma is thus the basis and norm for the prophetic speech that interprets it. Not all claims to Spirit-inspired speech prove faithful to the kerygma (1 Cor. 15:12). One might also say that only through theological controversy and testing is the meaning of the kerygma clarified in ever-new historical situations.

[13]Dorothee Sölle, *Political Theology*, trans. with an intro. by John Shelley (Philadelphia: Fortress Press, 1974), 23.

[14]J. Louis Martyn, "The Apocalyptic Gospel in Galatians," *Interpretation* 54 (July 2000): 252. This article distills Martyn's interpretation of Paul's letter in his magisterial *Galatians*, The Anchor Bible, vol. 33A (New York: Doubleday, 1997).

[15]Martyn, "The Apocalyptic Gospel," 254. For discussion of the soteriological and ethical implications of God's invasive action in 2 Corinthians discussed below, see James F. Kay, "2 Corinthians 4:3-6" through "2 Corinthians 6:1-13," in *The Lectionary Commentary: Theological Exegesis for Sunday's Texts*, vol. 2, *The Second Readings: Acts and the Epistles*, ed. Roger E. Van Harn (Grand Rapids: William B. Eerdmans, 2001), 243–64.

[16]See J. Louis Martyn, "Epistemology at the Turn of the Ages," in J. Louis Martyn, *Theological Issues in the Letters of Paul* (Nashville: Abingdon Press, 1997), 89–110, esp. 106–10.

[17]See James F. Kay, *Christus Praesens: A Reconsideration of Rudolf Bultmann's Christology* (Grand Rapids: William B. Eerdmans, 1994), 54–58 and 105–8.

[18]Bultmann, "The Word of God in the New Testament," *Faith and Understanding,* 1:307.

[19]Bultmann, "The Christology of the New Testament [1933]," *Faith and Understanding,* 1:278. See also "The Historical Jesus and the Theology of Paul [1929]," 1:242.

[20]Bultmann, "The Concept of Revelation in the New Testament [1929]," in *Existence and Faith: Shorter Writings of Rudolf Bultmann,* ed. and trans. Schubert M. Ogden (New York: Meridien Books, 1960), 80.

[21]Bultmann finds a similar pattern in the Fourth Gospel, where the paracletic Spirit functions in ways identical or parallel to Jesus himself. See Kay, *Christus Praesens,* 73–77.

[22]Alexandra R. Brown, *The Cross and Human Transformation: Paul's Apocalyptic Word in 1 Corinthians* (Minneapolis: Fortress Press, 1995), xviii.

[23]Karl Barth, "The Need and Promise of Christian Preaching [1922]," in *The Word of God and the Word of Man,* trans. with a new foreword by Douglas Horton, Harper Torchbooks ed. (New York: Harper and Brothers Publishers, 1957), 103. Italics slightly altered. For what follows, see James F. Kay, "Reorientation: Homiletics as Theologically Authorized Rhetoric," *The Princeton Seminary Bulletin* 24, no. 1 (February 2003): 20–24.

[24]Ibid., 122–25.

[25]Barth, "The Word of God and the Task of the Ministry [1922]," in *The Word of God and the Word of Man,* esp. 198–217.

[26]Eduard Thurneysen, "Die Aufgabe der Predigt [1921]," in *Aufgabe der Predigt,* ed. Gert Hummel, Wege der Forschung, vol. 234 (Darmstadt: Wissenschaftliche Buchgesellschaft, 1971), 108 and 111, alluding to Nietzsche's dictum, "Only where there are graves, are there resurrections." Italics original.

[27]"Barth gladly drove a stake into the heart of rhetoric and called upon the newly widowed homiletics not to mourn but to dance on the grave." Thomas G. Long, "And How Shall They Hear? The Listener in Contemporary Preaching," in *Listening to the*

Word: Studies in Honor of Fred B. Craddock, ed. Gail R. O'Day and Thomas G. Long (Nashville: Abingdon Press, 1993), 177.

[28]Karl Barth, *Homiletik: Wesen und Vorbereitung der Predigt* (Zürich: Theologischer Verlag, 1970). ET: Karl Barth, *Homiletics*, trans. Geoffrey W. Bromiley and Donald E. Daniels with a foreword by David Buttrick (Louisville: Westminster/John Knox Press, 1991). Barth's rhetorical interest is evident here when he writes, "Respect for the hearers and their particularity should allow the question of the 'How' of proclamation to appear large and important for us." *Homiletik*, 92. Barth reiterates this rhetorically-friendly position in calling for "some very fruitful and serious work" by an academically rigorous homiletics on "How, how shall we preach?" Barth, *God in Action: Theological Addresses*, trans. E. G. Homrighausen and Karl J. Ernst, with an introduction by Josias Friedl (Edinburgh: T & T Clark, 1936), 55–56.

[29]"The word 'announcement' [*Ankündigung*] has the advantage over 'proclamation' [*Verkündigung*] that in it God is the one who makes himself heard, who speaks, and not we, who simply have the role of announcing what God himself wants to say. This is what *epangelia* signifies in the New Testament. The word 'announcement' does not really carry with it a summons to human decision. A summons of this kind, which is taken solely between God and us, is in no sense constitutive for the task of preaching." Barth, *Homiletics*, 46. [GT, 32].

[30]Ibid., 51–53.

[31]"May it be that as we hear their word [i.e., the scriptural witnesses] we may hear the Word of him who alone can make it heard." Barth, *Homiletics*, 104.

[32]For discussion of "divine performance" in the preaching event, see Charles L. Bartow, *God's Human Speech: A Practical Theology of Proclamation*, with a foreword by Jana Childers (Grand Rapids: William B. Eerdmans, 1997).

[33]"All the action that takes place in preaching, which lies between the first advent and the second, is the action of the divine Subject." Barth, *Homiletics*, 47.

[34]Barth, *Homiletik*, 36.

[35]Barth, *Homiletics*, 49–50, 75–81, 88, and 102–4.

[36]Ibid., 49 and 102–3.

[37]Ibid., 98–106. Barth is challenging theologically stunted historical-critical exegesis, whether employed by "liberals" or "conservatives." In Barth's view, interpretation proceeding "as though the historical meaning of the text were its total sense" is "a dogma–not a church dogma but a pagan dogma–which recognizes only humanity and its world and functions, among which is religion." *Homiletics*, 99.

[38]Ibid., 49.

[39]Ibid., 102–6, 113, and 121.

[40]Ibid., 49 and 105.

[41]Ibid., 126.

[42]Ibid., 105. See also 126.

[43]Caren Algner, introduction to "Karl Barth, Sermon on Romans 15:5–13, 1933," in *Letter from the Karl Barth Archives*, no. 1 (1998): 3–6; and Busch, *Karl Barth*, 234–35.

[44]Karl Barth, "The Church of Jesus Christ: Sermon on Romans 15:5–13," trans. Charles Dickinson, *Letter from Barth Archives*, 7. Italics original.

[45]Ibid., 9. Italics original.

[46]Ibid., 11. Italics original.

[47]Barth, *Homiletics*, 121. The only exception Barth allows is when the scripture reading immediately precedes the sermon. A brief analysis of the passage may then occur before the sermon proper. See further, Kay, "Reorientation," 24–25.

[48]Ibid., 124. [GT, 104].

[49]Barth, *Homiletik*, 101. Italics original.

[50]Barth, *Homiletics*, 122–23.

[51]See, e.g., two Christmas sermons, "Unto You is Born this Day a Saviour [1954]" and "The Great Dispensation [1957]," in Karl Barth, *Deliverance to the Captives*, trans. Marguerite Wieser (New York: Harper and Brothers, 1961), 20–27 and 101–8.

[52]Hans-Dieter Bastian, "From the Word to the Words: Karl Barth and the Tasks of Practical Theology," trans. Richard Ulrich, in *Theology of the Liberating Word*, ed. Frederick Herzog (Nashville: Abingdon Press, 1971), 48.

[53]Ibid., 49. Does Barth's sermon at the Schlosskirche in Bonn, which admittedly does not mention the Aryan Laws, the Nazis, or "the Jewish question," mean that the "real situation" has dropped out of the equation?

[54]Ibid.

[55]"We are not concerned with an abolition of the Word-words dialectic in dogmatics, but with its heuristically necessary suspension in practical theology." Ibid., 51.

[56]For this discussion of Bultmann and his program, see further James F. Kay, "Bultmann, Rudolf," in *The Oxford Companion to Christian Thought*, ed. Adrian Hastings et al. (Oxford: Oxford University Press, 2000), 83–84. For a classic homiletic case for the liberal theological perspectives to which Bultmann was both heir and critic, see Harry Emerson Fosdick (1878–1969) in *The Modern Use of the Bible* (New York: Macmillan, 1924).

[57]For a critical assessment of the role of allegory in contemporary theology and preaching see Mark Ellingsen, *The Integrity of Biblical Narrative: Story in Theology and Proclamation* (Minneapolis: Fortress Press, 1990), 10–14 and 18. For the continuing homiletical possibilities of the fourfold model of exegesis, including the use of allegory, see Paul Scott Wilson, *God Sense: Reading the Bible for Preaching* (Nashville: Abingdon Press, 2001).

[58]For the sermon text, see Rudolf Bultmann, *This World and the Beyond: Marburg Sermons,* trans. Harold Knight (New York: Charles Scribner's Sons, 1960), 100–111. For background on *Kristallnacht,* see William L. Shirer, *The Rise and Fall of the Third Reich: A History of Nazi Germany* (New York: Simon & Schuster Inc., 1990), 430–35. For Bultmann's activities during the Nazi period, see Andreas Lindemann, "Neutestamentler in der Zeit des Nationalsozialismus: Hans von Soden und Rudolf Bultmann in Marburg," *Wort und Dienst* 20 (1989): 25–52.

[59]By saying that messianic hope "is by no means confined to Israel," as witness the beliefs of the "north Germanic tribes," "the Aryan Persians," or Karl Immermann (1796–1840), the German poet, Bultmann turns the tables on the Nazis by pointing out the "messianism" of their own ethnic heritage. Nevertheless, by arguing that the Old Testament, in effect, possesses *no less* significance than Aryan myths, Bultmann could also be heard as suggesting it has *no more.*

Chapter 3: Orators and Poets

[1]John P. Hoshor, "American Contributions to Rhetorical Theory and Homiletics," in *History of Speech Education in America: Background Studies,* ed. Karl R. Wallace (New York: Appleton-Century-Crofts, 1954), 149. For what follows, see further James F. Kay, "Reorientation: Homiletics as Theologically Authorized Rhetoric," *The Princeton Seminary Bulletin* 24, no. 1 (February 2003): 16–35. See also Don Wardlaw, "Homiletics and Preaching in North America," *Concise Encyclopedia of Preaching,* ed. William H. Willimon and Richard Lischer (Louisville: Westminster John Knox Press, 1995).

[2]John A. Broadus, A Treatise on the Preparation and Delivery of Sermons, 5th ed. (Philadelphia: Smith, English & Co., 1873), 30. Cf. the formulation of Alexandre Vinet, "Rhetoric is the genus, Homiletics the species." A. Vinet, *Homiletics; or The Theory of Preaching,* 2nd ed., trans. and ed. Thomas H. Skinner (New York: Ivison and Finney, 1854), 22.

[3]Wilbur Samuel Howell, "The New Rhetoric (1646–1800)," in *Eighteenth-Century British Logic and Rhetoric* (Princeton: Princeton University Press, 1971), 440–691. On Witherspoon's educational innovations, see Thomas Miller, preface to *The Selected Writings of John Witherspoon,* Landmarks in Rhetoric and Public Address (Carbondale and Edwardsville: Southern Illinois University Press, 1990), 19–24. George Campbell was principal of Marischal College, Aberdeen, and taught systematic theology and

pulpit eloquence. Hugh Blair was minister of St. Giles and the first Regius Professor of Rhetoric and Belles Lettres in Edinburgh. For a discussion of Campbell and Blair see Howell, *Eighteenth-Century British Logic and Rhetoric,* 577–612 and 647–671, respectively. See also, Lloyd F. Bizer, "Editor's Introduction," in George Campbell, *The Philosophy of Rhetoric* (Carbondale and Edwardsville: Southern Illinois University Press, 1988), vii–li, and, more recently, Arthur E. Walzer, *George Campbell: Rhetoric in the Age of the Enlightenment,* SUNY Series: Rhetoric in the Modern Era (Albany: State University of New York Press, 2003).

⁴John Witherspoon, "Lectures on Eloquence," in *The Selected Writings of John Witherspoon,* 231–318. For lecture fourteen on pulpit eloquence, see 295–300.

⁵Miller, preface to *The Selected Writings of John Witherspoon,* vii.

⁶Campbell, *The Philosophy of Rhetoric,* 98–99. See also Witherspoon, "Lectures on Eloquence," 295–309; and Hugh Blair, *Lectures on Rhetoric and Belles Lettres* (1819; reprint, with an introduction by Charlotte Downey, American Linguistics 1700–1900, (Delmar, New York: Scholars' Facsimiles and Pamphlets, 1993), 255–92. Blair's *Lectures* were first published in 1783.

⁷Nan Johnson, *Nineteenth-Century Rhetoric in North America* (Carbondale and Edwardsville: Southern Illinois University Press, 1991), 50–52, and emending Howell to include Richard Whately's (1787–1863) contributions within those of "the New Rhetoric." Cf. Howell's distinctions between the "old" and "new" rhetoric in *Eighteenth-Century British Logic and Rhetoric,* 441–47.

⁸Campbell, *The Philosophy of Rhetoric,* 1, noting Quintilian. Italics original. See also George Campbell, *Lectures on Systematic Theology and Pulpit Eloquence* (London: T. Cadell and W. Davies, Strand, 1807), 350. These lectures were first given in 1772–1773 in Aberdeen. Cf. Blair, *Lectures on Rhetoric and Belles Lettres,* 234: "To be eloquent, is to speak to the purpose. For the best definition which, I think, can be given of eloquence, is the art of speaking in such a manner as to attain the end for which we speak."

⁹Campbell, *The Philosophy of Rhetoric,* 1, noting "Tully," i.e., Marcus Tullius Cicero. Campbell holds that these distinct purposes can occur together, but one should be preeminent in a discourse. See also Campbell, *Lectures on Systematic Theology and Pulpit Eloquence,* 350.

¹⁰This distinction between the subject of a discourse and its aim or end is a commonplace. See Campbell, *Philosophy of Rhetoric,* 104–12; and Witherspoon, "Lectures on Eloquence," 247–48, 290–95.

¹¹Campbell, *Philosophy of Rhetoric,* 104–6. See also Campbell, *Lectures on Systematic Theology and Pulpit Eloquence,* 260.

¹²Campbell, *Philosophy of Rhetoric,* 104–6. As Campbell indicates elsewhere, he does not favor preaching dogmatic theology, as such. As befits a rhetorician of his era, he sees the ultimate end of every doctrine "in the performance of duty, or as a motive to it." The revelation of the truths of the gospel "was not given to gratify our curiosity, but to regulate our lives." Campbell, *Lectures on Systematic Theology and Pulpit Eloquence,* 467–68.

¹³Campbell, *Philosophy of Rhetoric,* 107, alluding to Titus 2:11–12. Cf. Campbell, *Lectures on Systematic Theology and Pulpit Eloquence,* 355–56: "The reformation of mankind is the great and ultimate end of the whole ministerial function, and especially of this particular branch, preaching or discoursing from the pulpit. But it is not necessary, that the ultimate end of the whole should be the immediate scope of every part."

¹⁴Campbell, *Philosophy of Rhetoric,* 108–9. Cf. Campbell, *Lectures on Systematic Theology and Pulpit Eloquence,* 522: "I acknowledge, that the whole of preaching either directly or indirectly points to persuasion."

¹⁵Blair, *Lectures on Rhetoric and Belles Lettres,* 282.

¹⁶Ibid., 282.

¹⁷Witherspoon, "Lectures on Eloquence," 297. Italics original. With more nuance, Campbell indicates "it is a matter of some consequence that, *in the opinion of those whom he addresseth,* he [the speaker] is both a wise and a good man." *Philosophy of Rhetoric,* 99. My

italics. With respect to the preacher, "there is little or no indulgence, in regard to his own failings, to be expected by the man who is professedly a sort of authorized censor, who hath it in charge to mark and reprehend the faults of others." *Philosophy of Rhetoric,* 100.

[18]Campbell, *Philosophy of Rhetoric,* 108. Campbell exclaims, "Happy the preacher whose sermons, by the blessing of Heaven, have been instrumental in producing even a few such instances!" 109.

[19]Ibid., 111.

[20]Ibid., 109–10.

[21]See Herbert W. Simons, ed., *The Rhetorical Turn* (Chicago: University of Chicago Press, 1990).

[22]See George A. Kennedy, *New Testament Interpretation through Rhetorical Criticism* (Chapel Hill: The University of North Carolina Press, 1984).

[23]Stephen H. Webb, *Re-figuring Theology: The Rhetoric of Karl Barth,* SUNY Series in Rhetoric and Theology (Albany: State University of New York Press, 1991).

[24]The rhetorical "turn to the listener(s)" is a characteristic feature of many other recent homiletical proposals. See, e.g., David Buttrick, *Homiletic: Moves and Structures* (Philadelphia: Fortress Press, 1987); Christine M. Smith, *Weaving the Sermon: Preaching in a Feminist Perspective* (Louisville: Westminster/John Knox Press, 1989); John S. McClure, *The Roundtable Pulpit: Where Leadership and Preaching Meet* (Nashville: Abingdon Press, 1995); Leonora Tubbs Tisdale, *Preaching as Local Theology and Folk Art* (Minneapolis: Fortress Press, 1997); and Lucy Atkinson Rose, *Sharing the Word: Preaching in the Roundtable Church* (Louisville: Westminster John Knox Press, 1997).

[25]David Buttrick, *A Captive Voice: The Liberation of Preaching* (Louisville: Westminster/John Knox Press, 1994), 3.

[26]Lucy Lind Hogan and Robert Reid, *Connecting with the Congregation: Rhetoric and the Art of Preaching* (Nashville: Abingdon Press, 1999). The authors accurately describe their book as "a basic *rhetoric* of preaching" (158). Italics original.

[27]Manfred Josuttis, "Homiletik und Rhetorik [1968]" in Josuttis, *Rhetorik und Theologie in der Predigtarbeit: Homiletische Studien,* (München: Chr. Kaiser Verlag, 1985), 9–28.

[28]See Gert Otto, *Predigt als Rede: Über die Wechselwirkungen von Homiletik und Rhetorik* (Stuttgart: Verlag W. Kohlhammer, 1976); *Predigt als rhetorische Aufgabe: Homiletische Perspektiven* (Neukirchen-Vluyn: Neukirchener Verlag, 1987); and *Rhetorische Predigtlehre: Ein Grundriss* (Mainz: Matthias-Grünewald-Verlag; Leipzig: Evangelische Verlagsanstalt, 1999). For a sermon by Otto, see "'Haves' and 'Have-Nots,'" trans. Jeffrey T. Myers, *Homiletic* 15, no. 2 (1990): 13–15.

[29]Among notable works are Rolf Zerfass, *Grundkurs Predigt,* 2 vols. (Düsseldorf, 1987–92); Karl-Fritz Daiber, *Predigt als religiöse Rede* (München, 1991); Peter Bukowski, *Predigt wahrnehmen: Homiletische Perspektiven* (Neukirchen-Vluyn: Neukirchener Verlag, 1992); Thomas Reschke and Michael Thiele, *Predigt und Rhetorik: Ein Querschnitt durch den Kern der Homiletik aus rhetorisch-praktischer Sicht,* with a foreword by Gert Otto, Studien zur Praktischen Theologie, 39 (St. Ottilien: EOS Verlag, 1992); and Klaus Müller, *Homiletik: Ein Handbuch für kritische Zeiten* (Regensburg: Verlag Friedrich Pustet, 1994).

[30]Otto, *Rhetorische Predigtlehre,* 7.

[31]Ibid.

[32]Otto, *Predigt als Rede,* 21, citing his first thesis from his 1970 "Thesen zur Problematik der Predigt," and echoing Johann Lorenz von Mosheim (1693–1755). Italics original. Cf. Karl Barth, *Homiletik: Wesen und Vorbereitung der Predigt* (Zürich: Theologischer Verlag, 1970), 99.

[33]Otto, *Predigt als Rhetorische Aufgabe,* 18–19, quoting thesis two from his 1970 "Thesen zur Problematik der Predigt." See also Fred B. Craddock, *As One without Authority,* 3d ed. (Nashville: Abingdon Press, 1979), 16.

[34]Hogan and Reid, *Connecting with the Congregation,* 13.

[35]Ibid., 9.

[36]Ibid., 11 and 12, quoting Karlyn Kohrs Campbell, *The Rhetorical Act*, 2nd ed. (Belmont, Calif.: Wadsworth, 1996), 9.

[37]Ibid., 16.

[38]Ibid., 55–56.

[39]Ibid., 55, quoting from "Character," by Susan K. Hedahl in *Concise Encyclopedia of Preaching*.

[40]The allusions are to Graham Greene, *The Power and the Glory* (London: William Heinemann, Ltd., 1940) and Walker Percy, *The Second Coming* (New York: Farrar Straus Giroux, 1980). Such allusions are not to commend either licentiousness or stupidity, but to confess with the Second Helvetic Confession that "the Word itself which is preached is to be regarded, not the minister that preaches; for even if he be evil and a sinner, nevertheless the Word of God remains still true and good" (5.004). Otherwise, who could preach–or endure listening to preachers–however "good"?

[41]Hogan and Reid, *Connecting with the Congregation*, 43–44. Italics original.

[42]Ibid., with citations from 7, 8, 9, and 11–12. The metaphor of God "playing on" the preacher like a trombone is an allusion of James Weldon Johnson taken from Richard Lischer, *The Preacher King: Martin Luther King, Jr. and the Word that Moved America* (Oxford University Press, 1995), 12.

[43]Hogan and Reid, *Connecting with the Congregation*, 108.

[44]Ibid., cf. 8 and 10. There appears here an oscillation between an "instrumental" rhetoric (that can allow for a trans-semiotic Agent as the subject matter) and a "critical" rhetoric that communally constructs the subject matter of preaching. By and large, the authors seem to prefer the former, as their acknowledged differences with Lucy Rose over argumentative persuasion may suggest. See 89–110, esp. 109. For the distinction between "instrumental" and "critical" rhetoric, see Rolf Zerfass, *Grundkurs Predigt*, 1:35–36, cited by Otto, *Rhetorische Predigtlehre*, 99–100.

[45]Hogan and Reid, *Connecting with the Congregation*, 8. Cf. King's biographer, "Martin Luther King, Jr., was a B+ preacher until he got caught up in something larger than himself." Richard Lischer, "Why I Am Not Persuasive," *Homiletic* 24, no. 2 (1999):16.

[46]Hogan and Reid, *Connecting with the Congregation*, 22.

[47]Ibid., 119. Italics original. See further 124–26. Other options include explanatory expository preaching; making possible an experience of provisional meaning; and presenting the storied-identity of God or Christ in the interest of Christian formation. In every case, these purposes of a sermon remain within the context of persuasion and are predicated on, or "controlled by," the preacher's rhetorical skills. See 16 and 115–31, esp. 118–19.

[48]Ibid., 124. Capitalization original. Kerygmatic approaches to preaching are discussed here without reference to Rudolf Bultmann, a lacuna also found in Rose, *Sharing the Word*, 37–56.

[49]Hogan and Reid, *Connecting with the Congregation*, 91. Original capitalized in bold face as a heading.

[50]Reid largely accepts this characterization; Hogan disputes it. My point is not to denigrate colleagues, but to identify the consistent tendency of their proposal.

[51]John Quincy Adams, *Lectures on Rhetoric and Oratory*, 2 vols. (1810; reprint, American Linguistics, 1700–1900, (Delmar, New York: Scholars' Facsimiles and Reprints, 1997), 1:322.

[52]Ibid., 1:322. Having recognized the difficulties, Adams then retreats with all deliberate speed "to apply the principles and method of Aristotle, so far as they can be applied, to this more recent species of public speaking." 1:324.

[53]Karl Barth, "The Strange New World within the Bible [1916]," in *The Word of God and the Word of Man*, trans. with a new foreword by Douglas Horton, Harper Torchbooks ed. (New York: Harper and Brothers, 1957), 34.

[54]Barth, *Homiletics*, trans. Geoffrey W. Bromiley and Donald E. Daniels (Louisville: Westminister/John Knox Press, 1991), 44.

[55]See Lucy Lind Hogan, "Rethinking Persuasion: Developing an Incarnational Theology of Preaching," *Homiletic* 24, no. 2 (1999): 11, albeit non-dialectically within a theology of glory.

[56]Hogan and Reid, *Connecting with the Congregation,* 13: "Effective preaching is effective rhetoric, and we cannot begin a theory of preaching pietistically devoid of an understanding of the art of rhetoric." Cf. Barth, *Homiletics,* 119: "To be sure a sermon is a speech. It has to be this. But in this speech we should not leave it up to the Holy Spirit (or some other spirit!) to inspire the words, no matter whether we have an aptitude for speaking or not." For Barth, the self-authentication of the Word of God and the work of the Holy Spirit are not put forward as "available mechanisms of theological self-exoneration" as they may have become for those evading the hard work of sermon preparation. See Ernst Lange, "Zur Theorie und Praxis der Predigtarbeit [1967]," in *Predigen als Beruf,* ed. Rüdiger Schloz (Stuttgart, 1976), 55.

[57]Barth, *Homiletics,* 44, with translation altered. Cf. Barth, *Homiletik,* 30.

[58]See Barth, *Church Dogmatics,* ed. G. W. Bromiley and T. F. Torrance (Edinburgh: T. and T. Clark, 1975), vol. 3, pt. 3; *The Doctrine of Creation,* ed. G. W. Bromiley and T. F. Torrance, trans. G. W. Bromiley and R. J. Ehrlich (Edinburgh: T. and T. Clark, 1960), 90–153; Otto Weber, *Foundations of Dogmatics,* 2 vols., trans. and annotated by Darrell L. Guder (Grand Rapids: William B. Eerdmans, 1981), 1:516–19; and Christopher Morse, *Not Every Spirit: A Dogmatics of Christian Disbelief* (Valley Forge, Pa.: Trinity Press International, 1994), esp. 219–20.

[59]Morse, *Not Every Spirit,* 219.

[60]Barth, *Church Dogmatics,* 3/3:138.

[61]Ibid.

[62]Cf. Otto, *Predigt als Rede,* 27: Italics original. See also Hogan and Reid, *Connecting with the Congregation,* 16. Provided this rhetorical claim is understood dialectically and not reductionistically, it can be affirmed theologically.

[63]Other theological routes to authorize a rhetorically attentive homiletics come to mind, including the Thomistic *convenientia* and the Calvinian *accommodare.* For discussion of the former, see John Milbank and Catherine Pickstock, "Truth and Touch," in *Truth in Aquinas* (London: Routledge, 2001); of the latter, see Ford Lewis Battles, "God Was Accommodating Himself to Human Capacity," *Interpretation* 31, no. 1 (1977): 19–38. For a proposal that draws on the theme of divine accommodation to authorize its contextual homiletic, see Tisdale, *Preaching as Local Theology and Folk Art,* 1997, 35–37. For a proposal that draws on divine accommodation to authorize *"a variety of possible sermon strategies,"* see Charles L. Bartow, *God's Human Speech: A Practical Theology of Proclamation* (Grand Rapids: William B. Eerdmans, 1997), 142. Italics original.

[64]A parallel to this judgment is found in Calvin's contention that the Word of God proscribes (Ex. 20:4) the use of graven images in worship (*Inst.* 1.11.1–4) and prescribes (Acts 2:42; 1 Cor. 11:20) frequent communion (*Inst.* 4.17.44), while leaving those matters neither prescribed nor proscribed by the Word of God (*adiaphora*) to the best judgment of the church. In regard to these latter matters, Calvin argues that the Word of God (1 Cor. 14:40) authorizes the church to make its own decisions touching upon decorum and order, sensitive "to the customs of each nation and age" (*Inst.* 4.10.30).

[65]For this background and text see James M. Washington, ed., *A Testament of Hope: The Essential Writings of Martin Luther King, Jr.* (San Francisco: Harper & Row, 1986), 253–58.

[66]Ibid., 253.

[67]Ibid., 253, 254, and 255, respectively.

[68]Ibid., 253.

[69]Ibid., 254.

[70]Ibid., 255.

[71]Ibid., 257.

[72]Ibid.

[73]Ibid., 257–58.

[74]W. Paul Ludwig, "The Poet and the Preacher," *Theology Today* 2, no. 3 (October 1945): 352–66, here esp. 352–54. I am grateful to Angela Dienhart Hancock, Ph.D. candidate at Princeton Theological Seminary, for calling Ludwig's essay to my attention.

[75]*Aristotle's Poetics,* trans. S. H. Butcher, with an introduction by Francis Fergusson. New York: Hill and Wang, 1961, (6:2), 61.

[76]Ludwig, "Poet and Preacher," 354–55.

[77]Ibid., 355–57.

[78]Ibid., 357–58. For an overview of the debates on the meaning of *katharsis* in Aristotle's *Poetics,* see Jonathan Lear, "Katharsis," in Amélie Oksenberg Rorty, ed., *Essays on Aristotle's Poetics* (Princeton: Princeton University Press, 1992), 315–40.

[79]Ludwig, "Poet and Preacher," 360–61.

[80]*Aristotle's Poetics* (7:2–3), 65.

[81]Ludwig, "Poet and Preacher," 362–64, and 366 on "divine-human drama."

[82]Ibid., 365

[83]Ibid., 366.

[84]Ibid. More recent biblical scholarship, while drawing on parallels between the Jesus of the Farewell Discourses and the heroes of Greek tragedies, disputes that Jesus is a tragic hero. The Fourth Gospel adapts the tragic genre so that the death that hangs over the career of the tragic hero corresponds to the resurrected glory that hangs over the career of Jesus. See George Parsenios, "No Longer in the World" (John 17:11): The Transformation of the Tragic in the Fourth Gospel," *Harvard Theological Review* 98, no. 1 (January 2005): 1–21.

[85]Ludwig, "Poet and Preacher," 365–66.

[86]Eugene L. Lowry, *The Homiletical Plot: The Sermon as Narrative Art Form* (Atlanta: John Knox Press, 1980), 16. See also his *Doing Time in the Pulpit: The Relationship between Narrative and Preaching* (Nashville: Abingdon Press, 1985), esp. 52–58 for a quick reprise of his first book, and *How to Preach a Parable: Designs for Narrative Sermons* (Nashville: Abingdon Press, 1989), where a further reprise appears on 23–26. *The Sermon: Dancing on the Edge of Mystery* (Nashville, Abingdon Press, 1997), offers a third reprise on 56–89, making some adjustments to Lowry's original proposal in dialogue with representatives of "the New Homiletic." The updates given in *The Sermon* are also found in the "Afterword" of the expanded edition of *The Homiletical Plot: The Sermon as Narrative Art Form,* with a foreword by Fred B. Craddock (Louisville: Westminster John Knox Press, 2001), 117–31.

[87]Scattered references to Aristotle appear in *Time in the Pulpit,* 23, 50, and 57, and the *The Sermon,* 56, 75, although in all of Lowry's books Aristotle's *Poetics* appear mediated through secondary sources. For Lowry's own indication of Aristotle's influence, see his "The Narrative Quality of Experience as a Bridge to Preaching," in *Journeys toward Narrative Preaching,* ed. Wayne Bradley Robinson (New York: The Pilgrim Press, 1990), 69.

[88]Lowry, *Homiletical Plot,* 23–24.

[89]Ibid., 25. Having characterized this plotted action as "essential" to a sermon, Lowry further nuances this claim by saying he is "providing the norm from which exceptions are made." In *The Sermon,* Lowry replaces his five-stage sequence with four stages of Conflict, Complication, Sudden Shift, and Unfolding. Now, (1) the "Good News" is no longer simply identified with or taken as the Sudden Shift, i.e., "Aha!, but may immediately follow it, or precede it immediately after the Complication or "Ugh!"; (2) the "Whee!" and the "Yeah!" are both subsumed under "Unfolding"; and, (3) the Sudden Shift need no longer be a "reversal" in Aristotle's sense, but only a "radical" change that can be less than "polar." See 81–85.

[90]Lowry, *Homiletical Plot,* 31. See also, 37.

[91]For comments along these lines see ibid., 23–24 and 64.

⁹²A further example of this delimitation of rhetoric by poetics is seen in Lowry's discussion of the "trust" necessary between a preacher and a congregation. Given his poetic frame of reference, the ethos arguments of rhetoric are transposed so that the trust in question becomes the listeners' confidence "in the preacher to resolve the issue [i.e. the homiletical bind] in light of the gospel." In other words, the character of the preacher is largely a matter of his or her adeptness as a narrative artist. See *Time in the Pulpit,* 68.

⁹³Lowry, *Time in the Pulpit,* 85. Italics original. Lowry's immediately adding, "And the Bible, through metaphor and parable, shows us how" does not redeem his claim from transferring to the creature and to creaturely language, as such, the power to render revelation present. The Bible and its forms are themselves creaturely. They only become instruments of revelation through the power of the Holy Spirit, and not through their own intrinsic power, literary or otherwise.

⁹⁴Lowry, *The Sermon,* 37. Italics original.

⁹⁵Ibid.

⁹⁶Ibid., 52. See also, 113–14.

⁹⁷Lowry, *Homiletical Plot,* 86–87. Similarly, in *Time in the Pulpit,* Lowry acknowledges "kairotic time" as "God's time" that in-breaks ordinary chronological time. See 32–38 and 63. Nevertheless, it is the preacher's task "to prompt the kairotic moment of revelation" (37). See also 35 and 64. See further *The Sermon,* 113: "Our task is, finally, to prompt, to evoke." The notion of a prompter is one familiar to the theatre, but it is inappropriately used here to characterize the creature's role vis-a-vis God. The testimony of scripture indicates that it is the Holy Spirit that prompts the creature in the kairotic moment—not the other way around (cf. Acts 8:26–39).

⁹⁸The Holy Spirit makes no appearance in Lowry's books until *The Sermon.* Here there are a couple of cameos, but never in such a way as to question the creature's capacity "to maximize the possibility of proclamation happening" or "to facilitate an unfolding." See 88–89 where these affirmations are juxtaposed with the claim that "the Spirit works with certainty." See also, 96 and esp. 100.

⁹⁹My exposition of Heidegger is largely based on the lucid studies of James M. Robinson, "The German Discussion of the Later Heidegger," in *The Later Heidegger and Theology,* ed. James M. Robinson and John B. Cobb, Jr. (New York: Harper & Row, 1963), 3–76, and of Paul J. Achtemeier, *An Introduction to the New Hermeneutic* (Philadelphia: The Westminster Press, 1969), esp. 26–54. I follow Achtemeier in capitalizing "Being," in contrast to "being," but that does not mean that Heidegger identifies or hypostasizes "Being" as "God."

¹⁰⁰Martin Heidegger, "The Thinker as Poet" [1947, orig. pub. 1954] in Martin Heidegger, *Poetry, Language, Thought,* trans. with an introduction by Albert Hofstadter (New York, Harper & Row, 1971), 5.

¹⁰¹Ibid., 4.

¹⁰²Heinrich Ott, "Four Decades of Theology in the Neighbourhood of Martin Heidegger," *Église et Théologie* 25 (1994): 95.

¹⁰³Ibid. See Martin Heidegger, *Being and Time: A Translation of Sein und Zeit,* trans. Joan Stambaugh (Albany: SUNY Press, 1996).

¹⁰⁴For what follows, see Achtemeier, *Introduction to the New Hermeneutic,* 41–54.

¹⁰⁵Martin Heidegger, "Language," in Heidegger, *Poetry, Language, Thought,* 210. Heidegger notes, "If attention is fastened exclusively on human speech, if human speech is taken simply to be the voicing of the inner man, if speech so conceived is regarded as language itself, then the nature of language can never appear as anything but an expression and an activity of man. But human speech, as the speech of mortals, is not self-subsistent. The speech of mortals rests in its relation to the speaking of language," 208.

¹⁰⁶Ott, "Four Decades of Theology," 97.

¹⁰⁷Ibid., 98.

¹⁰⁸"Idle talk" is discourse divorced from an understanding of its primordial subject matter. See Heidegger, *Being and Time,* 157–59.

[109]Robinson, "The German Discussion," 31, quoting Heinrich Ott, *Geschichte und Heilsgeschichte in der Theologie Rudolf Bultmanns,* vol. 19 of *Beiträge zur historischen Theologie* (Tübingen: J. C. B. Mohr [Paul Siebeck], 1955), 210–11, and Ott, *Denken und Sein: Der Weg Martin Heideggers und der Weg der Theologie* (Zollikon: Evangelischer Verlag, 1959), 7.

[110]Robinson, "The German Discussion," 46, quoting Ott, *Denken und Sein,* 173–74.

[111]Ibid., 53–54, quoting Ott's unpublished essay, "Sprache und verstehen als Grund problem gegenwärtiger Theologie" [1960].

[112]Robinson, "The German Discussion," 51.

[113]Heinrich Ott, "What Is Systematic Theology?," in *The Later Heidegger and Theology,* ed. Robinson and Cobb, 89.

[114]Gerhard Ebeling, "Verantworten des Glaubens in Begegnung mit dem Denken M Heideggers: Thesen zum Verhältnis von Philosphie und Theologie," in *Zeitschrift für Theologie und Kirche,* 2 (1961): 119–24.

[115]Ibid., 121. Philosophy and theology do not have two different "words," but their respective subject matters effectively result in two different modes of the word, thereby giving rise to both general and theological hermeneutics.

[116]Ibid., 122.

[117]Ibid., 122–24.

Chapter 4: From the New Hermeneutic to the New Homiletic

[1]David James Randolph, *The Renewal of Preaching* (Philadelphia: Fortress Press, 1969), 19. As Randolph later elaborates, "My quarrel with Broadus was not that he used rhetoric but that he made preaching a branch of rhetoric. He subsumed homiletics under rhetoric. I said then and I say now that preaching uses rhetoric but is theology. Rhetoric is in the service of theology in my view." Randolph, "The Renewal of Preaching in the 21st Century," in *The Renewal of Preaching in the 21st Century* (Babylon, N.Y.: Hanging Garden Press, 1998), 7.

[2]Fred B. Craddock, *As One without Authority,* 3d ed. (Nashville: Abingdon Press, 1979), 6. Craddock understands his work as set within "a hermeneutical frame of reference," 112.

[3]Ibid., 3, with further polemics on 143–44, and in Craddock, *Preaching* (Nashville: Abingdon Press, 1985), 178.

[4]Craddock, *As One without Authority,* 45. O. C. Edwards Jr. notes that the deductive outline does not stem from Aristotle as Craddock seems to suggest, or even from classical or patristic rhetoric in general. Edwards speculates it emerges in the Enlightenment. See Edwards, *A History of Preaching* (Nashville: Abingdon Press, 2004), 822, n.7.

[5]Craddock, *As One without Authority,* 26.

[6]Ibid., 52.

[7]Ibid.

[8]Gerhard Ebeling, *God and Word,* trans. James W. Leitch (Philadephia: Fortress Press, 1967), 16. Subsequently, Ebeling locates one of the origins of this theory of language in classical rhetoric whose subdivisions are based entirely upon the distinction between "the content of thought *(res)* and its formulation in words *(verba).*" While appreciative of classical rhetoric's contribution to "how language is to be used in real life," Ebeling finds its signifying theory of language "clearly inadequate to do justice to the problem of language with which we are faced at the present day." Ebeling, *Introduction to a Theological Theory of Language,* trans. R. A. Wilson (Philadelphia: Fortress Press, 1973), 137–44.

[9]Ebeling, *God and Word,* 17.

[10]Ibid., 17–18.

[11]Ibid., 19.

[12]Ibid., 26. For Craddock's comment, see *As One without Authority*, 112.

[13]Ebeling, *God and Word*, 19, 20–22, and 30. Thus, "we do not get at the nature of words by asking what they contain, but by asking what they effect, what they set going, what future they disclose." Gerhard Ebeling, *The Nature of Faith*, trans. Ronald Gregor Smith (Philadelphia: Fortress Press, 1961), 187.

[14]Fuchs studied with Bultmann and Heidegger in the 1920s in Marburg and served as a pastor during the Nazi period. He subsequently became a professor of New Testament at Marburg. His volume *Hermeneutik* (Bad Cannstatt: R. Müllerschön Verlag, 1954), conveniently marks the advent of a distinctive post-Bultmannian theological perspective. Ebeling attended Bonhoeffer's Confessing Church seminary at Finkenwalde and served as a pastor in Berlin. At Bonhoeffer's urging, he left Nazi Germany to finish his doctorate at Zürich. After the war, Ebeling taught first at Tübingen and from1956 principally at Zürich.

[15]In keeping with Lutheran theology, therefore, Bultmann's *Christus praesens*, the Christ who is present, plays an analogous role to that of the Holy Spirit in Reformed theology.

[16]Rudolf Bultmann, "Neues Testament und Mythologie: Das Problem der Entmythologisierung der neutestamentlichen Verkündigung [1941]," in *Kerygma und Mythos: Ein theologisches Gespräch*, ed. Hans Werner Bartsch (Hamburg: Reich & Heidrich, 1948), 51, omitting italics.

[17]Rudolf Bultmann, "Das befremdliche des christlichen Glaubens [1958]," in Bultmann, *Glauben und Verstehen: Gesammelte Aufsätze*, 4th ed., 4 vols (Tübingen: J. C. B. Mohr [Paul Siebeck], 1993), 3:207.

[18]Rudolf Bultmann, *History and Eschatology* (Edinburgh: The University Press, 1957), 151–52.

[19]See Rudolf Bultmann, *Jesus and the Word*, new ed., trans. Louise Pettibone Smith and Erminie Huntress Lantero (New York: Charles Scribner's Sons, 1958), and James F. Kay, <u>*Christus Praesens: A Reconsideration of Rudolf Bultmann's Christology*</u> (Grand Rapids: William B. Eerdmans, 1994), 93–97.

[20]Ebeling, *Nature of Faith*, 53–56.

[21]Ernst Fuchs, "Proclamation and Speech-Event," *Theology Today* 19, no. 3 (October 1962): 347.

[22]Ibid., 348.

[23]Ibid.

[24]Ernst Fuchs, "The New Testament and the Hermeneutical Problem," in *The New Hermeneutic*, ed. James M. Robinson and John B. Cobb Jr. (New York: Harper & Row, 1964), 123.

[25]Craddock, *As One without Authority*, 59.

[26]Fuchs, "The New Testament and the Hermeneutical Problem," 128–29. Italics original.

[27]Ebeling, *Nature of Faith*, 54, 56–57. Ebeling's interpretation of this cry of dereliction as one of faithfulness is reminiscent of Calvin. See *Institutes*, 1:519–20 (2.16.12).

[28]Here I am giving Ebeling's formulation of the problem in *Nature of Faith*, 57.

[29]Paul J. Achtemeier, *An Introduction to the New Hermeneutic* (Philadelphia: The Westminister Press, 1969), 141.

[30]Ibid., 142–45.

[31]Ebeling, "Word of God and Hermeneutics," trans. James W. Leitch (London: SCM Press, Ltd., 1963), 318. Emphases and italics original.

[32]Ibid., 326. From the standpoint of the doctrine of creation, humankind's destiny as a language bearer and as answerable to the summons of the Word-event is what it means to confess humanity as made "in the image of God." Ibid., 327. From the standpoint of redemption, the New Hermeneutic transposes the Chalcedonian language of the two natures of Christ as descriptive of the divine-human character of the linguistic event of revelation.

[33]Ibid., 311. Italics original.

[34]Ibid., 329–31.

[35]Craddock, *As One without Authority*, 133.

[36]Ibid., 3 and 45. See also, 143–44 and 59.

[37]Ibid., 163. See also 143–44. Cf. 153–54. See further, Randolph, *Renewal of Preaching*, 97: "The sermon should not be on a text but from a text. That is, the sermon should not be slapped onto a text, extraneous and superfluous to it, but should rather grow out of the text, organic to it, sharing its substance and shape." More recently, Thomas G. Long has called for sermons "not to replicate the text but to regenerate the impact of some portion of that text." This assumes, however, that we can know what that original impact was. See his *Preaching and the Literary Forms of the Bible* (Philadelphia: Fortress Press, 1989), 33. For a precursor of Long's proposal, see Craddock, *Preaching*, 178.

[38]Craddock, *As One without Authority*, 57. See also, 77, 125, and 162. By "inductive," Craddock means a movement from the particulars of experience to a general truth or conclusion, rather than beginning with a general truth and moving to particular applications. So understood, what is seemingly tossed aside is the exposition-application model of the sermon or the typical three-point sermon that begins with a stated proposition or theme, expounding and applying it point-by-point to the listeners. See 51–76, and esp. 57 citing Locke Bowman, Jr., *Straight Talk about Teaching in Today's Church* (Philadelphia: Westminster Press, 1967), 33–35.

[39]Craddock, *As One without Authority*, 77 and 124–25.

[40]Craddock can insist that "forms of preaching should be as varied as the forms of rhetoric in the New Testament," but this statement leaves unclear whether these New Testament forms should actually be repeated or used by the sermon and whether the same movement in the texts should reappear in recounting the movement from text to sermon–in the sermon. If these matters are not confusing enough, is Craddock excluding from consideration the various forms of rhetoric found in the Old Testament? See *As One without Authority*, 53.

[41]Eric O. Springsted, review of *Steps Along the Way: A Spiritual Autobiography*, by Diogenes Allen, *The Princeton Seminary Bulletin* 24, no. 1 (February 2003):141.

[42]See Anna Carter Florence, *Preaching as Testimony* (Louisville: Westminster John Knox Press, 2007).

[43]Craddock, *As One without Authority*, 100, 101, 103, and 143.

[44]Ibid., 152.

[45]Ibid., 104–5. Cf. Craddock, *Preaching*, 155–57, where the need for a theme statement is reiterated, albeit as derived from the entire interpretive act embracing text, listeners, and the negotiated distances between them. Craddock will go on to say, on 180, that sermonic form may be determined by "the pastor's sense of congregational need," thus signaling the primacy of rhetoric over poetics. Still, Richard L. Eslinger is largely correct that for Craddock "the interpretive payoff of every text is a proposition which then becomes the homiletic payoff of every sermonic form. Viewed from this perspective, the distance between a homiletics of induction and that of deduction closes considerably." See his *A New Hearing: Living Options in Homiletic Method* (Nashville: Abingdon Press, 1987), 125.

[46]Craddock, *As One without Authority*, 100.

[47]John A. Broadus, *A Treatise on the Preparation and Delivery of Sermons*, 5th ed. (Philadelphia: Smith, English and Co., 1873), 261–63.

[48]Thomas G. Long, *The Witness of Preaching* (Louisville: Westminister/John Knox Press, 1989), 82.

[49]Ibid.

[50]Craddock, *As One without Authority*, 108. Craddock acknowledges "what God is doing" can be declared in a sermon (127–28); what is less explicit is on what grounds the sermon itself is "something God is doing." In this regard, we find only one tangential reference to the Holy Spirit in Craddock's entire text, 107. Cf. Randolph,

who in citing Barth's definition of preaching, gives only half of it–the part referring to the human task, thereby lopping off the part about preaching as God's self-revelation. See his *Renewal of Preaching*, 29.

[51]Fred B. Craddock, *The Cherry Log Sermons* (Louisville: Westminister John Knox Press, 2001) 31–32.

[52]Ibid.

[53]Ibid., 33.

[54]Ibid., 34–35.

[55]Rebecca S. Chopp, *The Power to Speak: Feminism, Language, God* (New York: Crossroad, 1989), 31.

[56]Jürgen Moltmann, *Theology of Hope: On the Ground and Implications of a Christian Eschatology* (New York: Harper & Row, 1965), 65.

[57]Ibid., 67.

[58]Chopp, *The Power to Speak*, 12.

[59]Ibid., 13.

[60]Ibid.

[61]Ibid., 8.

[62]Peter C. Hodgson, *Jesus–Word and Promise, An Essay in Christology* (Philadelphia: Fortress Press, 1971), 262.

[63]Long, *The Witness of Preaching*, 60. My italics.

[64]Randolph, *Renewal of Preaching*, 28.

[65]Paul Tillich, "You Are Accepted," in *The Shaking of the Foundations* (New York: Charles Scribners' Sons, 1948), 153.

[66]Gerhard Ebeling, "Rudimentary Reflexions on Speaking Responsibly of God," *Word and Faith*, 334.

[67]Craddock, *As One without Authority*, 20–21.

[68]Gerhard Ebeling, "Worldly Talk of God," *Word and Faith*, 354.

[69]Ibid., 355. In my view, the power of the gospel (of God) is greater than the godlessness by which it is proclaimed, but this does not endorse casual godlessness as either faithful or fitting for preaching.

[70]John Riches, *A Century of New Testament Study* (Valley Forge, Pa.: Trinity Press International, 1993), 121.

Chapter 5: Preaching As Promissory Narration

[1]Robert W. Funk, *The Poetics of Biblical Narrative* (Sonoma, Calif.: Polebridge Press, 1989), 5.

[2]George A. Lindbeck, *The Nature of Doctrine: Religion and Theology in a Postliberal Age* (Philadelphia: The Westminster Press, 1984).

[3]Hans W. Frei, *The Eclipse of Biblical Narrative: A Study in Eighteenth and Nineteenth Century Hermeneutics* (New Haven: Yale University Press), 1974.

[4]Hans W. Frei, *The Identity of Jesus Christ: The Hermeneutical Bases of Dogmatic Theology* (Philadelphia: Fortress Press, 1975), hereafter cited as *IJC*.

[5]Charles L. Campbell, *Preaching Jesus: New Directions for Homiletics in Hans Frei's Postliberal Theology* (Grand Rapids: Eerdmans, 1997).

[6]Lindbeck, *Nature of Doctrine*, 18.

[7]Ibid.

[8]Ibid., 11.

[9]Ibid.

[10]Ibid., 9.

[11]For Frei's acknowledgment of Auerbach, see *IJC*, esp. xiii–xiv and Frei, *Eclipse*, esp. 1–16. For Auerbach's discussion of "realistic narrative," see *Mimesis: The Representation of Reality in Western Literature*, trans. Willard R. Trask (Princeton: Princeton University Press, 1953), 3–49, where biblical narratives are contrasted with the poems of Homer and the romance-fiction of Petronius. For characteristics of realistic narrative gleaned from Auerbach, see Frei, *Eclipse*, 1–16.

[12]For Frei's acknowledgment of the New Criticism, see both his "Remarks in Connection with a Theological Proposal," in *Theology and Narrative: Selected Essays*, ed. George Hunsinger and William C. Placher (New York: Oxford University Press, 1993), esp. 10–11, and "The 'Literal Reading' of the Biblical Narrative in the Christian Tradition: Does It Stretch or Will It Break?," in *The Bible and the Narrative Tradition*, ed. Frank McConnell (New York: Oxford University Press, 1986), esp. 62–68, 72–73.

[13]For brief overviews summarizing the tenets of the New Criticism, see, e.g., Karl Beckson and Arthur Ganz, *A Reader's Guide to Literary Terms: A Dictionary* (New York: The Noonday Press, 1960), 135–36. Without denying intramural tensions and distinctions, the names of such poets and critics as R. P. Blackmur, Cleanth Brooks, Kenneth Burke, John Crowe Ransom, Allen Tate, Robert Penn Warren, William K. Wimsatt, and Yvor Winters are often associated with this literary school and movement.

[14]For an exposition of Frei's "cultural-linguistic" turn, see Campbell, *Preaching Jesus*, 61–82.

[15]See Frei, *Types of Christian Theology*, ed. George Hunsinger and William C. Placher (New York: Oxford University Press, 1993), 140, where he ventures the historical generalization that there is a universal acceptance by all branches of the church of the literal sense of the Gospels. See also "Theology and the Interpretation of Narrative: Some Hermeneutical Considerations," in *Theology and Narrative*, 112, where Frei identifies the literal sense with what he calls elsewhere "realistic narrative." See further Campbell, *Preaching Jesus*, 83–111.

[16]For these characterizations see Julius Schniewind, "A Reply to Bultmann: Theses on the Emancipation of the Kerygma from Mythology," in Rudolf Bultmann, et al., *Kerygma and Myth: A Theological Debate*, ed. Hans Werner Bartsch, trans. Reginald H. Fuller (New York: Harper & Row, 1961), 67; Ernst Käsemann, "Blind Alleys in the 'Jesus of History' Controversy," in *New Testament Questions for Today*, trans. W. J. Montague (Philadelphia: Fortress Press, 1979), 44; Gerhard Ebeling, *Theology and Proclamation: Dialogue with Bultmann* (Philadelphia: Fortress Press, 1966), 65; and Ernst Steinbach, "Mythos und Geschichte," in *Mythos und Geschichte, Sammlung Gemeinverstädlicher Vorträger und Schriften aus dem Gebiet der Theologie und Religionsgeschichte*, vol. 194 (Tübingen: J. C. B. Mohr [Paul Siebeck], 1951), 20.

[17]Frei, *IJC*, xiii, 46, 48–50, 60, 63, and 124. Among the synonyms Frei employs is most commonly "the Gospel story," 49 et al., followed by "the Christian story," 57–59 and 62, "the New Testament narrative," 60, and "the New Testament story," 102. "Narrative" and "story" are often interchangeable for Frei.

[18]Ibid., 46. See also 51.

[19]For Bultmann, see *History of the Synoptic Tradition*, trans. John Marsh (New York: Harper & Row, 1963), 282–83, 306, 310–12 and *Theology of the New Testament*, 2 vols., trans. Kendrick Grobel (New York: Charles Scribner's Sons, 1951–1955), 1:86. For Frei, see *IJC*, 49–50 and 133–37. Matters become blurred when Frei continues to refer to myths as "stories" after binding the gospel narrative so tightly to this term. Cf. 50 with 56–57, 60, 62, and 139.

[20]Frei, *IJC*, 52, my italics. See also xiv, 82–83, 136, 139–40, 143, and 151. For what follows see further, James F. Kay, <u>*Christus Praesens: A Reconsideration of Rudolf Bultmann's Christology*</u> (Grand Rapids: William B. Eerdmans, 1994), 128–42.

[21]Ibid., xxx–xiv. See Auerbach, *Mimesis*, esp. 35–43 in relation to Mk. 14:66–72. On Frei's "rechristening" of myth as story, see *IJC*, 106, 114, 142, 243, 144, and 154. On 88, Frei does call mythical characters "storied," but this is apparently understood as not "realistically" so.

[22]Karl Barth, *Church Dogmatics* 4/1, *The Doctrine of Reconciliation*, trans. G.W. Bromiley (Edinburgh: T & T Clark, 1956), 335.

[23]Ibid., 336–37.

[24]Ibid., 3/2:445.

[25]Ibid., 4:1/337.

[26]"Saga in general is the form which, using intuition and imagination, has to take up historical narration at the point where events are no longer susceptible as such of historical proof. And the special instance of biblical saga is that in which intuition and imagination are used but in order to give prophetic witness to what has taken place by virtue of the Word of God in the (historical or pre-historical) sphere where there can be no historical proof." Ibid., 508.

[27]Frei, *IJC,* xiv.

[28]Ibid., 37–38.

[29]Ibid., 41–43, omitting italics.

[30]Ibid., 43–44 and 91–101. Frei recognizes that the self's identity is not only the product of its enacted intentions, but also of its responses to the enacted intentions of others or to unintended occurrences as well. For further discussion of Frei's "intention-action" model of identity as derived from the Oxford analytic philosopher Gilbert Ryle (1900–1976), see Campbell, *Preaching Jesus,* 23–25. For criticism of Frei's self-manifestation model, see Ronald F. Thiemann, *Revelation and Theology: The Gospel as Narrated Promise* (Notre Dame: University of Notre Dame Press, 1985), 182–83, n. 1. Thiemann argues that the intention-action model is adequate for describing the perdurability of the self and needs no supplementation by self-manifestation identity descriptions.

[31]Frei, *IJC,* 88.

[32]Ibid., 109–11. See also 82–83, 103, 108, 115, 127, and 144–45. Frei also calls Jesus' obedience "perfect." See 102–3 and 146.

[33]Ibid., 121.

[34]Ibid., 127. Mark, of course, neither depicts the birth of Jesus, nor, if we follow the shorter ending at 16:8, the Risen Lord. Given Frei's harmonization of the Gospels in the interest of a unified plot and characterization, such gaps have no literary or theological importance for him.

[35]Ibid., 128–32.

[36]Ibid., 133–37.

[37]Ibid., 109–10.

[38]To take one example of how this harmonization works, Frei claims that Jesus' obedience in the temptation scene (Lk. 4:1–13) is immediately enacted in his preaching at the Nazareth synagogue (Lk. 4:16–30). Since the Gospel of Mark refers only in passing to the temptation (1:12–13), omitting Jesus' dialogue with the devil, and since both Mk. 6:1–6 and Mt. 13:53–58 place Jesus' preaching in the synagogue only later in their Gospels, in stories quite different from Luke's and in contexts removed from the temptation scene, "the Gospel narrative" is really that of Luke alone. Cf. Frei, *IJC,* 111.

[39]Ibid., vii.

[40]Ibid., 145.

[41]Ibid, 145–46. See also 8, 13–15, 17, 26, 36, 147–52, and 154–55.

[42]My analysis here of Campbell's homiletic has been assisted by the unpublished paper of Charles Hardwick, "Preaching Jesus–or Not? An Analysis of the Sermons of Hans Frei, Charles Campbell, and Walter Brueggemann in Light of Campbell's Postliberal Paradigm for Preaching," 2004.

[43]Campbell, *Preaching Jesus,* 197, quoting Lindbeck, *Nature of Doctrine,* 118.

[44]Hardwick, "Preaching Jesus–or Not?" 7.

[45]Campbell, *Preaching Jesus,* 227.

[46]Ibid., 233–34. As David Lose points out, "faith" in postliberalism "is closer to the Aristotelian notion of virtue or *habitus* than it is to the biblical sense of trusting confidence." *Confessing Jesus Christ: Preaching in a Postmodern World* (Grand Rapids: William B. Eerdmans, 2003), 121.

[47]Campbell, *Preaching Jesus,* 216–19. See further Charles L. Campbell, *The Word before the Powers: An Ethic of Preaching* (Louisville: Westminster John Knox Press, 2002).

[48]Frei, *IJC,* vii.

[49]Ibid., 145.

[50]Cf. Campbell, *Preaching Jesus*, 18–22, for a positive evaluation of Frei's "Anselmian proof." For discussion of Anselm's ontological argument, see Karl Barth, *Anselm: Fides Quarens Intellectum, Anselm's Proof of the Existence of God in the Context of his Theological Scheme*, trans. Ian W. Robertson (London: SCM, 1960), esp. 132–61.

[51]Rudolf Bultmann, "On the Question of Christology," in *Faith and Understanding*, ed. Robert W. Funk, trans. Louise Pettibone Smith (Philadelphia: Fortress Press, 1987), 128.

[52]Philipp Melanchthon, *Melanchthon on Christian Doctrine: Loci Communes 1555*, ed. and trans. Clyde L. Manschreck, with an introduction by Hans Engelland (Oxford: Oxford University Press, 1965; reprint ed. Grand Rapids: Baker, 1982), 158.

[53]That Frei does not recognize that this is where his proposal logically leads is indicated by his criticism along similar lines of D. Z. Phillips, *Faith and Philosophical Inquiry* (New York: Schocken, 1979). In Phillips, Frei discovers, "The sensus literalis here is logically equivalent to sheer repetition of the same words. That is hardly how it has functioned in the Christian interpretive tradition," and, I might add, especially in preaching. See Frei, *Types of Christian Theology*, 46–55.

[54]Campbell, *Preaching Jesus*, 202–3.

[55]Frei rarely preached, but see *IJC*, 168–73 for his "A Meditation for the Week of Good Friday and Easter."

[56]Ibid., x.

[57]Jürgen Moltmann, *Theology of Hope: On the Ground and Implications of a Christian Eschatology* (New York: Harper & Row, 1965), 103–4.

[58]Ernst Käsemann, "On the Subject of Primitive Christian Apocalyptic," in *New Testament Questions for Today*, trans. W. J. Montague (Philadelphia: Fortress Press, 1979), 125–31.

[59]Christopher Morse, *The Logic of Promise in Moltmann's Theology* (Philadelphia: Fortress Press, 1979), esp. 67–81, which are summarized here. See also J. L. Austin, *How to Do Things with Words*, ed. J. O. Umson (Cambridge: Harvard University Press, 1962); Donald D. Evans, *The Logic of Self-Involvement: A Philosophical Study of Everyday Language with Special Reference to the Christian Use of Language about God as Creator* (London: SCM Press, 1963); and John R. Searle, *Speech Acts: An Essay in the Philosophy of Language* (London: Cambridge University Press, 1969). For further developments of the lines Morse has sketched, see Ronald F. Thiemann, *Revelation and Theology*, and Lose, *Confessing Jesus Christ*, esp. 156–67, where a critical appropriation of Morse and Thiemann is ventured with the aim of moving the discussion forward in the context of postmodernism.

[60]For this reason, Barth's preference for the term *epangelia* (promise) over that of *kerygma* in order to eliminate human response as a constitutive dimension of preaching is questionable.

[61]Bultmann, TNT, 1:319, cf. *TdNT*, 319. See similarly *TNT*, 1:302 and 2:240–41.

[62]Rudolf Bultmann, "New Testament and Mythology: The Problem of Demythologizing the New testament Proclamation [1941]," in Bultmann, *New Testament and Mythology and Other Basic Writings*, ed. and trans. Schubert M. Ogden (Philadelphia: Fortress Press, 1989, 110–11, and Bultmann, *Jesus Christ and Mythology* (New York: Charles Scribner's Sons, 1958), 68.

[63]See "New Testament and Mythology," 114 and 116–17; TNT 2:238, and *Jesus Christ and Mythology*, 75–76. For Bultmann's use of this analogy in his preaching, see *This World and the Beyond*, 34, 80–81, and 132.

[64]Morse, *The Logic of Promise*, 77.

[65]Ibid.

[66]Hardwick, "Preaching Jesus–or Not?," 13–32.

[67]Ibid., 16, analyzing Frei, "Untitled Sermon on John 15:1–8," 1988 (?) TMS (photocopy), 34. Hans Wilhelm Frei Papers, Record Group No. 76, Special Collections, Yale Divinity School Library, Yale University, New Haven, Connecticut.

[68]Fleming Rutledge, "Believing Without Seeing," in *The Bible and The New York Times* (Grand Rapids: William B. Eerdmans, 1998), 138–44.

69Ibid., 140–43.
70Ibid., 144.

Conclusion: Preaching and Theology

1A. Vinet, *Homiletics; or The Theory of Preaching*, 2nd ed., trans. and ed. Thomas H. Skinner (New York: Ivison and Finney, 1854), 36.

2Ibid., 37.

3Ibid.

4For preaching as worship, see Hughes Oliphant Old, *Themes and Variations for a Christian Doxology* (Grand Rapids: William B. Eerdmans Publishing Company, 1992), 48, 56, 70–72, 99, 119–120, and 132. Richard Lischer notes that "in the ecclesiastical Latin of the fourth century, four hundred years before it was exclusively associated with preaching, *praedicare* meant 'to praise,' 'to celebrate.'" *Theology of Preaching*, 13, citing Domenico Grasso, *Proclaiming God's Message* (Notre Dame, Ind.: Univ. of Notre Dame Press, 1965), 244.

5See further, Geoffrey Wainwright, *Doxology: The Praise of God in Worship, Doctrine, and Life* (London: Epworth Press, 1980), 218–83.

6Christopher Morse, *Not Every Spirit: A Dogmatics of Christian Disbelief* (Valley Forge, Pa.: Trinity Press International, 1994), 53–54.

7"Gays and Riverside," *The Christian Century* 102 (1985): 576–77.

SELECT BIBLIOGRAPHY

Anglican

Babin, David E. "Towards a Theology of Liturgical Preaching." *Anglican Theological Review* 52 (1970): 228–39.

Rice, Charles L. *The Embodied Word: Preaching as Art and Liturgy.* Minneapolis: Fortress Press, 1991.

Whiteley, Raewynne. "Word and Sacrament, Preaching and Eucharist: Reformation Roots and Contemporary Contributions to a Liturgical-Theological Anglican Homiletic." Ph.D. diss., Princeton Theological Seminary, 2002.

African American

Forbes, James. *The Holy Spirit and Preaching.* Nashville: Abingdon Press, 1989.

LaRue, Cleophus J. *The Heart of Black Preaching.* Louisville: Westminster John Knox Press, 2000.

Mitchell, Henry H. "The Holy Spirit and Holistic Preaching." In *Celebration and Experience in Preaching,* 145–51. Nashville: Abingdon Press, 1990.

_____."Toward a Theology of Black Preaching." In *African American Religious Studies: An Interdisciplinary Anthology,* edited by Gayraud Wilmore. Durham, N.C.: Duke University, 1989.

Taylor, Gardner C. *How Shall They Preach.* Elgin, Ill.: Progressive Baptist Publishing House, 1977.

Asian American

Kim, Eunjoo Mary. "A Theology of Preaching." In *Preaching the Presence of God: A Homiletic from an Asian American Perspective,* 48–76. Valley Forge: Judson Press, 1999.

Eastern Orthodox

Stylianopoulis, Theodore G., ed. *God's Living Word: Orthodox and Evangelical Essays on Preaching.* Brookline, Mass.: Holy Cross Orthodox Press, 1983.

Evangelical

Coggan, Donald. *Preaching: The Sacrament of the Word.* New York: Crossroad, 1988.

English, Donald. *An Evangelical Theology of Preaching.* Nashville: Abingdon Press, 1996.

Stott, John R. W. "Theological Foundations for Preaching." In *Between Two Worlds: The Art of Preaching in the Twentieth Century*, 92–134. Grand Rapids: William B. Eerdmans Publishing Company, 1982.

Feminist

Bond, L. Susan. *Trouble with Jesus: Women, Christology and Preaching*. St. Louis: Chalice Press, 1999.

Chopp, Rebecca S. *The Power to Speak: Feminism, Language, God*. New York: Crossroad, 1989.

Florence, Anna Carter. *Preaching as Testimony: Towards a Women's Preaching Tradition and New Homiletical Models*. Louisville: Westminster John Knox Press, 2007.

Smith, Christine M. *Weaving the Sermon: Preaching in a Feminist Perspective*. Louisville: Westminster/John Knox Press, 1989.

Hispanic

González, Justo L., and Pablo A. Jiménez, eds. *Púlpito: An Introduction to Hispanic Preaching*. Nashville: Abingdon Press, 2005.

Liberal

Fosdick, Harry Emerson. *The Modern Use of the Bible*. New York: Macmillan, 1924.

Liberation Theology

González, Justo, and Catherine G. Gunzález. *Liberation Preaching: The Pulpit and the Oppressed*. Nashville: Abingdon Press, 1980.

González, Justo, and Catherine G. Gunzález. *The Liberating Pulpit*. Nashville: Abingdon Press, 1994.

Smith, Christine M. *Preaching as Weeping, Confession, and Resistance: Radical Approaches to Radical Evil*. Louisville: Westminster/John Knox Press, 1992.

Lutheran and "Law-Gospel"

Bonhoeffer, Dietrich. *Worldly Preaching: Lectures on Homiletics* edited and translated by Clyde E. Fant. New York: Crossroad, 1991.

Bultmann, Rudolf. "New Testament and Mythology: The Problem of Demythologizing the New Testament Proclamation [1941]." In *New Testament and Mythology and Other Basic Writings*, edited and translated by Schubert M. Ogden, 1–43. Philadelphia: Fortress, Press, 1984.

_____. "Preaching: Genuine and Secularized." Translated by Harold O. J. Brown. In *Religion and Culture: Essays in Honor of Paul Tillich*, edited by Walter Leibrecht, 236–42. New York: Harper & Brothers, 1959.

Forde, Gerhard. *The Preached God: Proclamation in Word and Sacrament.* Grand Rapids: Eerdmans, 2007.

_____. *Theology Is for Proclamation.* Philadelphia: Fortress Press, 1990.

Lischer, Richard. *A Theology of Preaching: The Dynamics of the Gospel.* Rev. ed. Durham, N.C.: The Labyrinth Press, 1992.

Lose, David J. *Confessing Jesus Christ: Preaching in a Postmodern World.* Grand Rapids: William B. Eerdmans Publishing Company, 2003.

Sittler, Joseph. *The Doctrine of the Word.* Philadelphia: Muhlenberg Press, 1948.

Stuempfle, Herman G. *Preaching Law and Gospel.* Philadelphia: Fortress Press, 1978.

Wilson, Paul Scott. *Preaching and Homiletical Theory.* St. Louis: Chalice Press, 2004.

Wingren, Gustaf. *The Living Word: A Theological Study of Preaching and the Church.* Philadelphia: Muhlenberg Press, 1960.

New Hermeneutic

Craddock, Fred B. *As One without Authority.* 3d ed. Nashville: Abingdon Press, 1979.

_____. "A Theology of Preaching." In *Preaching*, 51-65. Nashville: Abingdon Press, 1985.

Ebeling, Gerhard. *Theology and Proclamation: Dialogue with Bultmann.* Philadelphia: Fortress Press, 1966.

Fuchs, Ernst. "Proclamation and Speech-Event." *Theology Today* 19, no. 3 (October 1962):341–54.

Mezger, Manfred. "Preparation for Preaching–the Route from Exegesis to Proclamation." In *Translating Theology into the Modern Age,* edited by Robert W. Funk. New York: Harper, 1965.

Michaelson, Carl. "Communicating the Gospel." *Theology Today* 14, no. 3 (October 1957):321–34.

Randolph, David James. *The Renewal of Preaching.* Philadelphia: Fortress Press, 1969.

Sittler, Joseph. *The Anguish of Preaching.* Philadelphia: Fortress Press, 1966.

Postliberal

Brueggemann, Walter. *Finally Comes the Poet: Daring Speech for Proclamation.* Minneapolis: Fortress Press, 1989.

158   *Preaching and Theology*

Campbell, Charles L. *Preaching Jesus: New Directions for Homiletics in Hans Frei's Postliberal Theology*. Grand Rapids: William B. Eerdmans Publishing Company, 1997.

_____. *The Word before the Powers: An Ethic of Preaching*. Louisville: Westminster John Knox Press, 2002.

Ellingsen, Mark. *The Integrity of Biblical Narrative: Story in Theology and Proclamation*. Minneapolis: Fortress Press, 1990.

Pasquarello, Michael III. *Christian Preaching: A Trinitarian Theology of Proclamation*. Grand Rapids: Baker Academic, 2006.

Willimon, William H. *Theology and Proclamation*. Nashville: Abingdon Press, 2005.

Process Theology

Suchocki, Marjorie Hewitt. *The Whispered Word: A Theology of Preaching*. St. Louis: Chalice Press, 1999.

Williamson, Clark M., and Ronald J. Allen. *A Credible and Timely Word: Process Theology and Preaching*. St. Louis: Chalice Press, 1991.

Reformed

Bartow, Charles L. *God's Human Speech: A Practical Theology of Proclamation*, with a foreword by Jana Childers. Grand Rapids: William B. Eerdmans Publishing Company, 1997.

Barth, Karl. *Church Dogmatics*. Vol. 1., part 1, *The Doctrine of the Word of God*. Edited by G. W. Bromiley and T. F. Torrance. Edinburgh: T. & T. Clark, 1975.

_____. *The Göttingen Dogmatics: Instruction in the Christian Religion*. Vol. 1. Edited by Hannelotte Reiffen. Translated by Geoffrey W. Bromiley. Grand Rapids: William B. Eerdmans Publishing Company, 1991.

_____. *Homiletics*. Translated by Geoffrey W. Bromiley and Donald E. Daniels. Louisville: Westminster/John Knox Press, 1991.

_____. *The Word of God and the Word of Man*. Translated with a new foreword by Douglas Horton. New York: Harper & Brothers Publishers, 1957.

Bohren, Rudolf. *Preaching and Community*. Translated by David E. Green. Richmond, Va.: John Knox Press, 1965.

Buttrick, David. "A Brief Theology of Preaching." In *Homiletic: Moves and Structures*, 449–59. Philadelphia: Fortress Press, 1987.

_____. *Preaching Jesus Christ: An Exercise in Homiletic Theology*. Philadlephia: Fortress Press, 1988.

Forsyth, P. T. *Positive Preaching and Modern Mind*. New York: A. C. Armstrong & Son, 1907.

Ott, Heinrich. *Theology and Preaching: A Programme of Work in Dogmatics, Arranged with Reference to Questions 1-11 of the Heidelberg Catechism.* Translated by Harold Knight. Philadelphia: Westminster Press, 1965.

Resner, André, Jr. *Preacher and Cross: Person and Message in Theology and Rhetoric.* Grand Rapids: William B. Eerdmans Publishing Company, 1999.

Ritschl, Dietrich. *A Theology of Proclamation.* Richmond: John Knox Press, 1960.

Von Allmen, Jean-Jacques. *Preaching and Congregation.* Translated by B. L. Nicholas. London: Butterworth Press, 1962.

Willimon, William H. *Conversations with Barth on Preaching.* Nashville: Abingdon Press, 2006.

Roman Catholic

DeLeers, Stephen V. "'Written Text Becomes Living Word': Official Roman Catholic Teaching on the Homily, 1963–93." Papers of the Annual Meeting, Academy of Homiletics, Santa Fe, New Mexico, 1996.

Fichtner, Joseph. *To Stand and Speak for Christ: A Theology of Preaching.* New York: Alba House, 1981.

Grasso, Domenico. *Proclaiming God's Message: A Study in the Theology of Preaching.* Notre Dame: Nortre Dame University Press, 1965.

Hilkert, Mary Catherine. *Naming Grace: Preaching and the Sacramental Imagination.* New York: Continuum, 1997.

Rahner, Hugo. *A Theology of Proclamation.* New York: Herder, 1968.

Semmelroth, Otto. *The Preaching Word: On the Theology of Proclamation.* Translated by John Jay Hughes. New York: Herder & Herder, 1965.

Schmaus, Michael. *Preaching as a Saving Encounter.* Translated by J. Holland Smith. Staten Island, N.Y.: St. Paul, Alba House, 1968.

Theology in Preaching

Allen, Ronald J. *Preaching Is Believing: The Sermon as Theological Reflection.* Louisville: Westminster John Knox Press, 2002.

Carl, William J., III. *Preaching Christian Doctrine.* Philadelphia: Fortress Press, 1984.

Cooper, Burton Z., and John S. McClure. *Claiming Theology in the Pulpit.* Louisville: Westminster John Knox Press, 2003.

Hughes, Robert G., and Robert Kysar. *Preaching Doctrine for the Twenty-first Century.* (Minneapolis: Fortress Press, 1997).

Wilson, Paul Scott. "Theology in the Sermon." In *The Practice of Preaching,* 82–97. Nashville: Abingdon Press, 1995.

INDEX OF NAMES

INDEX OF SCRIPTURE REFERENCES

Bultmann - kerygma - Decision
Bauth   - proclamation of G's promisse
                    + anglia

- und
  Aristotle
      rhetoric
      poetic
      science

all systems of understanding -

hearing the word
in context
pg 57

" outward means
   of the Spirits inward work "
                        p. 17

CPSIA information can be obtained
at www.ICGtesting.com
Printed in the USA
FFOW02n0854240314
4415FF

look @ Buechner - gospel as tragedy, comedy etc